IRREVERENT guide to Rome

3rd Edition

By
Sylvie Hogg

Wiley Publishing, Inc.

other titles in the

IRREVERENT GUIDE

series

Irreverent Amsterdam

Irreverent Boston

Irreverent Chicago

Irreverent Las Vegas

Irreverent London

Irreverent Los Angeles

Irreverent Manhattan

Irreverent New Orleans

Irreverent Paris

Irreverent San Francisco

Irreverent Walt Disney World®

Irreverent Washington, D.C.

About the Author

Born in California, **Sylvie Hogg** first came to Rome as a screaming toddler and returned 20 years later as a distracted student of classical archaeology. After living and working in Rome for several years—during which time she developed unnatural obsessions with umbrellas, pines, and tufa; a serious prosciutto habit; and a huge crush on 17th-century artist Gian Lorenzo Bernini—Sylvie now resides in New York City, making several trips to Italy, her favorite place in the world, throughout the year. She is also the author of Frommer's *Rome Day by Day.*

Published by:
Wiley Publishing, Inc.

111 River St.
Hoboken, NJ 07030-5774

ISBN-13: 978-0-7645-9886-9
ISBN-10: 0-7645-9886-4

Interior design contributed to by Marie Kristine Parial-Leonardo

Editor: Cate Latting
Production Editor: Suzanna R. Thompson
Cartographer: Roberta Stockwell
Photo Editor: Richard Fox
Production by Wiley Indianapolis Composition Services

For information on our other products and services or to obtain technical support, please contact our Customer Care Department within the U.S. at 800/762-2974, outside the U.S. at 317/572-3993 or fax 317/572-4002.

Wiley also publishes its books in a variety of electronic formats. Some content that appears in print may not be available in electronic formats.

Manufactured in the United States of America

5 4 3 2 1

Acknowledgments

Thanks to my family (and especially Dad, for your support and complicity); to my Roman brother, Fabrizio, and my expat girls—Anne L., Jennifer C., Claire H., and Emily C.—for sharing so many of the experiences that have shaped this book; to Fulvia and Pierluigi—*siete grandi;* to the Dartmouth Classics department; to Frank Bruni; and last, but not least, to the lovely Cate Latting at Frommer's, for her patience, stamina, and steady hand through the treacherous shoals of target page count.

A Disclaimer

Prices fluctuate in the course of time, and travel information changes under the impact of the varied and volatile factors that influence the travel industry. We therefore suggest that you write or call ahead for confirmation when making your travel plans. Every effort has been made to ensure the accuracy of information throughout this book and the contents of this publication are believed correct at the time of printing. Nevertheless, the publishers cannot accept responsibility for errors or omissions, for changes in details given in this guide, or for the consequences of any reliance on the information provided by the same. Assessments of attractions and so forth are based upon the author's own experience and therefore, descriptions given in this guide necessarily contain an element of opinion, which may not reflect the publisher's opinion or dictate a reader's own experience on another occasion. Readers are invited to write to the publisher with ideas, comments, and suggestions for future editions.

Your safety is important to us, however, so we encourage you to stay alert and be aware of your surroundings. Keep a close eye on cameras, purses, and wallets, all favorite targets of thieves and pickpockets.

CONTENTS

INTRODUCTION

Most people who've never been to Rome before have the wrong idea. Many think "Rome" and imagine a concrete jungle with officious gray palaces, mean-spirited Fiats barreling down narrow alleys, and somewhere in there, the Colosseum. Maybe it's the way the name conjures ideas of a masculine empire, the Catholic church, and Italian bureaucracy, but what most visitors do not expect is the intimacy and accessibility of *Roma.* Sure, the city's monuments were built with all the lofty ideals man has ever conceived, and sure, Rome's undulating topography nearly quakes with historical and religious import, but unlike most other major world cities, none of this grandeur is forbidding. Of course, if you only stay for 2 days and try to see everything on the postcard rack, you'll be too addled by the crowds and dizzy from the variety of offerings to find Rome a congenial place. But if you linger and venture off the beaten tourist track, you'll discern the inviting smile of Rome and grin right back.

"It is no accident that one small village on the Tiber was chosen to rule the world," a glory-drunk Messala (Stephen Boyd) said in *Ben-Hur.* In the Eternal City, brace yourself for a walloping of formidable heritage. Everyone who has ever ruled Rome, from Romulus to Mussolini, has taken it upon himself to tweak the urban landscape, with little reverence for the previous era. Almost everything the ancient Romans erected was felled by the popes in the Middle Ages and the Renaissance; the marble of pagan temples was recycled to embellish Catholic churches. (Yet for the Church's controversial role in the ancient city's state

Map 1: Rome Neighborhoods

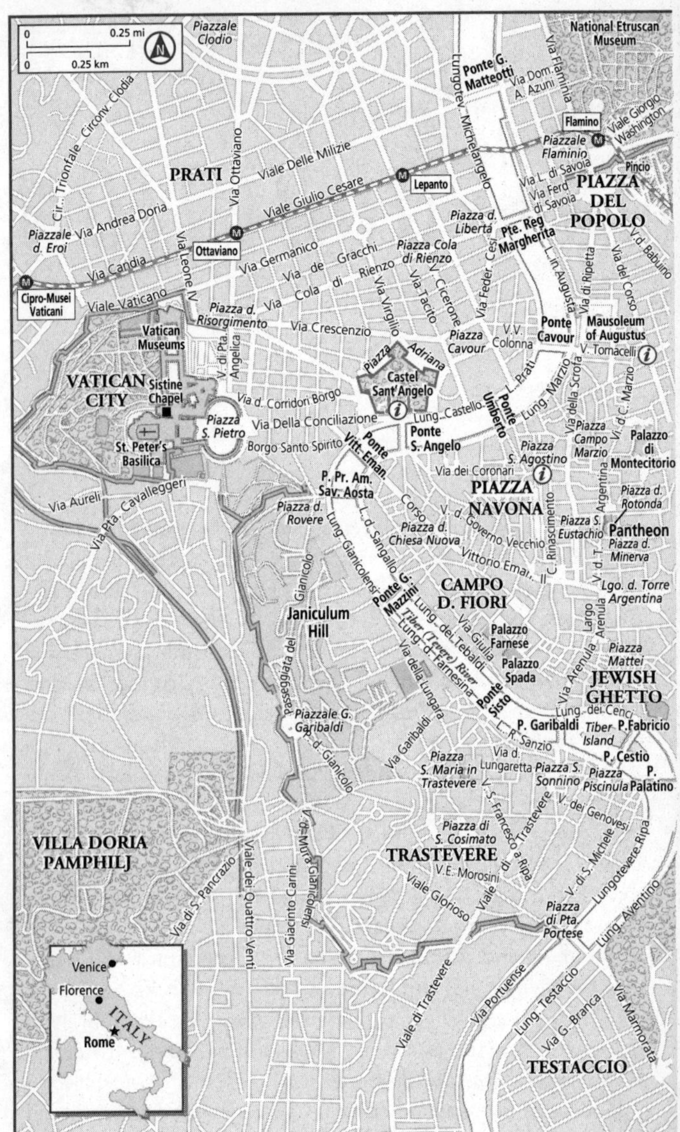

Information
City Walls
Metro A
Metro B
Railway
National Gallery of Modern Art
Galleria Borghese
VILLA BORGHESE/ PARIOLI
VIA VENETO
Spanish Steps
PIAZZA BARBERINI
National Roman Museum
Termini Station
Trevi Fountain
Teatro dell'Opera
Santa Maria Maggiore
SAN LORENZO
Vittorio Emanuele Monument
Capitoline Museums
ANCIENT ROME
Roman Forum
San Pietro in Vincoli
Golden House of Nero
Colosseum
PALATINE HILL
AVENTINE HILL
San Giovanni in Laterano
Baths of Caracalla
To the Appian Way

of ruin, it's thanks to the existence of the Vatican that Rome was spared bombing in World War II.) Even the short-lived Savoia monarchs left their mark, having the temerity to build the garish, glacial Vittoriano at Piazza Venezia, in the heart of Rome's well-established *centro storico.* For his part, Il Duce bulldozed ruins and medieval churches in the 1930s to create Via dei Fori Imperiali, the ultimate showcase of past, and potential, Italic glory. Every era has done its best to redirect the history of Rome; dark ages, political upheaval, barbarians, floods, and plagues have tried to break Rome's stride. But the urbs learned early on to roll with the punches, adding so many layers of history to the city's millennial character that there's now a 6m (20-ft.) difference between the ancient and modern street levels. Just like good leftover lasagna, the disparate flavors and textures have melded together, making the whole that much more sublime.

Milan is more sophisticated, Florence is more refined, and Venice is in a magical league all its own—but as Italian cities go, Rome is the one that satisfies all criteria in the "myth of Italy." Shouting, gesticulating people act out their everyday dramas while leaning against Renaissance palaces and baroque fountains that in other cities would be fenced and off-limits. Sexy, stiletto-heeled women flash by on Vespas, only to be honked at by irate nuns driving cargo vans of who-knows-what. Good food and fine wines are abundant and affordable, playing perhaps the most important role in modern life—after soccer, that is. Crosses and papal insignias are everywhere, but in spite of (or, perhaps, because of) the imposing presence of the Vatican across the river, the only people in Rome's 400 churches seem to be the tourists who've come to check out the Caravaggio altarpiece or Bernini sculpture inside.

In terms of beauty, Rome has the kind of looks that make you say "damn!"—the kind of intangible savoir-faire that makes a woman *hot* as opposed to just pretty. The charm of Rome is greatly enhanced by the fact that the city is not perfectly groomed. Rome's imperial mantle is threadbare in places, and her baroque finery needs a trip to the cleaners, but that just adds to her irresistible appeal. Rome's position halfway down the Italian peninsula, smack in the middle of the Mediterranean, gives the city a warm, flattering light, lots of sunshine, and—thanks to a serendipitous marine effect—rich blue skies despite a serious smog problem.

However, Rome is not all good times and glamour. Superficial problems include rampant graffiti, petty theft, litter, and pollution from vehicle emissions, which threatens not only inhabitants' lungs, but priceless monuments, the cleaning of which inevitably compromises the original art. But what can you do? Put a Plexiglas case around Trajan's Column? You could, but the Romans won't. A deeper issue is Rome's struggle for its own, modern identity. The juggling act that 21st-century Rome is forced to perform—clinging to its traditions and trying to be a vital European capital—isn't easy. The laurels of the Eternal City's illustrious history are in plain view, everywhere, and on a daily basis; modern Romans can't help but feel daunted by the achievements of their forebears. Its hip and energetic current mayor, Walter Veltroni, has tried to make Rome not just a top travel destination but also an important world capital for the new millennium—he's inaugurated several new contemporary cultural spaces, and perhaps not coincidentally, it's under his administration that so many of Rome's bars and restaurants have gotten their modern, minimalist makeovers. But there's something unconvincing about all these trappings of modernity when this is still a town where young people live with their parents well into adulthood. But instead of getting too frustrated and glum about this state of affairs, as some northern populaces might, Romans do their best to shrug it off and focus on the next great meal. Sputter though it may, the engine of progress in Rome, as in the rest of Italy, is moving forward. The smoking ban, for instance, which went into effect in January 2005 in Italian bars and restaurants, is a huge stride.

The Eternal City is a feast for the senses, but it can easily become sensory overload if you try to gulp it down too quickly. Certainly, the chaos of Rome would be completely insufferable if it weren't for the breathing room provided by ubiquitous *piazze,* the delight provided by whimsical fountains, or the palpable priority—despite their seemingly frenetic pace—that natives put on taking time for the simple things. When in Rome, enjoy the *dolce far niente* (the "sweet doing of nothing"), the food and wine, as well as the passionate pageantry of Roman street life. Don't just take pictures of Rome, dive into the fray.

Rome rewards the imaginative, the passionate, the nostalgic, and those who take it at an easy pace. Give yourself time to wander the backstreets of the *centro storico* and to reel before the ruins flanking Via dei Fori Imperiali at sunset, and I guarantee you'll fall hopelessly in love. Centuries of writers have tried to put their finger on it, but the complex character of Rome ultimately eludes the pen. Henry James put it best when he wrote that, in trying to put Rome into words, "one exposes oneself to the perilous likelihood of talking nonsense about it." Whatever it is, welcome to the most spellbinding city in the world.

YOU PROBABLY DIDN'T KNOW

How to get into Roman character... When on the stage of Rome, pretend you're auditioning for a remake of *La Dolce Vita.* Be glamorous yet blasé. Observe your surroundings not with the wide, smiling eyes of a tourist, but with the jaded squint of a decadent movie star who's taking a long drag on a cigarette. Wear the brooding countenance of someone who has been wronged, but who is silently, methodically plotting his revenge. Periodically jerk your head around as if pestered by the unrelenting flash of the paparazzi, and always, *always* wear sunglasses. You think I'm kidding? Just look at the dramatic vignettes that unfold when Romans are all by themselves—waiting at stoplights on their scooters, or at the grocery store buying cornflakes. These are a people who work through the full gamut of human emotions daily, if not hourly, with no apparent provocation. And why shouldn't they ham it up? With so many gorgeous things to gawk at in their hometown, locals know they're always in someone's sightlines—and for all they know, you could be the next Fellini.

How can I look less like a tourist?... Well, the first clues are the map and guidebook you're holding. Here's a trick for you—hide both in the folds of an Italian newspaper (*Il Messaggero,* the Roman everyman's rag, is a good bet), sneaking furtive glances at the reference literature only when absolutely necessary. Most Americans also need a serious makeover to blend in with the Roman species. Start with some big, outlandish sunglasses—in fact, pile on all the flashy accessories you can find. Wear tight clothes and banish all stonewashed jeans, khakis, and "sport sandals" from your wardrobe. If teenaged, procure yourself a brightly colored Invicta backpack and then scribble the names of your favorite bands all over it in black marker. If female, be a slave to the trends, no matter how ridiculous they are—Roman women manage to be fashion victims with flair. Wear lotsa eyeliner, and master walking on cobblestones in stilettos—it's all in the toe. The shoe-resenting scowl that will eventually find its way onto your face will help you look like the local women. If you're a middle-aged man hoping to camouflage yourself in Italy, simply outfit yourself in a *National Geographic*–photographer type vest, available cheap at the street markets. Guys of all ages can also go with the sporty chic of pseudo-technical sailing apparel, as many Romans seem to think they're on some kind of standby crew for the America's Cup.

The truth about *caffè* and cappuccino... Italians may do a lot of things that confound logic, but not so with regards to their coffee—which is why Starbucks hasn't opened up shop in Rome and probably never will. Why would anyone pay 4€ ($5) for a burnt cappuccino when they can get a real one for .70€ (90¢) at any old bar down the street? For the record, a real cappuccino is made with full-fat milk, and the milk is only steamed ever so slightly, not frothed into stiff submission by some kid in a green apron; as Dante himself once said, "a green apron does not a *barista* make." Many Americans walk into Roman bars and ask for a "latte," then act confused when they're served a plain glass of milk. (Well, here's a news bulletin for you—*latte* means milk in Italian. If you want espresso in it, ask for a *caffellatte.*) Remember, Starbucks-ese is not spoken in Italy: Terms like "non-fat" and "soy" will only draw blank stares, and steer clear of "venti" unless you really mean to order 20 coffees. Finally, there's no "x" in the word *espresso.*

"Prego," the all-purpose word... You don't actually need to know any Italian to get by in Rome, but the language is fun, and the locals, unlike the French, are charmed by even your most pathetic stabs at basic phrases like *grazie* ("thank you"—pronounced "*graht*-see-eh," not "grodzy," or "gracias," as most Americans believe), *buon giorno* ("good morning" or "good day," before 3pm), or *buona sera* ("good evening" after 3pm). *Ciao* is "hi" or "bye" (when it's the latter, *ciao-ciao-ciao-ciao* rings harried and important). *Mamma mia* can be interjected whenever you please to express frustration, incredulity, shock, relief, endorsement, even glee. *Madonna* is, ironically enough, used like the English "Jesus." *Prego* (literally, "I pray") is perhaps the most useful word of all: It can mean "You're welcome," "Please go ahead of me," "May I take your order," or in some cases, "I didn't understand a word of what you just said in your garbled American accent; please repeat." If all of that seems too advanced, you can always adopt *"Aoh!"*—a uniquely Roman utterance whose one, two, or three syllables can be friendly or hostile, as in: "*Aoh!* Good to see ya!" or "*Aoh!* Stop staring at my wife's cleavage!"

How to swear like an Italian... As useful as *prego* is, there comes a time in your Roman holiday when you'll need more powerful language. At the core of the Roman expletive lexicon is another five-letter word that begins with a P: *porco* (pig). One of the most common phrases you'll hear on the street is *"Porco dio"* (God is a pig), uttered in times of distress, anger, or failure. Biblical traitors *(porco Giuda),* prostitutes *(porca puttana),* even the first woman *(porca Eva)* are all fair game. Here are some examples for you to try around town. **Situation 1:** You only have 1 day to see the Colosseum, and it's closed because of a museum workers' strike. You say: *"Porca miseria"* (pig misery). **Situation 2:** You spill red wine on your white linen pants. You say: *"Porco di quel porco"* (pig of that pig). **Situation 3:** You realize your taxi driver has just stiffed you 20€ ($25), and he's already driving down the street. In this case, there's no need for *porco*—just shout *"Mortacci tua!"* (in Roman slang, "your dead people") and throw your right arm up for effect.

How to spot pickpockets... The streets and public transportation in Rome are crawling with gypsies and other sleight-handed miscreants, but Romans never get pickpocketed. How is this? The city's petty thieves prey on you, the unwitting tourist, who, bless you, are dumb enough to leave your wallet in your jeans pocket. Gypsies (called *rom* here) make up the vast majority of the pickpocket population, and they're pretty easy to recognize. Young women wearing loose, mismatched floral garments, their uncombed hair tied back, try to distract you with their babes-in-arms, cardboard pleas for charity, or newspapers, under which their hands work deftly at undoing your money belt or reaching into your pocket. The other 5% of street thieves are plainclothes pickpockets, who might be dressed like totally respectable businessmen but whose "business" is riding crowded Metro trains (and especially bus 64) and slipping away with wads of tourists' cash. The good news is that these thieves aren't violent, and it's a good bet that no one will ever "mug" you in Rome. Just keep your bags close to your body—no need for paranoid clutching, though—and an I-am-not-a-victim attitude about you, and you'll likely make it through your visit without having to cancel your credit cards.

How to resist caving to jet lag on your first day... Most people arrive in Rome the morning after an overnight flight, disoriented, tired, and in need of a shower. In most cases, however, your hotel room won't be ready until at least 1pm. (Those whose flights arrive at 11am have a great advantage over the 7am crowd, so always try to book a flight with a later departure.) Pack a change of clothes in your carry-on luggage or near the top of your suitcase, use the hotel's lobby bathroom to freshen up, grab a *caffè,* and hit the town. Don't attempt anything too ambitious (for example, the Vatican) on your first day; instead, visit a few squares and churches in the *centro storico* and get some lunch on a side street near Piazza Navona or on Campo de' Fiori. After lunch, you can take a shower in your now-ready hotel room, but resist the urge to conk out on the bed. The trick is to keep moving. Stroll in the sunlight for a few more hours, get an *aperitivo* at dusk, and then you'll be ready for dinner. You might be exhausted by the end of your meal, but you won't have wasted the day, and you'll sleep well, perfectly primed for Rome time.

Do drink the water!... Ever since ancient times, when aqueducts brought 38 million gallons of H_2O into the city daily, Romans have enjoyed cold, clean, abundant *acqua.* It's perfectly acceptable (and safe) to stop at one of those low hydrants—known as *fontanelle* or *nasoni* (literally, big noses)—all over the city and take a sip of water. Block the spigot with your finger, and water will spurt out the hole in the top of the curved pipe. If you have an empty bottle with you, you can save money (and the environment) by filling up there. Locals don't, but who cares?

Where can I go to the bathroom?... For a city with tourist attractions every 5 feet, Rome sure has a shortage of public restrooms—or so it would seem. We, however, have a secret for you. Rome also has cafes every 5 feet, which are required by law to allow non-customers to use their facilities. (They're also required to provide a glass of tap water to any thirsty person who enters.) Just ask politely for the *bagno,* to which they'll reply, *"In fondo a destra"* (in the back, to the right). Cafe toilets tend not to be stocked with rolls of Quilted Northern, so grab a napkin from the bar on your way in and don't be shocked if cleanliness could be improved upon.

First come, not first served... If you're one of those people who thinks of line-jumpers as sociopaths on a par with, say, the Unabomber, you're in for some blood boiling in Rome. "Why are all these people cutting in line, when I'm obviously next?" you'll wonder, as all the locals blatantly violate your custom of waiting one's proper turn. I hate to say it, but this is one cultural difference that doesn't seem to be going away even in the age of globalization. Queue-jumpers come in all shapes and sizes, but none are more skilled perpetrators of this heinous act ("What? There were people here before me?") than the city's old ladies. At the post office, the gelato shop, even museums, Romans are like carrion birds, circling and squawking to create distraction, all the while ready to swoop when the next agent becomes available. Politeness, unfortunately, is punished with an even longer wait, and the people behind the counter don't help matters by keeping track of who got there first. So when you find yourself in one of those all-too-frequent situations in which the line is not clearly defined, assert yourself. Put on your blinders—do not, under any circumstances, acknowledge the presence of any other customers around you, and maintain eye contact at all times with the cashier/server, so that when they scan the crowd for the next vulture, you'll be ready.

A word on bus etiquette... If you plan to take public transportation in Rome, here are some unwritten rules you should be aware of. First of all, tickets must be validated (time-stamped) as soon as you board buses and trams—for the Metro, stamp your ticket at the turnstiles at the station's entrance. Of course, the validating machines are out of order half the time, in which case you're supposed to find a pen and write on your ticket the time at which you boarded. Next, if you find an empty seat, by all means take it, but you'll be expected to give it up to nuns, melodramatic old ladies who never should have left the house in the first place, and kids. If you're not sure where to get off, ask a melodramatic old lady—recognizable by her non-specific state of distress and drooping suntan support hose.

How to avoid becoming roadkill... Despite the relentless stream of cars, Vespas, and buses coming at you like a plague of locusts, crossing the street in Rome isn't nearly as dangerous as it looks. In fact, Romans do it all the time and typically survive. With a few tips you, too, can be an intrepid pedestrian. On major thoroughfares, stick to the designated pedestrian stripes, and if there's a stoplight, do wait until your light turns green—though this is no guarantee that the intersection will be safe. As crazy as it sounds, your best bet for getting across a busy street is just to step out and start striding confidently. Don't dart, and don't freeze up halfway through, even if a cargo van does appear to be about to flatten you. Romans drivers are amazingly expert swervers and last-minute brakers. Go at a determined pace, holding your palm up in an "I think we both know you're gonna stop for me" kind of way, and the traffic will ultimately slow down, though they may shout blasphemies at you as you cross. Alternatively, follow a nun or a priest—not only will drivers screech to a halt to let these holy people pass, they'll even cross themselves as you walk by, which is cool.

What's the deal with all the police?... Between the *Carabinieri, Polizia,* traffic cops, fiscal police, firemen, and Swiss Guard, Rome has more costumed characters than Disneyland. Unlike Mickey and Donald, however, a lot of these guys carry Uzis, which can be understandably disconcerting for tourists. (However, when you discover that most of these forces' squad cars are Fiat Panda 1.4-liter hatchbacks, the intimidation factor pretty much disappears.) Central Rome's incredibly dense police presence, in front of government buildings, embassies, banks, and tourist attractions, is a bit of a holdover from the 1970s and 1980s (the so-called *anni di piombo*—"leaden years"), when terrorism among political parties was rampant. These days, so many armed guards probably aren't necessary, but whatever the case, Rome is the safest big city you'll likely ever encounter—violent crime is virtually unheard of in the center of town.

What does SPQR mean?... When you're in the *Urbs Aeterna* (Eternal City), you'll see these four letters everywhere. And if you paid attention in Latin class, you already know that SPQR stands for *Senatus Populusque Romanus,* which means "the Senate and People of Rome." The city government has long attached this abbreviation to any kind of municipal property or municipally approved public works, including monuments, lampposts, sewer lids, garbage cans, taxis—even Russell Crowe's shoulder in *Gladiator.* Latin dorks can have all kinds of fun in Rome tracking down inscriptions and translating them, whether carved into imperial triumphal arches or plaques at the Vatican parking garage.

How to tame the Italian stallion... Ladies, the rumors you've heard are true—Roman men of all ages are blatant oglers and forward as can be in handing out compliments to women they encounter on the street, in a bar, or at the tomb of Pope John Paul II. It usually works like this: You're walking along, minding your own business, and you hear a call of *"Bella!"* (beautiful), *"Biondina!"* (blondie), or

"Ammazza, quanto sei bona!" (damn, how hot you are!). You make the mistake of looking around to see who it is, and—wouldn't you know, out of all the beautiful male specimens in Rome—the guy who's just hit on you is either 18 and awkward, or 60 and grizzled. In either case, it can make newcomers feel very uncomfortable. In truth, although they have no inhibitions about flexing their machismo in public, these boys tend to back down pretty easily, raised as they are by the often-intimidating Italian *mamma.* A somewhat amused glare, as if to say, "Dream on, pal," from beneath your sunglasses (essential armor in these situations) should get rid of them—although the best defense of all is not even acknowledging their presence. If they persist, do as the *romane* (Roman women) do and exaggerate a bit. A forceful and bitchy *"Mi lasci stare"* (leave me alone) will usually do the trick.

Miao, bella!... Some say they came from Egypt with Cleopatra in the 1st century B.C.; some say they were brought from Turkey in the Middle Ages to kill rats that carried the plague. Whatever the case, cats have been living in and around Roman ruins for centuries. In 1988, the Roman government passed a law allowing cats to live where they are born, resulting in a proliferation of cat colonies, especially around the Colosseum, the Pantheon, and the Area Sacra at Largo Argentina. Living the good life, the strays rely on *gattare* (feline caregivers, usually female) to bring them meals of plain pasta, and even lasagna on holidays. An authentic souvenir of Rome, live cats (spayed or neutered and vaccinated) are available for adoption at the **Torre Argentina Cat Sanctuary** (Tel 06/687-21-33; www.romancats.com). If at any time during your stay in Rome a black cat should cross your path, superstition dictates that you must turn around—360 degrees, on feet or wheels—to rid yourself of the curse before continuing on your way.

ACCOMM

ODATIONS

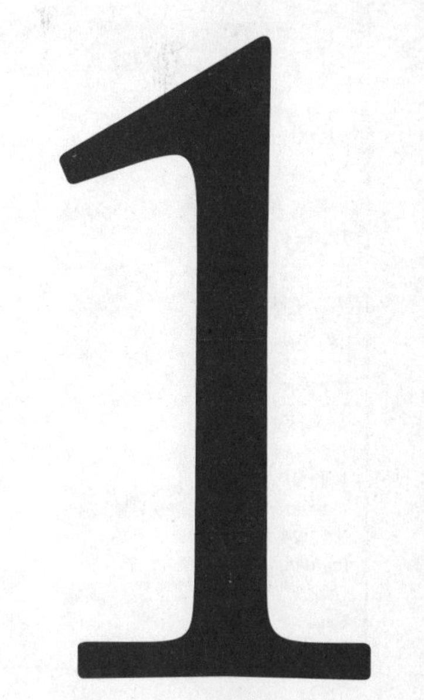

Map 2: Rome Accommodations Orientation

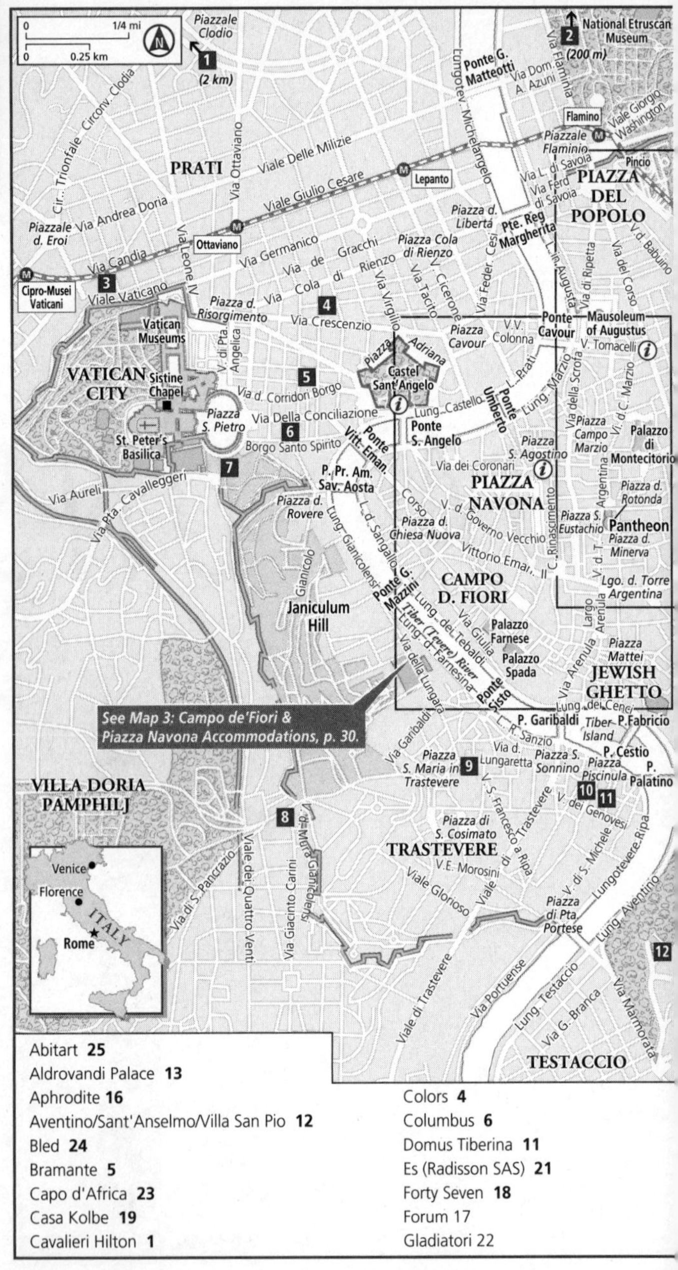

Grand Hotel del Gianicolo **8**
Hilton Rome Airport **26**
Hotel/Hostel des Artistes **15**
Lord Byron **2**
Oceania **14**
Residenza Paolo VI **7**
Santa Maria **9**
Spring House **3**
Trastevere House **10**
Verona **20**

Basic Stuff

The formula for the prototypical Roman hotel used to be wall-to-wall conglomerate marble tiles, smoke-stained vintage prints of local landmarks, and disinterested staff. The dawn of the third millennium, however, has brought much-needed decor updates and total refurbishments to hotels citywide. Granted, many government-rated five-star hotels still look like something out of a Lil' Kim video, and one-stars are still spartan, but those in the middle have benefited from the ambitious makeovers of international design teams. Paint is fresh, and mattresses are firm—the chintz factor, however, continues to be a problem at many properties. On the whole, Roman hotels have never looked so good. And they damn well better, considering the prices. Even in the budget range, this isn't a cheap-sleeps kind of town. Compounded by the strength of the euro, hotel rates in Rome are staggeringly high, by anyone's standards, and will likely take up more than half of your daily budget. The good news is that most everything else you've come to Rome for—eating, drinking, touring—is wonderfully inexpensive, with many of the city's most spectacular sights free of charge. While there is a definite premium on accommodations in the heart of the old city, spending the extra money to stay in the *centro storico* pays off in spades—in addition to charm, don't underestimate the value of convenience in this sometimes stressful city, whose public transportation network is no Paris Metro or London Underground. Truly central lodging means that you'll see and do more of what Rome has to offer and be more relaxed while you're at it. The cheapest and most abundant accommodations are always going to be around the train station, but if you plan to eat and drink out a lot, having a hotel in the *centro storico* will save you a bundle on cab fare. (Because who can figure out the night bus, anyway?)

When to Book & When to Go

Do yourself a favor and book well in advance—the last thing you want to do is show up in Rome in high season without a reservation. Plan ahead (at least 2 months, if possible), and you'll thank me later. (Do know, however, that if you try to book a single night somewhere, most Roman inns will tell you they're fully booked even if they're not—they just hate to book rooms for fewer than 2 nights.)

Rome is extremely popular and always packed with pilgrims, history buffs, gourmands, *dolce vita* seekers, and flocks of package-tour sheep. The first high season goes from Easter through July, and the second runs from September through Christmas season, with a slight lull in November. For those two-thirds of the year, lower-end inns fill up quickly, but if money is no object, you're in luck. A glut of new luxury-class hotels (and a drop-off in the luxury-class tourist flow) means that many of those five-star rooms are left vacant and may be offered at slightly discounted rates.

The highest hotel rates are in May, June, July, September, October, and around any big religious event or national holiday. Easter, April 25, May 1, and December 8 are big holidays for travel in Italy, and Rome fills to the brim with Italian tourists, who traditionally visit their country's *città d'arte* (cities of art) on those three-day weekends. If you show up without a reservation during one of those long weekends, you may face the equally distasteful options of (a) forking over 500€ ($625) for a room in a luxury hotel, or (b) sleeping at the train station. If you want to avoid the crowds and get a somewhat better deal, your best bet may be to plan a trip during the short low seasons—November, January, February, and August—which are not Rome's best months weather-wise. Even then, you may have trouble finding vacancies or reasonably priced rooms. Some upper-range hotels post special offers on their websites year-round, although significant discounts are generally only available during the "dust bowl" season (late Jan–Feb, when it's rainy and cold, and hoteliers are starving for business).

Enjoy Rome (Via Marghera 8A; Tel 06/445-18-43; Mon–Fri 8:30am–2pm and 3:30–6pm, Sat 8:30am–2pm), a free service run by amiable English-speakers, can often find you a place to stay, whether it's a hotel (up to three stars), an apartment, or a dorm bed. **Free Hotel Reservation Service** (Tel 06/699-10-00; daily 7am–10pm) has a multilingual staff and is also worth a shot. The service also has desks at the Fiumicino airport and the Termini train station, the former a less stressful experience for the weary traveler than the latter. Ragged arrivals at Termini will be assaulted by young men wearing homemade TURIST INFORMATION badges. These touts are not staff members of the Tourist Board; they work for private hotels and hostels and will do their best to get you to book a room with them. As you might imagine, many of the places they offer are pretty dodgy—simply mutter a beleaguered "no, *grazie,*" and they'll leave you alone.

Alternatives to the hotel scramble are apartment rentals and bed-and-breakfast accommodations, which are springing up everywhere these days, and religious inns, which are run by curfew-enforcing holy men and women. Any accommodations-related questions or complaints can be directed to the **APT** (Azienda di Promozione Turistica di Roma) at Via Parigi 11, 00185 Rome (Tel 06/488-99-253; fax 06/488-99-238).

European Hotels for Beginners

If you've never been to Europe before, there are a few things you should know about lodging on the Continent. If a hotel advertises a double, queen, or king bed, what they mean—and expect you to intuit—is that it's just two twins shoved together. First-timers are also frequently alarmed by the Lilliputian size of most bathrooms—even in top-rated hotels—as well as the absurd plumbing contraptions they call showers in many European inns. Although the shower-curtain concept is slowly catching on, there is often no barrier between where you shower and the rest of the bathroom, which means that you'll flood the place every time you bathe, soaking the toilet paper through to the cardboard. (As ridiculous as it sounds, this is totally standard practice.) Finally, what they expect you to use to dry off with is often more tablecloth than towel in terms of absorbency.

Next, if your hotel rate includes breakfast, that's not necessarily a big selling point—especially in two- or three-star places. Whatever breakfast they offer will not be a bacon-and-eggs buffet extravaganza—nah, just a stale croissant and burnt coffee. Skip whatever they have and get a real cappuccino with the locals at the bar down the street. Finally, if you're visiting in summer and are lucky enough to have a room with air-conditioning, remember that most midrange hotels will charge you an extra 10€ ($13) or so per day for using it. Don't want to splurge on canned air? Ask the reception staff for a *ventilatore* (fan).

Is There a Right Address?

If you're visiting Rome properly, you won't be spending much time in your room. Ideally, though, you should stay somewhere that's convenient to the sights, the highest concentration of restaurants, shopping, and nightlife. For all of these things, plus loads of atmosphere, there is no better location than the ***centro storico*** (the heart of the old city, around **Piazza Navona,** the **Pantheon,** and **Campo de' Fiori**). The *centro storico* has a few lavish hotels, but accommodations here tend to be small—from 10 to 100 rooms—and family-run. No uniformed bellhops here; if you're lucky, the receptionist will look up from the desk when you walk in. Services may be scant, but these hotels fill up quickly because, frankly, they have the right addresses. Street noise can be a problem at many *centro storico* hotels and *pensioni* (small, often family-run establishments), though courtyard-facing rooms are often quiet—ask for a *camera silenziosa* (translated as "silent room") if you don't want to be kept awake by guitar-playing drunks until 3am. Bordering the *centro storico* to the northeast (and considered by some to be part of it), the **Tridente** is the area between the Spanish Steps and the Tiber. A bit less authentic than the *centro storico* proper but equally pricey, the Tridente has plenty of accommodations, with neighbors like Fendi and Chanel, on its pretty, well-maintained streets.

As much as we love the old city, not everyone wants to deal with the chaos (er, liveliness) of the *centro storico* or its inflated prices. Though not totally in the heart of things, the **Vatican** area (the medieval Borgo and affluent Prati quarters) is a good compromise in terms of location and relative peace and quiet. The concentration of government-rated five-star hotels around **Via Veneto** leads the uninitiated to think that this is *the* area to stay. Sure it is, if being mere yards from the Hard Rock Cafe and far removed from the real pulse of the city is your idea of a sweet pad. Nowadays, a heavy tourist population from the United States, Japan, and Germany reigns supreme on the Via Veneto, blissfully unaware that the sweet life up and moved from this pretty street decades ago. The **Celio** neighborhood, south of the Colosseum, has several exceptional hotels—some with dramatic views over the ruins—but if you want street life, forget it. When the sun goes down, the Celio is as dead as a defeated gladiator. **Monti,** the tangle of medieval streets above the Forum and below Via Cavour, offers some charming accommodations, with equally charming local flavor. Bargain central starts at the middle of Via Cavour and continues east up the Esquilino to the area around Piazza Vittorio and Termini. Both sides of **Termini** overflow with budget accommodations, but keep in mind that what you save in hotel costs, you lose in atmosphere, and convenience—although an argument can be made for staying in the Termini area if you are only in town for a few days and plan to arrive and leave by train.

History buffs and art lovers can stay anywhere in Rome and feel satisfied. Gastronomes will be best positioned near the **Pantheon, Piazza del Popolo, Piazza Navona,** and **Campo de' Fiori.** To avoid spending too much on cab fare, night owls are advised to stay in the Navona and Campo areas, within walking distance of some great *enoteche,* bars, and *discoteche,* though the serious club scene is south of the center, in the **Testaccio** and **Ostiense** areas, which have only a handful of hotels. If you'd prefer to be where crafts shops and taverns outnumber tourist hordes, find a room at one of the few hotels and B&Bs in **Trastevere,** just across the river from the *centro storico.*

Now Starring

Before you dive into the fray, know that you do have a few laws and guidelines on your side for a change. All hotels in Italy are rated on a **five-star system** (with five stars being the highest class) and, as ordered by the Italian government and the Italian State Tourist Board, each hotel must prominently display the number of stars on its facade. The stars indicate what kinds of amenities the hotel offers, though plenty of four-stars are as ritzy as five-stars, and some two- and three-star establishments are extremely friendly or offer surprising views. Four- and five-stars all have dataport connections, as do many of the refurbished three-stars. Remember that law requires all Italian hoteliers to post maximum room rates in a public area and show you their available rooms upon request.

The Lowdown

New inns on the block... With their staggered blocks of colored windows, the facades of the brand-new **Abitart** look like gigantic screen shots of Tetris. Guest rooms in the boutique-y, design-led inn have wildly disparate themes—a suite on one floor is done up in a surrealist De Chirico motif, while another floor's suite looks like a '70s shag pad—and the in-house restaurant, Estrobar, clearly aims to be the Next Big Thing for Roman scenesters. Abitart's location, in the post-war Ostiense quarter, is a hotbed of exciting urban requalification projects (and minutes from the city's best nightclubs), but it's a world away from the charm of the *centro storico.* Most rooms at the **Forty Seven,** which occupies a 1930s *palazzo* in the thickest, greenest part of Rome's archaeological territory, have views of Romanesque churches, Republican temples, or historic hills. Decor is textbook hotel-contemporary—soothing but unimaginative—and the building's relatively late date means that rooms, and especially bathrooms, are more spacious than at most Roman inns. The coup de grâce here, however, is the roof terrace and bar, with stunning 270-degree views of the Palatine, Capitoline, and Aventine hills, plus the Circus Maximus, Tiber Island, Trastevere, and the Janiculum.

Edgy escapes for paparazzi-plagued VIPs... For those who like to sleep in style but aren't ready to shack up with the usual grande dames, a few hotels in Rome fit the bill. A favorite of visiting writers and poets, the Art Nouveau **Locarno** oozes character. It's decorated entirely with antiques from the early 20th century, including an original wrought-iron cage elevator and etched glass, Tiffany-style lamps. Rooms in the hotel's east wing are far preferable to those in the main building. Top models invade Rome at the end of July to take part in the "Donne Sotto le Stelle" fashion show at the Spanish Steps, and you may well see a few leggy types moodily lurking in the lobby of the **Gregoriana** down the street. Style mavens have long been attracted to the 19-room Gregoriana for its privacy (there are no public rooms) and its William Morris florals, but the hotel's recent, and somewhat sterile, deco makeover has left some cold. Minimalist to the point of calling three steel hangers on a bar (with no closet) a "wardrobe," the **Es** hotel (opened in 2002 as an independent but bought by the Radisson–SAS group in 2004) is by far the most ambitious modern inn in Rome. The south-of-Termini location is a bit seedy, but the 235-room hotel is a world unto itself, with an outdoor rooftop pool (and adjacent cafe, Zest; see the Nightlife chapter) and fitness club with all kinds of gimmicky beauty treatments, like *enoterapia* (wine baths). Also relatively new on the scene is the **Aleph,** a government-rated five-star "concept" extravaganza near Piazza Barberini. In the red and black lobby (designed by Adam Tihany to represent Dante's *Inferno*), eye-catching statuary includes caged marble lions and stylized warriors that look like they've been lifted from the Oceania wing of the local natural history museum. Upstairs, the guest rooms also bear the stamp of "modern design" (though in a much less visually assaulting way) and are less expensive than those at other luxury hotels in town. Take a time warp back to the 1500s at the **St. George,** in a Bramante-built *palazzo* on the picturesque Via Giulia. The hotel interior, with cathedral ceilings, antique furnishings, and cardinal-red accents, has a sumptuous Renaissance feel. (At press time, the hotel is closed for renovations; whether the interiors will look the same when it reopens in early 2006 remains to be seen.) In a beautifully renovated former schoolhouse on a dead-end road just south of the Colosseum, the three-year-old **Capo d'Africa** isn't exactly sexy, but its bright, spacious doubles have pretty contemporary accents, and many of the bathrooms have windows.

Swank and central... The neoclassical **Hotel de Russie** has a prime spot at the edge of Piazza del Popolo, on one of the most elegant streets in town. Spacious rooms feature neutral decor, with light green walls and dark wood furniture, but the real gem here is the interior garden created by the hotel's U-shaped footprint. Lush terraces with mossy fountains back up against the Pincio Hill; below, Bar Stravinskij and the Le Jardin du Russie restaurant are a favorite asylum for paparazzi-hounded VIPs. The **Grand Hotel de la Minerve** (formerly the Crowne Plaza) is the most centrally located government-rated five-star in town, 45m (150 ft.) from the back of the Pantheon. The 1930s lobby is awash in architectural bowers of green and blue and the hotel's large rooms have an appealing blend of modern comfort and "ancient" vestiges, like exposed wood beam ceilings and lamps with amphora-shaped bases. For impeccable service and understated luxury in the Spanish Steps shopping zone, the **Inghilterra** is your best bet.

The grande dames... If Jessica Simpson ever came to Rome, she would probably stay at the **Westin Excelsior,** which wrote the book on over-the-top luxury hotel decor—Oriental rugs contrast with leopard-print chairs, Louis XIV furniture and crystal vases clutter the lobby, and gilt and chintz from floor to ceiling could actually send you into a seizure. Between the Via Veneto and Spanish Steps is the discreet **Eden,** which consistently earns top ratings in all the travel magazine reader surveys for its attentive service and understated elegance. Perched regally atop the Spanish Steps, the **Hassler Villa Medici** is the oldest grande dame of them all, with small but luxurious rooms. The Hassler is the only privately owned government-rated five-star hotel in the city (and one of very few in Europe).

Dirt cheap and dead central... If you can forgo most creature comforts, the immensely popular government-rated two-stars near Campo de' Fiori, Piazza Navona, and the Pantheon are some of the best places to stay in Rome. Frills are few to nonexistent, but the value for location simply cannot be beat; try to book well in advance. All located in the heart of the old city, where the liveliest restaurant and bar action is, the **Abruzzi, Campo de' Fiori, Della**

Lunetta, Navona, Pomezia, Smeraldo, and **Sole al Biscione** (our personal favorite) are separately managed but pretty similar in price, amenities (hardly any), and convenience (loads). Across the piazza from the Pantheon, the newly upgraded Abruzzi isn't quite the steal it was in its dingier days, but a few rooms have magnificent views of the ancient temple. The Campo' de Fiori, Lunetta, Pomezia, Smeraldo, and Sole are all a stone's throw from the buzz of Campo de' Fiori, the city's most popular meeting place. The Navona is near the famous baroque piazza of the same name. Most rooms are the epitome of European quirky (cramped and dark, with sagging mattresses and strange bathroom fixtures), though some are spacious, with more modern touches. All but the Abruzzi and Navona have interior gardens or roof terraces open to all guests.

Best cheap sleeps... One of the best bets for sociable, budget-minded travelers, the Vatican-area **Colors** hotel and hostel has a friendly international staff, communal kitchen and laundry facilities, and a small terrace. Colors has other floors with brand-new private doubles and modern decor. It's convenient to many sights, and the quiet residential street won't keep you up at night. Decidedly less tranquil, the charmless Termini area, surrounding the city's main train station, has loads of cheap hotels. A stand-out here is the government-rated three-star **Aphrodite,** which has all modern amenities, a rooftop terrace, and a fitness room. The **Hotel des Artistes** is a friendly, family-run *pensione* where you can get a double room with a private bathroom. It has personal touches like fresh-cut flowers in all the rooms, and all rooms are nonsmoking. The Hostel des Artistes, which is actually the fifth floor of the hotel, has dormlike and private rooms, all of which share bathrooms in the hall; if you're low on cash, you can get a bed for about 25€ ($31) per night. Not far from Termini, in the Piazza della Repubblica area, **Oceania** offers a clean, cozy setup behind a nondescript exterior. Besides sizable rooms, the hotel also has amenities you rarely see in a government-rated two-star, like dataports and satellite television. Near Santa Maria Maggiore, just south of Termini, the family-run **Verona** has a gorgeous interior courtyard, sparse doubles, and a few triples and quads suitable for families or groups. The accommodations at **Casa Kolbe,** on a rustic, quiet street at the base of the ancient Palatine hill, are spartan remnants of the hotel's days as an abbey. But the rooms are still comfy, and many look out onto a pretty courtyard.

Where to drop after you shop... Many boutique hotels are clustered around the Via Condotti retail zone, providing a convenient home base for those whose objectives in Rome are more Prada than Pantheon. **La Lumière** has spacious, bright rooms furnished in a country style—upholstery in ivories, blues, and mauves, and blond-wood flooring. The marble bathrooms all have whirlpools. Prices are surprisingly low for the location and amenities. In a former convent on the artists' street of Via Margutta, the funky **Hotel Art** has reception stations that resemble giant blobs of mozzarella, and the lobby, a very recognizable former chapel, has a bar where the altar should be. Nearby, the **Margutta** is basic but cheerful, and an incredible bargain in this part of town. (If you stay here, be sure to check out the house at Via Margutta 51—where Gregory Peck's character, Joe Bradley, lived in *Roman Holiday.*) Amid the bustling, chic cafes of Via della Croce, the **Panda** is a well-kept, government-rated two-star lair with a five-star address.

Luscious love nests... If Zelda Fitzgerald were alive today and in the throes of a passionate affair with Leonard Nimoy, they would stay at the **Valadier,** near Piazza del Popolo. Part Art Deco and part 1970s space age, the rooms look like vintage 007 shag pads, with blond-wood and black-lacquer furniture, beds set at 45-degree angles, padded (soundproofed) walls, and mirrored ceilings. The **Sole al Pantheon,** with some rooms that look out onto the Pantheon, exudes a subtle romance, with terra-cotta floors and hand-painted coffered ceilings. The **Raphaël** is in a quiet, ivy-draped corner a few alleys away from Piazza Navona and has a sultry *luxe* look, with velvet couches in the foyer, original Renaissance art, and suffused lighting throughout. The luxurious rooms at **Casa Howard,** near the Spanish Steps, have sexy, French- and Asian-inspired interiors and canopy beds, but bathrooms at this boutique inn are down the hall. Away from the hustle of the *centro,* in posh Parioli, the **Lord Byron** feels luxurious, romantic, and exclusive. Relax in the sunny garden or have a drink at the roof bar, where you can gaze over the umbrella pines of Villa Borghese to the snow-capped peaks of the Appennines.

Rooms with a view... Almost every room in Rome has a view of something interesting: a quiet, cobbled alley; a filigreed fountain; or someone's laundry line. Nab one of the Colosseum-facing rooms at the all-new, boutique-y **Gladiatori,** and you're in for one of the most coveted views in the city, especially after dark. Guests at this former hunting lodge built over the ancient gladiators' barracks can avail themselves of the roof bar, where the evening panorama is sublime. The **Forum** also has a rooftop restaurant and bar that has spectacular views of the ancient ruins, but from the east, which means your eyes have to travel over the traffic of Via dei Fori Imperiali before you can contemplate the ruins. The only hotel that looks onto the Trevi Fountain is the **Fontana.** The rushing water of the fountain can be soothing, but it's drowned out by the din of tourists. The upscale **Sole al Pantheon** and the dirt-cheap **Abruzzi** both face the Pantheon, but it's the government-rated three-star **Albergo del Senato** that's closest to the ancient temple. From the newly opened rooftop terrace, a view of the Pantheon's dome will leave you simply speechless. If you're willing to splurge, the classic Roman address for views is the **Hassler Villa Medici,** overlooking the Spanish Steps and *centro storico.* The **Ponte Sisto** has some great views of the Tiber, Trastevere, and the Gianicolo from its picture windows. Guest rooms here are larger than average, and bathrooms have colored marble.

Closer to God are thee... Religious holidays, beatifications, canonizations, and papal death watches are all a big cha-*ching* for Roman tourism. Amid the glut of hotels that have lined up around Catholic pilgrimage sites to cash in on the rites of the faithful, there are a few clean, honest souls. **Bramante,** located in a 16th-century building that was once the residence of architect Domenico Fontana, is one of the original pilgrim hotels. It was converted into an inn for visiting Catholics during the 1870s and began admitting regular old tourists in 1960. Just blocks from St. Peter's, the hotel has 16 small but cozy rooms. Located directly across St. Peter's Square from the pope's apartment in the Vatican, the **Residenza Paolo VI** trumps all when it comes to proximity to the Holy See—no wonder, then, that the hotel's dramatic roof terrace was the preferred perch for TV anchors' broadcasts during the papal election of April 2005. Decor inside, however, has a fussy piety to it that can be best described as "cardinal chic." Not content to look like a nun's boudoir, **Spring House,** just around the corner from the entrance of the Vatican Museums, has red leather seating in the lobby; bright, color-washed guest rooms; and a cozy bar (which can be hard to come by in this neighborhood). The **Columbus,** on the grand, Fascist-era Via della Conciliazione that leads to St. Peter's, is housed in a 15th-century *palazzo* that was once the home of pope Julius II. Dark wood-beamed ceilings and faded ocher frescoes preserve the hotel's Renaissance time-warp feel. Clear across town, the **Bled** is just down the street from the relic gold mine of Santa Croce in Gerusalemme. Sure, it's an unsettling name for a hotel and the oddly isolated building looks like a house in a horror B-movie, but rooms are comfy.

Bring the bambinos... For the most part, hotel rooms in Rome tend to be on the small side, and if you're traveling with kids, you may have trouble finding ample lodging. Kids will be more likely to enjoy summertime sightseeing in Rome if there's a promise of a swim back at the hotel. On a hill above the Vatican, the **Cavalieri Hilton** is a haven with two pools and big, American-style rooms. The **Grand Hotel Parco dei Principi,** next to the Villa Borghese park, has a pool and family-friendly suites. Another option near the Villa Borghese is the **Aldrovandi Palace**—parents love its airy elegance; kids love the kidney-shaped pool. On the west side of town, the family- and business-oriented **Grand Hotel del Gianicolo** has a pool and is between Trastevere and Rome's largest park, Villa Doria Pamphilj. Back in the heart of the old city, the midrange **Ponte Sisto** has big bathrooms, breakfast served in the courtyard, and plenty of room for kids to run around, but no swimming facilities.

Sleep in heavenly peace... While the majority of rooms in Rome have been soundproofed to dull out the buzzing of cars, *motorini,* and tourists, it's still often hard to find respite from the din. On an alley around the corner from Piazza Navona, **Due Torri** is one of the quieter hotels in the *centro storico.* The hotel was originally built in 1518 as a residence for cardinals and bishops, who most certainly couldn't be disturbed by the revelry of sinners. Nearby, the boutique-y **Residenza Canali** has somewhat fussy rooms but a great location off Via dei Coronari. The exclusive, residential Aventine Hill is home to some of the quietest inns in Rome, set among trees, churches, and monasteries. The hotel trio **Aventino/Sant'Anselmo/Villa San Pio** has aristocratic decor and over 100 peaceful rooms, though very few cafes and restaurants are around. A real treasure in Trastevere is the chalet-style **Santa Maria,** built on the site of a 15th-century cloister and housed within its own private courtyard.

Make your own bed... Vacation apartment rentals and B&B-style accommodations have caught on in recent years, meaning accommodations-seekers on a budget now have a ton more to choose from in the *centro storico.* The **Rental in Rome** agency (www.rentalinrome.com; 75€/$94 and up per night for double occupancy, depending on size and location) has a mother lode of apartments at all the most sought-after addresses, including several that are right on Piazza Navona and the Spanish Steps. (You can even rent rooms in a delightful 17th-century "castle" in Rome's southern suburbs and eat breakfast with the prince who still lives there!) Rome's B&Bs are handled by the **Bed and Breakfast Association** (Piazza del Teatro di Pompeo 2; Tel 06/687-73-48; fax 06/687-48-81; www.b-b.rm.it). Among them, **Casa Banzo** is an exceptional B&B near Campo de' Fiori, with black-and-white marble floors, vaulted ceilings, and large picture windows. **Trastevere House** is a B&B with a cozy, Mediterranean feel; **Domus Tiberina** (also in Trastevere, and run by the same friendly young people) was once the single-family residence of international journalists before being converted into a B&B in 2002.

I have a 7am flight—are there any hotels near the airport?... The only hotel located at Rome's Fiumicino Airport is the all-new **Hilton Rome Airport.** The hotel has a business center, a health club, and an indoor pool. But it's expensive, so unless you really plan to take advantage of the hotel amenities, it's probably better to stay at your hotel in the *centro* and treat yourself to a nice 5am taxi ride.

Map 3: Campo De' Fiori & Piazza Navona Accommodations

Map 4: Spanish Steps, Piazza Del Popolo & Via Veneto Accommodations

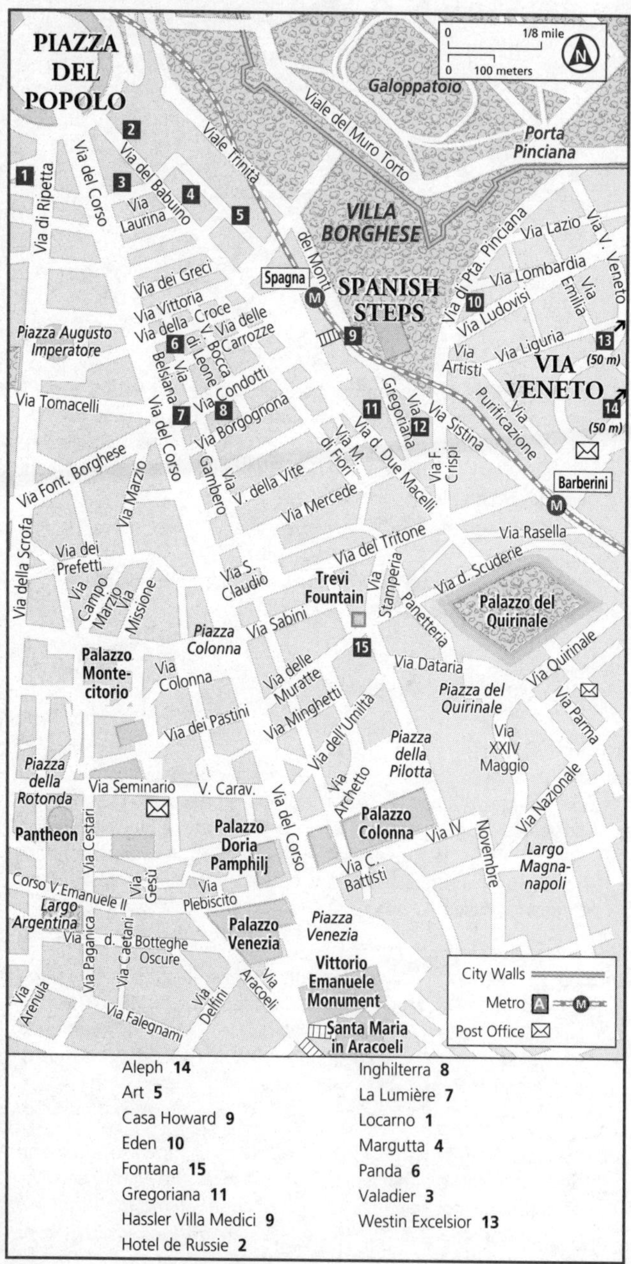

- Aleph **14**
- Art **5**
- Casa Howard **9**
- Eden **10**
- Fontana **15**
- Gregoriana **11**
- Hassler Villa Medici **9**
- Hotel de Russie **2**
- Inghilterra **8**
- La Lumière **7**
- Locarno **1**
- Margutta **4**
- Panda **6**
- Valadier **3**
- Westin Excelsior **13**

The Index

$$$$$	450€ and up
$$$$	300€–450€
$$$	200€–300€
$$	100€–200€
$	100€ and below

Prices ratings are based on the lowest price quoted for a standard double room in high season; most hotels include the IVA, or value-added tax (9%–19%) in their quoted rates, but be sure to ask before you book. All hotels take major credit cards except where noted below.

Note: 1€ = US$1.25.

The following abbreviations are used for credit cards:

AE	American Express
DC	Diners Club
DISC	Discover
MC	MasterCard
V	Visa

Abitart (p. 22) OSTIENSE Brand new hotel with slick modern Italian design and themed suites, from the "Picasso" to the "Deconstructed." Huge discounts off rack rates are often available.... *Tel 06/454-3191. Fax 06/4543-19899. www.abitarthotel.com. Via P. Matteucci 10–12, at Via Ostiense, 00154. Metro Piramide. Buses 23 or 271. 14 rooms. AE, DC, MC, V. $$$*

See Map 2 on p. 16.

Abruzzi (p. 24) PANTHEON Recently renovated government-rated two-star hotel with views of the Pantheon.... *Tel 06/679-20-21. Fax 06/697-88-076. www.hotelabruzzi.it. Piazza della Rotonda 69, at Via dei Pastini, 00186. Buses 30, 40, 46, 64, 70, 87, 116, 492, or 571. Tram 8. 25 rooms. AE, DC, MC, V. $$*

See Map 3 on p. 30.

Albergo del Senato (p. 27) PANTHEON Well-priced government-rated three-star within spitting distance of the Pantheon. Stupendous, up-close-and-personal view of the dome from the new rooftop garden.... *Tel 06/678-43-43. Fax 06/699-40-297. www.albergodelsenato.it. Piazza della Rotonda 73, at Via dei Pastini,*

00186. Buses 30, 40, 46, 64, 70, 87, 116, 492, or 571. Tram 8. 56 rooms. AE, DC, MC, V. $$$

See Map 3 on p. 30.

Aldrovandi Palace (p. 28) VILLA BORGHESE Government-rated four-star oasis for families and business travelers down the street from the U.S. ambassador's gorgeous compound; lush garden and swimming pool add to suburban feel.... *Tel 06/322-3993. Fax 06/322-1435. www.aldrovandi.com. Via Ulisse Aldrovandi 15, at Via M. Mercati, 00197. Tram 19. 135 rooms. AE, DC, MC, V. $$$$*

See Map 2 on p. 16.

Aleph (p. 23) PIAZZA BARBERINI An extravaganza of Dante-inspired design near Via Veneto, with rooms priced below the norm for government-rated five-star hotels. Lobby bar is popular with young movers and shakers.... *Tel 06/422-901. Fax 06/422-90-000. www.boscolohotels.com. Via di San Basilio 15, near Via Bissolati, 00187. Metro Barberini. Buses 52, 53, 62, 63, 80, 95, 116, 175, 492, or 630. 96 rooms. AE, DC, MC, V. $$$$*

See Map 4 on p. 31.

Aphrodite (p. 25) TERMINI Modern rooms at this brand-new government-rated three-star feature lots of polished travertine, showers have colorful mosaics, and the rooftop terrace and fitness room are unusual bonuses for this part of town.... *Tel 06/491-096. Fax 06/491-579. www.accommodationinrome.com. Via Marsala 90, at Via Milazzo, 00185. Metro Termini. 48 rooms. AE, DC, MC, V. $–$$*

See Map 2 on p. 16.

Art (p. 26) SPANISH STEPS Bright, friendly, design-heavy government-rated four-star on the quiet and lovely Via Margutta.... *Tel 06/328-71-11. Fax 06/360-03-995. www.hotelart.it. Via Margutta 56, near Via Alibert, 00187. Metro Spagna. 46 rooms. AE, DC, MC, V. $$$$*

See Map 4 on p. 31.

Aventino/Sant'Anselmo/Villa San Pio (p. 29) AVENTINE Three attractive and serene hotels with formal decor, near orange groves and rose gardens on the Aventine hill.... *Tel 06/574-35-47. Fax 06/578-36-04. www.aventinohotels.com. Piazza Sant'Anselmo 2, at Via di Sant'Anselmo, 00154. Bus 95. 100+ rooms. AE, DC, MC, V. $$–$$$*

See Map 2 on p. 16.

Bled (p. 28) ESQUILINO Once you get past the name and horror-movie look of the building, you can have a very relaxing stay at this cozy inn near Santa Croce in Gerusalemme.... *Tel 06/702-78-08. Fax 06/702-79-35. Via Santa Croce in Gerusalemme 40, at Via Statilia, 00185. Metro Manzoni. 47 rooms. AE, DC, MC, V. $$*

See Map 2 on p. 16.

Bramante (p. 27) VATICAN Modest pilgrim inn turned charming, intimate government-rated three-star in the medieval Borgo area near the Vatican.... *Tel 06/688-06-426. Fax 06/681-33-339. www.hotelbramante.com. Vicolo delle Palline 24, at Borgo Pio, 00193. Metro Ottaviano. 16 rooms. AE, DC, MC, V. $$–$$$*

See Map 2 on p. 16.

Campo de' Fiori (p. 24) CAMPO DE' FIORI Room decor—and comfort level—vary widely at this inexpensive, centrally located inn.... *Tel 06/688-06-865. Fax 06/687-60-03. www.hotelcampodefiori.com. Via del Biscione 6, off Campo de' Fiori, 00186. Buses 30, 40, 46, 64, 70, 87, 116, 492, or 571. 28 rooms. Some rooms have shared bathroom. AE, DC, MC, V. $$*

See Map 3 on p. 30.

Capo d'Africa (p. 23) COLOSSEUM A contemporary, bright haven in an Art Nouveau schoolhouse a stone's throw from the Colosseum.... *Tel 06/772-801. Fax 06/772-80-801. www.hotelcapodafrica.com. Via Capo d'Africa 54, at Via dei Querceti, 00184. Metro Colosseo. Buses 60, 75, 175, or 271. Tram 3. 64 rooms. AE, DC, MC, V. $$$–$$$$*

See Map 2 on p. 16.

Casa Banzo (p. 29) CAMPO DE' FIORI The comfortable rooms in this B&B have vaulted ceilings and are decorated with antiques; all have private bathrooms. Closed February, July, and August.... *Tel 06/683-39-09. Fax 06/686-45-75. Piazza Monte di Pietà 30, off Via Giubbonari, 00186. Buses 30, 40, 46, 64, 70, 87, 116, 492, or 571. 3 rooms. No credit cards. $–$$*

See Map 3 on p. 30.

Casa Howard (p. 26) SPANISH STEPS One of the first boutique hotels in Rome, with five luxuriously appointed, tasteful rooms and warm, personalized service. Bathrooms are down the hall, and there's a Turkish *hammam* open to all guests for an extra 25€ ($31).... *Tel 06/69924555. www.casahoward.com. Via Capo Le Case 18, at Via dei Due Macelli, 00187. Metro Spagna. Buses 62, 175, or 492. 5 rooms. AE, DC, MC, V. No private bathrooms. $$–$$$*

See Map 4 on p. 31.

Casa Kolbe (p. 25) PALATINE Quiet government-rated two-star inn on one of Rome's lovely, untrodden streets near the Palatine.... *Tel 06/679-88-66. Fax 06/699-41-550. Via di San Teodoro 44, at Via del Velabro, 00186. Buses 30, 95, or 170. 63 rooms. Some rooms have shared bathroom. No credit cards. $*

See Map 2 on p. 16.

Cavalieri Hilton (p. 28) MONTE MARIO Away from it all, on the northern outskirts of the city, with great panoramic views of St. Peter's. Other amenities include on-site tennis courts, a gym, and a pool.... *Tel 06/350-91. Fax 06/350-92-241. www.cavalieri-hilton.it. Via Cadlolo 101, 00136. 375 rooms. AE, DC, MC, V. $$$-$$$$$*

See Map 2 on p. 16.

Colors (p. 25) VATICAN Friendly and clean home-away-from-home for budget travelers, with kitchen, terrace, and washing machine. One floor has shared/dorm-style accommodations, and a brand-new lower floor has modern, nicely appointed doubles, all with private bath.... *Tel 06/687-40-30. Fax 06/686-79-47. www.hotelcolors.com. Via Boezio 31, at Via Terenzio, 00193. Metro Ottaviano. Buses 23, 81, 87, 271, or 492. 21 rooms. Some rooms have shared bathroom. No lift. $*

See Map 2 on p. 16.

Columbus (p. 28) VATICAN A monastery before it was transformed into lodging for tourists and Vatican VIPs, this government-rated four-star retains much of its original, 16th-century woodwork and frescoes.... *Tel 06/686-54-35. Fax 06/686-48-74. www.hotelcolumbus.net. Via della Conciliazione 33, at Via Scossacavalli, 00193. Buses 40, 62, or 64. 92 rooms. AE, DC, MC, V. $$$*

See Map 2 on p. 16.

Domus Tiberina (p. 29) TRASTEVERE Comfy Mediterranean-style B&B in the quieter southern half of Trastevere, a stone's throw from Tiber Island.... *Tel 06/580-30-33. Fax 06/581-36-48. www.domustiberina.com. Via in Piscinula 37, near Piazza in Piscinula, 00153. Buses 23, 271, or 280. Tram 8. 10 rooms. AE, DC, MC, V. $$*

See Map 2 on p. 16.

Due Torri (p. 28) PIAZZA NAVONA Once the residence of clergymen, this quiet inn tucked in an alley has kept its old-world charm (read: some rooms are cramped).... *Tel 06/687-69-83. Fax 06/686-54-42. www.hotelduetorriroma.com. Vicolo del Leonetto 23, at Via del Cancello, 00186. Buses 30, 70, 87, 280, 492, or 628. 26 rooms. AE, DC, MC, V. $$-$$$*

See Map 3 on p. 30.

Eden (p. 24) SPANISH STEPS/VENETO Quiet elegance at this Veneto-area government-rated five-star keeps discerning travelers loyal.... *Tel 06/478-121. Fax 06/482-15-84. www.hotel-eden.it. Via Ludovisi 49, at Via di Porta Pinciana, 00187. Metro Spagna. Buses 52, 53, 63, 95, or 116. 121 rooms. AE, DC, MC, V. $$$$$*

See Map 4 on p. 31.

Es (Radisson SAS) (p. 23) ESQUILINO/TERMINI Hulking, minimalist hotel in the up-and-coming (but still seedy) Esquilino neighborhood. Rooms are small, but the huge, single-pane windows change color at night, and the rooftop pool is super-glam.... *Tel 06/444-841. Fax 06/443-41-396. www.rome.radissonsas.com. Via F. Turati 171, at Via Rattazzi, 00185. Metro Vittorio. Bus 70. 235 rooms. AE, DC, MC, V. $$$$$*

See Map 2 on p. 16.

Fontana (p. 27) TREVI FOUNTAIN Front rooms and roof terrace at this modest government-rated three-star face the massive Trevi Fountain; rear rooms lack the view but have A/C.... *Tel 06/678-61-13. Fax 06/679-00-24. www.fontanahotel.com. Piazza di Trevi 96, 00187. Metro Barberini. Buses 62, 85, 95, 116, 175, or 492. 24 rooms. A/C in rear rooms; ceiling fans in front rooms. AE, DC, MC, V. $$–$$$*

See Map 4 on p. 31.

Forty Seven (p. 22) ANCIENT ROME New government-rated four-star with views of ruins and churches in the heart of ancient Rome. Contemporary decor is asexual, but there's a stupendous panorama from the roof terrace.... *Tel 06/6787816. Fax 06/69190726. www.fortysevenhotel.com. Via Petroselli 47, at Piazza della Bocca della Verità, 00186. Buses 30, 95, or 170. 61 rooms. AE, DC, MC, V. $$$–$$$$*

See Map 2 on p. 16.

Forum (p. 27) COLOSSEUM/ROMAN FORUM The lobby might be a little too 1950s men's club, and the elevator might make too many suspicious noises, but the view from the roof garden over the Roman Forum inspires only reverence.... *Tel 06/679-24-46. Fax 06/678-64-79. www.hotelforumrome.com. Via Tor de' Conti 25, off Via Cavour, 00184. Metro Colosseo. Buses 60, 75, 84, 85, 87, 175, 271, or 571. 80 rooms. AE, DC, MC, V. $$$*

See Map 2 on p. 16.

Gladiatori (p. 27) COLOSSEUM A 16th-century hunting lodge built over the ancient barracks of the gladiators, now a boutique hotel done up in subdued tones and classic furnishings. The view from the rooftop terrace over the Colosseum is to die for.... *Tel 06/775-91-380. Fax 06/700-56-38. www.hotelgladiatori.it. Via Labicana 125, at Via dei Normanni, 00184. Metro Colosseo. Buses 85 or 87. Tram 3. 17 rooms. AE, DC, MC, V. $$$*

See Map 2 on p. 16.

Grand Hotel de la Minerve (p. 24) PANTHEON This classy government-rated five-star, refurbished in 1990 by Italian star architect and interior designer Paolo Portoghesi, is well positioned at the back of the Pantheon.... *Tel 06/695-201. Fax 06/679-41-65. www.grandhoteldelaminerve.com. Piazza della Minerva 69, 00186. Buses 30, 40, 64, 70, 87, 116, 492, or 571. 134 rooms. AE, DC, MC, V. $$$$$*

See Map 3 on p. 30.

Grand Hotel del Gianicolo (p. 28) JANICULUM/MONTEVERDE This attractive but dated government-rated four-star is a quiet haven (with swimming pool) near Villa Pamphilj, Rome's largest public park. Pool is available to non-guests for 20€ ($25) on weekdays, 30€ ($38) on weekends.... *Tel 06/58333405. Fax 06/58179434. www.grandhotelgianicolo.it. Viale delle Mura Gianicolensi 107, near Porta San Pancrazio, 00152. Bus 870. 40 rooms. AE, DC, MC, V. $$–$$$$*

See Map 2 on p. 16.

Gregoriana (p. 23) SPANISH STEPS In an extensive 2004 remodel, this modish inn near the top of the Spanish Steps traded its William Morris florals and leopard prints for a sleeker, colder Art Deco look.... *Tel 06/679-42-69. Fax 06/678-42-58. www.hotel-gregoriana.it. Via Gregoriana 18, at Via Sistina, 00187. Metro Spagna or Barberini. 19 rooms. AE, DC, MC, V. $$$*

See Map 4 on p. 31.

Hassler Villa Medici (p. 24) SPANISH STEPS A government-rated five-star hotel in the fanciest part of town (atop the Spanish Steps). Rooms are small but incredibly luxurious, and service is discreet.... *Tel 06/699-340. Fax 06/678-99-91. www.hotel hasslerroma.com. Piazza Trinità dei Monti 6, 00187. Metro Spagna. 100 rooms. AE, DC, MC, V. $$$$$*

See Map 4 on p. 31.

Hilton Rome Airport (p. 29) FIUMICINO AIRPORT Massive, new 517-room hotel connected by covered overpass to Fiumicino Airport. Kids under 12 stay free.... *Tel 06/652-58. Fax 06/652-56-525. www.hilton.com/hotels/ROMAPTW. Via Arturo Ferrarin 2, 00050. 517 rooms. AE, DC, MC, V. $$$–$$$$*

See Map 2 on p. 16.

Hotel de Russie (p. 24) PIAZZA DEL POPOLO From its location right on Piazza del Popolo, to its simple but sophisticated decor, to its private Mediterranean-style terrace/garden, the Hotel de Russie has it all.... *Tel 06/328-881. Fax 06/328-88-888. www. roccofortehotels.com. Via del Babuino 9, at Piazza del Popolo, 00187. Metro Spagna, Flaminio. 125 rooms. AE, DC, MC, V. $$$$$*

See Map 4 on p. 31.

Hotel/Hostel des Artistes (p. 25) TERMINI Three brothers run this very nice, very informal hotel/hostel on the north side of Termini. Rooms are unique, modern, inexpensive, and completely nonsmoking. Breakfast is included only for the guest rooms with private bathrooms.... *Tel 06/445-43-65. Fax 06/446-23-68. www.hoteldesartistes.com. Via Villafranca 20, at Via Vicenza, 00185. Metro Castro Pretorio. 32 rooms. Some rooms have shared bathroom. AE, DC, MC, V. $–$$*

See Map 2 on p. 16.

Inghilterra (p. 24) SPANISH STEPS Henry James and Mark Twain slept here (though not together). This luxurious spot wins your heart with all the small details.... *Tel 06/699-811. Fax 06/6992-2243. http://hoteldinghilterra.warwickhotels.com. Via Bocca di Leone 14, at Via Borgognona, 00187. Metro Spagna. 98 rooms. AE, DC, MC, V. $$$$*

See Map 4 on p. 31.

La Lumière (p. 26) SPANISH STEPS This new boutique hotel features large, comfy rooms with all the modern amenities, including dataports and whirlpools. Priced very reasonably considering stratospheric rates at nearby hotels.... *Tel 06/693-80-806.*

Fax 06/692-94-231. www.lalumieredipiazzadispagna.com. Via Belsiana 72, at Via Condotti, 00187. Metro Spagna. 10 rooms. AE, DC, MC, V. $$$

See Map 4 on p. 31.

Locarno (p. 23) PIAZZA DEL POPOLO "Deluxe" double rooms in the east wing of this Art Nouveau inn have a Gatsby-esque glamour. The dark and cramped "standard" doubles in the main building are shabbier, but all guests have access to a small, attractive patio in the back.... *Tel 06/361-08-41. Fax 06/321-52-49. www.hotellocarno.com. Via della Penna 22, off Via Ripetta, 00186. Metro Flaminio. 48 rooms. AE, DC, MC, V. $$$*

See Map 4 on p. 31.

Lord Byron (p. 26) VILLA BORGHESE/PARIOLI Romantic, government-rated five-star getaway in leafy Parioli. The in-house restaurant, Sapori del Lord Byron, is one of the best tables in town.... *Tel 06/3220404. Fax 06/3220405. www.lordbyronhotel.com. Via Giuseppe de Notaris 5, opposite Villa Borghese, near Viale Bruno Buozzi, 00197. Bus 52. 32 rooms. AE, DC, MC, V. $$$–$$$$*

See Map 2 on p. 16.

Lunetta (p. 25) CAMPO DE' FIORI Nothing special about the rooms or amenities at this government-rated two-star, but the prime location makes it ideal for night owls on a budget.... *Tel 06/686-10-80. Fax 06/689-20-28. Piazza del Paradiso 68, at Via del Biscione, 00186. Buses 30, 40, 46, 62, 64, 70, 87, 116, 492, or 571. 40 rooms. AE, DC, MC, V. $$*

See Map 3 on p. 30.

Margutta (p. 26) PIAZZA DEL POPOLO Amazing bargain for this part of town, just down the street from Gregory Peck's apartment in *Roman Holiday*.... *Tel 06/322-3674. Fax 06/320-0395. www.hotelmargutta.it. Via Laurina 34, at Via Margutta, 00187. Metro Flaminio. 24 rooms. AE, DC, MC, V. $–$$*

See Map 4 on p. 31.

Navona (p. 25) PIAZZA NAVONA/PANTHEON Hard to believe this is only a government-rated one-star hotel. Keats and Shelley were once boarders on the upper floors, and ancient ruins are in the basement. The rooms are bright and spacious.... *Tel 06/686-42-03. Fax 06/688-03-802. www.hotelnavona.com. Via dei Sediari 8, off Corso Rinascimento, 00186. Buses 30, 40, 46, 62, 64, 70, 87, 116, 492, or 571. 21 rooms. Some rooms have shared bathroom. AE, DC, MC, V. $–$$*

See Map 3 on p. 30.

Oceania (p. 25) REPUBBLICA Handsome government-rated two-star with friendly service, near the Baroque churches of the Quirinale.... *Tel 06/482-46-96. Fax 06/488-55-86. www.hoteloceania.it. Via Firenze 38, at Via XX Settembre, 00184. Metro Repubblica. 9 rooms. AE, DC, MC, V. $–$$*

See Map 2 on p. 16.

Panda (p. 26) SPANISH STEPS Utilitarian with a barely perceptible hint of charm, this government-rated two-star's selling point is its value for location.... *Tel 06/678-0179. Fax 06/699-42151. www.hotelpanda.it. Via della Croce 35, at Via Belsiana, 00187. Metro Spagna. 28 rooms. AE, DC, MC, V. $–$$*

See Map 4 on p. 31.

Pomezia (p. 25) CAMPO DE' FIORI Basic government-rated two-star, perfect for the cheapskate who wants centralissimo lodging.... *Tel/fax 06/686-1371. hotelpomezia@libero.it. Via dei Chiavari 13, near Vicolo dei Chiodaroli, 00186. Buses 30, 40, 46, 62, 64, 70, 87, 116, 492, or 571. Tram 8. 25 rooms. No A/C. AE, DC, MC, V. $$*

See Map 3 on p. 30.

Ponte Sisto (p. 27) CAMPO DE' FIORI Fantastic midrange hotel has views of the Tiber River and Ponte Sisto and is within walking distance of Trastevere and the Ghetto. Surprisingly large bathrooms.... *Tel 06/686-311. Fax 06/686-31-801. www.hotelpontesisto.it. Via dei Pettinari 64, near Via Giulia, 00186. Buses 23, 271, or 280. Tram 8. 106 rooms. AE, DC, MC, V. $$$–$$$$*

See Map 3 on p. 30.

Raphaël (p. 26) PIAZZA NAVONA Romantic inside and out. An ivy-draped *palazzo* gives way to a gorgeous lobby filled with antiques.... *Tel 06/682-831. Fax 06/687-89-93. www.raphaelhotel.com. Largo Febo 2, at Via dell'Anima, 00186. Buses 30, 40, 46, 62, 64, 70, 87, 116, 492, or 571. 70 rooms. $$$$–$$$$$*

See Map 3 on p. 30.

Residenza Canali (p. 28) PIAZZA NAVONA Tiny but elegant inn with exposed wood beam ceilings, mosaic bathrooms, and an intimate terrace, just off Rome's main antiques strip.... *Tel 06/454-39-416. Fax 06/454-39-598. www.travel.it/roma/residenzacanali. Via dei Tre Archi 13, off Via dei Coronari, 00186. Buses 70, 81, 87, 280, or 492. 6 rooms. AE, MC, V. $$–$$$*

See Map 3 on p. 30.

Residenza Paolo VI (p. 27) VATICAN As close as laypeople can get to sleeping at the Vatican—snag a room at this pious government-rated three-star overlooking St. Peter's Square for the best view of beatifications, canonizations, and Sistine Chapel smoke puffs.... *Tel 06/684870. Fax 06/6867428. www.residenzapaolovi.com. Via Paolo VI 29, at Piazza San Pietro, 00193. 27 rooms. AE, DC, MC, V. $$$*

See Map 2 on p. 16.

Santa Maria (p. 29) TRASTEVERE One-story, chalet-style accommodations in hotel-starved Trastevere. Recently remodeled rooms are small but charming, arranged around a courtyard with orange trees.... *Tel 06/589-46-26. Fax 06/589-48-15. www.htlsantamaria.com. Vicolo del Piede 2, between Piazza Santa Maria* *in Trastevere and Via della Pelliccia, 00153. Buses 23, 271, or 280. Tram 8. 19 rooms. AE, DC, MC, V. $$$*

See Map 2 on p. 16.

Smeraldo (p. 25) CAMPO DE' FIORI Budget lodging, weak on character, strong on location.... *Tel 06/687-59-29. Fax 06/688-05-495. www.smeraldoroma.com. Vicolo dei Chiodaroli 9, at Via dei Chiavari, 00186. Buses 30, 40, 46, 62, 64, 70, 87, 116, 492, or 571. Tram 8. 50 rooms. AE, DC, MC, V. $$*

See Map 3 on p. 30.

Sole al Biscione (p. 25) CAMPO DE' FIORI Rooms are basic, but the central location can't be beat, and a fantastic multilevel interior garden is perfect for wine-sipping and postcard-writing. Popular with student groups, the Sole can also be noisy.... *Tel 06/688-06-873. Fax 06/689-37-87. www.solealbiscione.it. Via del Biscione 76, at Piazza del Paradiso, 00186. Buses 30, 40, 46, 62, 64, 70, 87, 116, 492, or 571. Tram 8. 60 rooms. No A/C. No credit cards. Some rooms have shared bathroom. $–$$*

See Map 3 on p. 30.

Sole al Pantheon (p. 26) PANTHEON In operation as an inn since the 15th century, the Sole al Pantheon is a quaint but fully modern government-rated four-star.... *Tel 06/678-04-41. Fax 06/69-94-06-89. www.hotelsolealpantheon.com. Piazza della Rotonda 63, at Via del Pantheon, 00186. Buses 30, 40, 64, 70, 87, 116, 492, or 571. 25 rooms. AE, DC, MC, V. $$$$–$$$$$*

See Map 3 on p. 30.

Spring House (p. 28) VATICAN A government-rated three-star with a modern look, near the Vatican Museums.... *Tel 06/397-20-948. Fax 06/397-21-047. www.springhousehotelrome.it. Via Mocenigo 7, at Via Candia, 00193. Metro Ottaviano. 35 rooms. $–$$$*

See Map 2 on p. 16.

St. George (p. 23) CAMPO DE' FIORI/VATICAN Formerly known as the Cardinal, an upscale, airy inn with Renaissance interiors and ancient ruins in the ground floor bar. Reopening in early 2006 after complete renovation.... *Tel 06/686611. Fax 06/68661230. www.stgeorgehotelrome.com. Via dei Bresciani 36, at Via Giulia, 00186. Buses 23, 40, 62, 64, 116, 271, or 280. 71 rooms. AE, DC, MC, V. $$$*

See Map 3 on p. 30.

Trastevere House (p. 29) TRASTEVERE On the quieter southern side of Trastevere, but still close to the action, this B&B has a cozy Mediterranean feel.... *Tel/fax 06/588-3774. http://trastevere house.hotel-roma.net. Vicolo del Buco 7, off Via della Luce, 00153. Buses 23, 271, or 280. Tram 8. 11 rooms. No A/C, no phone in rooms. AE, DC, MC, V. $–$$*

See Map 3 on p. 30.

Valadier (p. 26) PIAZZA DEL POPOLO/SPANISH STEPS Probably the only convent-turned-brothel-turned-hotel in Rome. An inn with a decor identity crisis but still sexy, the Valadier boasts a rooftop garden and a swank piano lounge.... *Tel 06/361-19-98. Fax 06/320-15-58. www.hotelvaladier.com. Via della Fontanella 15, at Via del Babuino, 00187. Metro Spagna. 48 rooms. AE, DC, MC, V. $$$–$$$$*

See Map 4 on p. 31.

Verona (p. 25) TERMINI This government-rated two-star has basic rooms and a lovely courtyard. Parking included.... *Tel 06/487-12-44. Fax 06/488-42-12. www.hotelverona-roma.com. Via Santa Maria Maggiore 154, at Via Cavour, 00184. Metro Termini. 33 rooms. AE, DC, MC, V. $$–$$$*

See Map 2 on p. 16.

Westin Excelsior (p. 24) VENETO The most ornate of the Via Veneto hotels, boasting scads of statues, wall-to-wall marble, and silk-paneled corridors.... *Tel 06/470-81. Fax 06/482-62-05. excelsior.hotelinroma.com. Via Veneto 125, at Via Boncompagni, 00187. Metro Barberini. Buses 52, 53, 63, 116, or 490. 327 rooms. AE, DC, MC, V. $$$$$*

See Map 4 on p. 31.

D I N

I N G

2

Map 5: Rome Dining Orientation

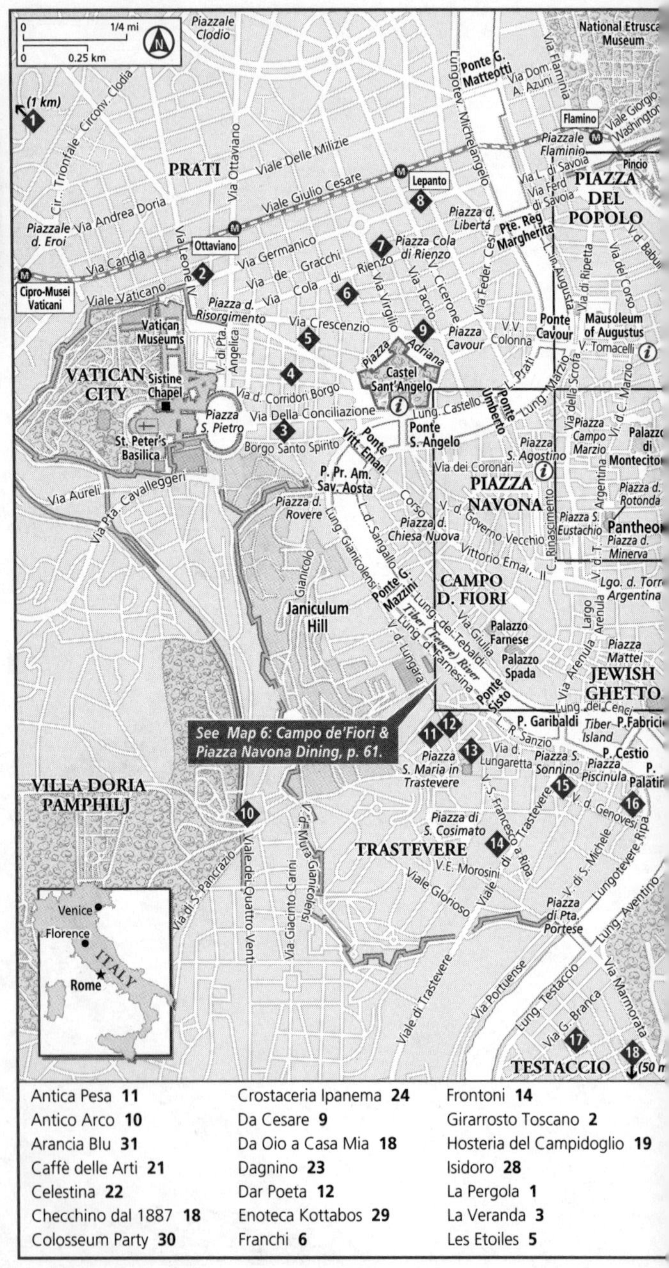

Antica Pesa **11**
Antico Arco **10**
Arancia Blu **31**
Caffè delle Arti **21**
Celestina **22**
Checchino dal 1887 **18**
Colosseum Party **30**
Crostaceria Ipanema **24**
Da Cesare **9**
Da Oio a Casa Mia **18**
Dagnino **23**
Dar Poeta **12**
Enoteca Kottabos **29**
Franchi **6**
Frontoni **14**
Girarrosto Toscano **2**
Hosteria del Campidoglio **19**
Isidoro **28**
La Pergola **1**
La Veranda **3**
Les Etoiles **5**

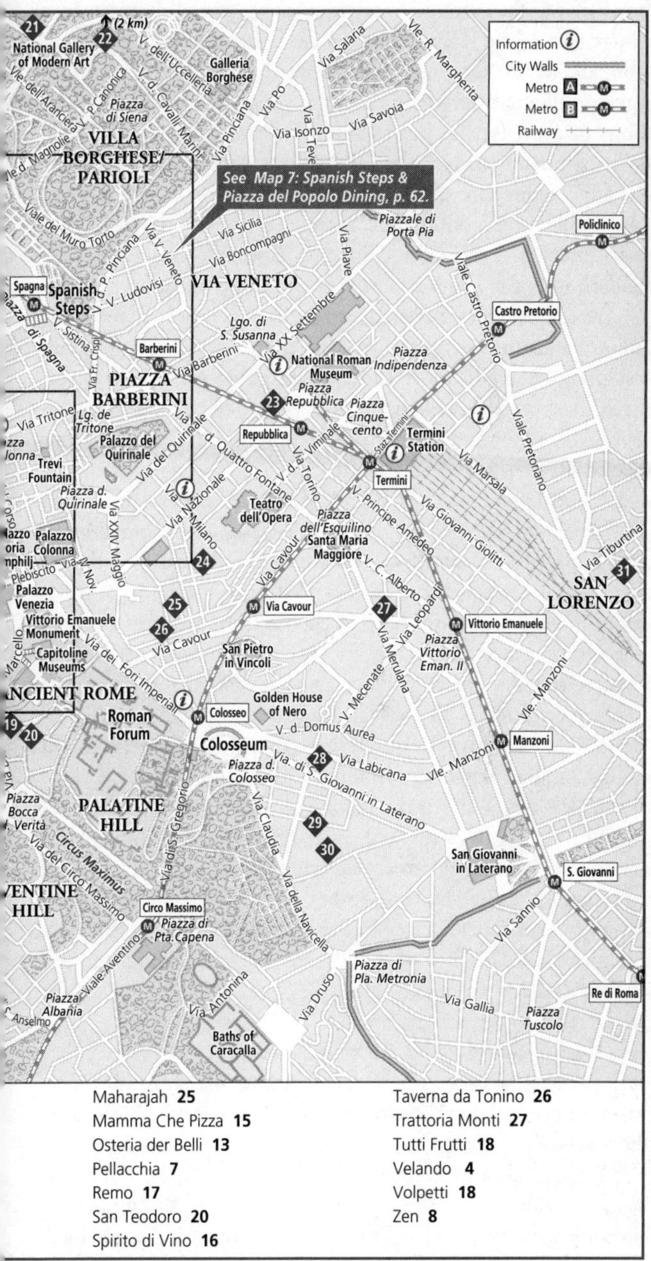

Maharajah 25
Mamma Che Pizza 15
Osteria der Belli 13
Pellacchia 7
Remo 17
San Teodoro 20
Spirito di Vino 16
Taverna da Tonino 26
Trattoria Monti 27
Tutti Frutti 18
Velando 4
Volpetti 18
Zen 8

Basic Stuff

It is banal in the extreme to say that eating and drinking out are a huge part of the Roman experience. This is the capital of Italy, after all, whose national pride is its culinary tradition. With three million natives who dine out at least twice a week and platoons of tourists who need to be fed year-round, Rome overflows with *ristoranti, osterie,* and *trattorie,* which can be fantastic but fairly redundant in terms of menu and atmosphere.

Somewhere around 2002, it seems that every young Roman restaurateur had the same epiphany: Give thy restaurant sleek, modern interiors and a fusion menu, and the masses will come. The result? A glut of over-designed dining rooms with overly ambitious culinary combinations. While not every modern restaurant succeeds, most Romans are ga-ga for this new aesthetic. And who can blame them? It used to be that every restaurant in Rome was called *"taverna"* this or *"antica"* that. Few strayed from the red-and-white-checked tablecloth canon of decor, and lights were too bright. Bills of fare were stubbornly provincial and identical all over town—spaghetti *alla carbonara,* roast lamb, grilled swordfish. You ate well, and inexpensively, but there wasn't a whole lot of variety. With this new crop of modern eateries, there's a bit more to choose from. But just a bit.

Don't expect a whole lot of international options in Rome—Italians are very fierce in their conviction that their culinary tradition is the best in the world, and what passes for "fusion" in this town is often something as "avant-garde" as adding Sicilian vegetables to a northern dish like polenta. Traditionalists who crossed the pond expressly for that classic Italian dining room with red-and-white-checked tablecloths needn't worry—old-guard *osterie,* where boisterous waiters serve up hearty, home-style, time-tested pasta and meat dishes, are still the norm. Luckily, too, this is a town where even the plebs are born rather blunt food critics. No one is shy about matter-of-factly stating *fa schifo* ("this is disgusting") if taste or texture are off, which keeps chefs honest.

If your idea of going out to dinner is scarfing down a plate of pasta, having a glass of wine, and getting the check all within 45 minutes, you're in the wrong town. Mealtime in Rome, as in the rest of Italy, isn't just about eating. It's an important social event, to be taken at a relaxed pace. That doesn't mean that you have to order five courses (one of the bigger myths about Italian dining customs)—Italians are capable of eating a salad and a lamb chop and still spending 5 hours at the table. Linger. Soak up the atmosphere (and the alcoholic *digestivo* they're sure to offer if they like you). Waiters will never pressure you to leave, even if there are 10 parties waiting for your table. And when you do ask for the check, prepare to wait about 20 minutes for them to actually bring it to you.

Now, about that check: Returning visitors will find that, thanks to the euro, Roman restaurants aren't quite the steal they used to be. Nonetheless, even with the weak dollar, Rome's quality dining is still a bargain compared with eating out in other major cities, especially considering the price of wine. Cheap labor keeps domestic *vino* inexpensive, so order some more of that Chianti Classico already—you're not driving!

Ristorante Etiquette 101

Exceptions are noted in "The Index," but Rome isn't really a reservations town—the idea being that eating well should be easy, not something you have to plan weeks in advance. If you want to reserve a table, calling at lunchtime the same day is usually sufficient. At most places, if you show up around 8:30pm, you'll probably be seated immediately. Arrive later, and you may have to wait 20 minutes or so. Whatever you do, do *not* show up at a Roman restaurant before 8pm—the dining room will be depressingly empty. Those accustomed to eating earlier can stave off hunger with an *aperitivo* (snack and drink) at some lovely little outdoor cafe around 6 or 7pm.

Bread *(pane)* is not free; it will show up on the bill at around 1€ to 2€ ($1.25–$2.50) per person, so if you're feeling carb-phobic or just cheap, intercept the waiter before he plops it down on the table. If you want some olive oil with your bread, simply ask for it. (Italians don't do this, but you won't be regarded as a freak if you do. You will, however, be regarded as a freak if you ask for butter.) Then they'll ask you what you want to drink—the standard combo is *vino* (of course!) and *acqua minerale* (mineral water): You can request *liscia* (still), *frizzante* (sparkling), or, locals' favorite compromise, *Ferrarelle* (this is a brand name but is also understood to mean water with just a touch of fizz). Do opt for the mineral water, as it does wonders for your digestion and helps regulate your *vino* intake. All but the simplest restaurants have some kind of wine list, but the *vino della casa* (house wine) is usually quite drinkable (and at 7€/$8.75 a liter, you can't really complain). If you like cocktails with your dinner, well, too bad; it's simply not done in Rome. Multilingual menus are everywhere, which is very helpful, although the translations can be pretty amusing (one Roman restaurant will bring you "creeps with ricotta and spinach" for 12€/$15). The typical Roman menu is divided into antipasti (appetizers—including bruschetta, pronounced "brusketta," not "brushetta"), *primi* (pasta or risotto), and *secondi* (meat or fish), with *contorni* (vegetables or salads) and *dolci* (desserts) tacked on the back pages. Mix and match as you wish—the old practice of ordering every course is passé, and Roman waiters in the third millennium are happy to accommodate your requests to have dishes brought in unorthodox order (salad before pasta, for example). At some point during your stay, be sure to try an antipasto of fresh *mozzarella di bufala* and prosciutto. It's as integral to your Roman experience as seeing the Sistine Chapel, and probably just as spiritually moving.

Only in Rome

Many classics of Italian cuisine—lasagna, eggplant *alla parmigiana*—are hard to find on Roman menus. Other staples of Italian-American cooking—spaghetti with meatballs, garlic bread—simply don't exist on this side of the Atlantic. What you will find on most menus are five or six traditional Roman pastas and meat dishes, simple creations fashioned out of the freshest ingredients. For the adventurous eater, many menus offer dishes that make use of the *quinto quarto*—scraps from the slaughterhouse floor or, if you will, hot dog ingredients. In the past, down-at-the-heel Romans had only these entrails to work with, so they created specialty dishes that still have a faithful following among locals. From the eyeball to the esophagus, right on down to the spleen, all organs are fair game. Be on the lookout for pasta *alla pajata* (red sauce with intestines from an unweaned calf—yep, mother's milk still inside), *coda alla vaccinara* (braised oxtail in *ragù,* or meat sauce), *trippa* (tripe), *animelle* (a medley of fried glands), and *coratella* (heart and who the hell knows what else). It sounds disgusting, but as long as you don't know what it is, you enjoy it immensely. (So, forget you read this section.)

Safely out of *quinto quarto* territory are such local pasta sauces as *amatriciana* (tomatoes, pecorino cheese, and pork jowl), carbonara (egg, pecorino, and pancetta), and *arrabbiata* ("angry," fresh tomatoes with garlic and cayenne pepper). Rome's time-honored Jewish cuisine includes deep-fried delicacies like *filetti di baccalà* (fried cod filets), *carciofi alla giudìa* (Jewish-style artichokes), and *fiori di zucca* (zucchini blossoms with mozzarella and sometimes anchovies). Classic Roman *secondi* (meat or fish entrees) include saltimbocca (veal scaloppine with sage and prosciutto), all manner of *maiale* (pork), *filetto di manzo* (beef filet), and grilled or baked sea bass, swordfish, bream, turbot, and calamari. Poultry is a rarity.

Vegetarians will have no trouble eating well in Rome. Every day, chefs from around the city raid the outdoor markets for eggplant, artichokes, asparagus, tomatoes, porcini, zucchini, and more, all of which inevitably wind up as *contorni* (vegetable side dishes) or as the focus of a pasta or risotto dish. Meat-free *primi,* such as *tonnarelli cacio e pepe* (pasta with sheep's cheese and pepper) or even a simple spaghetti *al pomodoro* (with a tomato and basil sauce) are extremely common, even at the priciest establishments. Kids, upset stomachs, and other fussy eaters can always ask for pasta *in bianco* (with a mild but tasty sauce of butter or olive oil and *parmigiano*).

When to Eat—& Drink

Prima colazione (breakfast) is usually just a cappuccino and a *cornetto* (a croissant or jam-filled pastry that may taste really good or, equally often, like cardboard), which can be taken up until 11am; the single easiest way to quickly identify yourself as a tourist in Rome is to order a cappuccino any time after noon. For Italians, coffee drinks with a lot of milk are for breakfast only—not as a late-day treat, and most certainly not for after-dinner. Sure, the *barista* will serve you one whenever you like, but that doesn't mean he'll approve of your bizarre lifestyle choices. More common in the afternoon is a simple *caffè* (a shot of espresso) or a *macchiato*—espresso with a splash of steamed milk. In the summer, most bars have mass quantities of presweetened *caffè freddo* (iced espresso) on hand, a great way to cool down and jolt up at the same time. Lunch starts at around 12:30pm and can often last until 3:30pm. Because breakfast is so small, lunch is traditionally the main meal of the day, although more and more Romans are taking lunch on the go. (Even so, many shops will be closed 2–4pm.) If you've got a busy sightseeing itinerary and don't want to stop for a sit-down meal, any *alimentari* (grocery/deli) will make sandwiches on the spot. When in Rome, you'll want to make the *aperitivo* hour (snacks and wine or cocktails at a bar or cafe, around 6:30pm; see the Nightlife chapter) part of your daily schedule—it's a great way to unwind and meet people. Romans don't start showing up for dinner until after 8:30pm, and most restaurants will seat diners until 10:30pm (and *pizzerie* will take you even later). Note that very few Roman restaurants, unlike their counterparts in other world cities, have a bar area where you can just come and have a drink either before or totally separate from your meal—that's what the *aperitivo* is for.

The Lowdown

Starbucks could learn a thing or two... An essential part of Italian culture, coffee bars are a dime a dozen in Rome. Romans stop in at the "bar" all the time, as much for the caffeine as for the chance to socialize and rehash the previous day's soccer results. Wherever you go, the coffee is nearly always great and always espresso bean–based. If you ask for a *caffè americano,* it won't taste like what you're used to at home—it'll just be espresso with more water. And don't even think of brandishing any of that offensive Starbucks-ese—words like "nonfat" and "soy" will only draw blank stares, and if you ask for a *latte,* you'll just get a glass of milk. (*Caffellatte* is the proper name of the coffee drink.) Locals, however, pretty much stick to the classics, starting the day with a cappuccino and taking several more breaks for *caffè* (espresso) throughout the day. Coffee at the bar is served in ceramic cups with saucers and taken standing up. To-go orders—not this country's forte—are put in non-heat-resistant plastic cups with improvised lids. Prices are fairly consistent throughout town—.50€ (65¢) for a *caffè* and .65€ (81¢) for a cappuccino, though prices go up in the thickest tourist areas and double if you want to take your coffee sitting down. One of the most important features in a Roman bar is the omnipresent mirror behind the counter—do as the Romans do and check out your look before flirting with that cute *barista,* and always tip .10€ to .15€ (13¢–19¢) when placing your order. Around the corner from the Pantheon, **Sant'Eustachio**'s presweetened *gran caffè* attracts locals from early morning to the wee hours. The northeast side of Piazza della Rotonda also boasts **Tazza D'Oro,** a larger coffee bar, where to-die-for *granita di caffè* (an espresso slush with layers of thick whipped cream) is slung by surly *baristi.* While Sant'Eustachio and Tazza d'Oro are justifiably famous in Rome, you'll find a much friendlier, community feel at any of the local bars on Rome's less-touristed sidestreets. Unless you're a regular (or can act like one), ingratiate yourself at the Roman bar by paying for your coffee before you order it.

Local heroes... Lodged against Monte Testaccio, across the square from a former slaughterhouse, **Checchino dal 1887** is Rome's quintessential *quinto quarto* restaurant—*the* place to go if you want to splurge on a traditional Roman meal. The menu is strong on specialties like *rigatoni con pajata* (veal intestines engorged with cow's milk) and *coda alla vaccinara* (oxtail), but there are also plenty of non-offal dishes to choose from. The paparazzi love to loiter around the outdoor tables at **I Due Ladroni (The Two Thieves),** the eternally *in* spot for show biz types, where grey-haired film producers and TV hosts come to flaunt their 20-something actress girlfriends. Entertaining clientele aside, the classy but casual restaurant serves up top-notch, unfussy Italian fare, and service is charming and professional. An under-the-radar favorite is **Matricianella,** a trusty trat near the Pantheon with a homey dining room, classic Roman cuisine, and a strong cult of devotees. A bit out of the way, on the Gianicolo hill above Trastevere, **Antico Arco** is the darling of many a guidebook writer but still an excellent choice when you want to spend a little more for all-around dining pleasure. Rounding out the field is **Dal Bolognese,** where jaded hotel concierges have been sending well-heeled Americans since time immemorial. Its location on elegant Piazza del Popolo, and cuisine from the Emilia-Romagna region (including lasagna, unusual in Rome), are hard not to like, but the steady flow of the luxury hotel set has left the restaurant a little soulless.

Hip, trendy—and the food's good, too... The **'Gusto** gourmet triumvirate occupies an imposing, Fascist-era building on the northern side of Piazza Augusto Imperatore. 'Gusto itself is a restaurant and pizzeria (two different dining rooms with two different menus) in a buzzy, soaring space slightly reminiscent of high school wood shop, with blocky, unfinished wooden tables, white paper table liners, and industrial-looking ducts overhead. Black-clad staff is friendly (and much better looking than most customers), and there's a ton to choose from on the reasonably priced pizzeria menu; the restaurant menu is more expensive and eclectic. Attached to the back of 'Gusto is a small, always lively wine bar; adjacent is **Osteria della Frezza,** a wine-and-cheese cafe/bistro kind of place where drinks can easily turn into dinner. The *osteria* has a sit-down dining room, but the front room, with its checkered floors and club chairs, is where all the action is. Settle in with a big glass of Barolo and sample one of the hundred-plus cheeses from their *"formaggeria"* menu, nibble on *cicchetti* (tapas-style samplings of their pasta, veggie, and meat dishes), or order full-sized *primi* and *secondi.* A 19th-century throwback, **Fiaschetteria Beltramme** draws quite a few celebs; there's no phone number, so be prepared to queue, but the trendy vibe and the mouthwatering food—hearty classics like *tonnarelli cacio e pepe*—are well worth the wait. Not far from Termini, family-run **Trattoria Monti** is an intimate, beguiling blend of contemporary style and hearty cuisine from the Marche region. Before setting off on an all-nighter in the *centro,* the young, see-and-be-seen crowd meets up at affordable **Maccheroni** for great pasta, Argentine-style steak, and occasional live music. When those same hipsters have a hot date, they reserve a table at romantic **Il Bacaro,** on the same square. If the paparazzi are chasing you around again, do as celebs do and duck into the courtyard of the **Hotel de Russie** (see the Accommodations chapter) for lunch or an *aperitivo.* If a sandwich and a beer or glass of wine at lunch are all you're after, you can't beat the garlicky pizza bread panini at **Taverna del Campo,** in the midst of all the market activity at Campo de' Fiori. Bring your oversized sunglasses and plenty of attitude.

Modern grub... One of the more unique and successful creations to be spawned by Rome's modern restaurant craze is **Obikà,** an innovative "mozzarella bar" near the Pantheon. Sleek design touches are warmed by exposed red brick and some antiqued columns, and you can feast till the cows—or buffalos—come home on endless permutations of the freshest, highest quality mozzarella, paired with cured meats and vegetables. Near Campo de' Fiori, **Crudo** takes its name and eponymous ethos ("raw") a bit too seriously, staunchly refusing to cook anything. But the striking space—a vast salon with unfinished cement walls and floors, 1960s furniture upholstered in white and red leather, and a huge mural of a snarling wolf—is always packed with Roman scenesters noshing on oysters (and, of course, anything with wasabi). For modern Euro-fabulousness, check out **Supperclub,** a spinoff of the original joint in Amsterdam. Its white interiors strike quite a contrast with its prime location near the 1,900-year-old Pantheon—but just like the ancient Romans, here you eat lying down, get a massage, and listen to great music (only nowadays of the chill-out variety; no lyre-strumming).

Dining alfresco... Just about every restaurant in Rome spills out onto a sidewalk or square in warm weather. As far as charm is concerned, your best bet for an alfresco experience is in the *centro storico* or Trastevere. In an ivy-draped piazza near Piazza Navona, **Santa Lucia** counts Sophia Loren as a regular, but who wouldn't feel glamorous dining on Neapolitan specialties in such a setting? Nearby, the lovely little trattoria **Osteria del Gallo** is perfect for languorous lunching—try their unique ravioli with *porcini* and shrimp sauce. The clientele at **Pierluigi** isn't getting any younger, but the chef still has his taste buds. Try the amazing *soppressata di polipo* (octopus "*salame*") or the *tagliata di manzo* (tender beef strips with arugula). Patrons at the outdoor tables pretty much have the piazza to themselves, and what's more, one of the waiters thinks he's Elvis. A worthy detour from the restaurant zone, **San Teodoro** has excellent seafood dishes (and somewhat dubious '80s interior decor); if you go, be sure to eat outside—its quiet location above the Forum makes this an especially memorable spot for an evening meal. (**Hosteria del Campidoglio,** a few doors down, has the better real estate, with more jaw-dropping views of the Capitoline and Forum from its alfresco tables, but the food isn't as imaginative or as consistently good.) People go to lunch at **Caffè delle Arti,** at the national modern art gallery, more for the setting—right in the heart of Villa Borghese—than for the food, but the salads are praiseworthy. A no-frills favorite on Rome's busiest pedestrian square (Campo de' Fiori), **Hostaria Romanesca** does a gloriously juicy *pollo ai peperoni* (stewed chicken with peppers).

When the moon hits your eye like a big pizza pie... Pizza abounds in Rome and makes for some of the best-value informal dining in town. In fact, this staple of Italian cuisine is such an important part of Roman culture that many natives cannot say the word "pizza" without miming the shape of a dinner plate with their hands—which can spell trouble if they happen to be driving and talking on the cellphone at the same time. If you're on the go and need to grab a quick bite, look for one of the many good-value *pizza al taglio* establishments around the city—often the only option for late-afternoon eats, since all other normal restaurants will be closed. The dough at these snack-bar-style places is thicker than it would be in a round Roman pie, but beware those cost-cutting proprietors who use animal lard *(strutto)* instead of olive oil (ingredient lists are posted by law behind the counter). For the good stuff, with great toppings, check out **Mamma Che Pizza,** a pizza-by-the-slice joint in Trastevere, where the pizza always comes fresh from the oven instead of sitting for hours while the fat from the mozzarella congeals. Inventive toppings include provolone with truffles. (And, in case you still question their cred, the walls are adorned with framed certificates from pizza-making competitions.) Traditional round pizza in Rome is taken sitting down and after 8pm (though a few places that cater to American tourists serve it at lunch). Do know that, in terms of tastiness, not all pizza in Rome is created equal, but it's all priced about the same—6€ to 8€ ($7.50–$10) for a 10-inch pie. Also in Trastevere, eternally packed **Dar Poeta** (sit-down, dinner only) is hard to find, but worth your perseverance. In fact, why every pizzeria in the city hasn't sent spies to infiltrate the kitchen here and get the secret recipe is still a mystery (maybe they can't find the place). Get here at 8pm sharp or be prepared to wait up to an hour for a table. Back across the river, right in the heart of the *centro storico,* is the equally popular **Pizzeria La Montecarlo,** where it always feels like a party. The crowds waiting outside may seem daunting, but the cheerful, green-shirted staff is amazingly efficient at getting parties seated. North of the center, in snooty Parioli, **Celestina** is a stylish but down-to-earth pizzeria where soccer player and celebrity sightings are frequent (not that you'd recognize the weatherman from RAI UNO, though). Spit-and-sawdust **Remo** is the pizzeria of choice for the salt-of-the-earth Romans of Testaccio. Go to **PizzaRé,** near Piazza del Popolo, for good old Naples-style (thick-crusted) pizza; stay for the air-conditioning.

Favorite enotecas... Wine bars have experienced a boom in recent years—and for good reason: Who doesn't love to sit and sip a host of local and regional wines by the glass or bottle while enjoying the best antipasti Italy has to offer? Intimate and lively **Cul de Sac,** just off Piazza Navona, has simple wooden booths, shelves displaying the enoteca's overwhelming variety of wines (offered by the glass or bottle), and winking waiters. Snack or build a full meal from its extensive a la carte menu, with everything from escargot to onion soup to cheeses you've never heard of. On the ground floor of a 16th-century *palazzo* just east of the Pantheon is **Casa Bleve,** the latest venture by Roman wine guru Anacleto Bleve. With vaulted ceilings, terra-cotta floors, marble statues, and a gluttonous spread of gourmet delights, the place has the look and feel of a Renaissance buffet. A haven for weary shoppers near the Spanish Steps, the always-chic **Enoteca Antica di Via della Croce** serves wine by the glass and plates of meats, olives, and cheeses at its long, dark bar. (Settling the bill here is an honor-based affair: Each order is scribbled on a yellow Post-It and handed to you, and you—who may well be drinking heavily—are trusted to keep track of these and present them all at the cashier window near the door when you leave.) **Enoteca Kottabos,** a cavernous space with exposed brick arches and vaulted terra-cotta ceilings, takes its name from a gas of an ancient drinking game—like jai alai with liquid, *kottabos* players would fling wine across the room and try to catch it in their chalices. That the enoteca does not permit the playing of this game is a bit of a buzzkill. And for those times when you just want a wine bar where you can drink and get loose without those fancy plates of aged Parmigiano-Reggiano interfering, try the **Vineria** (see the Nightlife chapter) or **Taverna del Campo.**

Chowin' down near the Colosseum... Tourist traps with an overpriced *menu turistico* and questionable street-vendor fare plague the food scene in the immediate environs of the Colosseum and Forum, but you don't have to wander too far to get to some much better places. Popular with priests and gluttonous locals, **Taverna da Tonino** serves up succulent roast lamb and other savory *secondi*—at dinner only—at really low prices. The dining room is small, and they don't take bookings, so come early. At pasta heaven **Isidoro,** you'll need several stomachs to enjoy the full delights of the *assaggini misti* (pasta tasting menu). Despite its proximity to the ruins, the scene is mostly locals. Longing to relive the banquets of Roman imperial times? **Colosseum Party** is an ancient Roman-themed cabaret, complete with prancing palace concubines, sparring gladiators, amphitheater seating, and precious marbles. It is, for the most part, a poor man's Caesar's Palace, with one major advantage over the Vegas casino—Caesar might have actually set foot here.

Taking a bite out of Trastevere... As more and more foreigners discover the area and descend on its myriad restaurants, Trastevere by night has lost much of its neighborhood atmosphere, but you can still find great eats here, as well as oodles of charm. On one of the liveliest little squares in the area, the inexpensive **Osteria der Belli** gets it right every time with its garlicky sauté of clams and mussels, spaghetti *alla pescatora* (a tomato and garlic sauce with little marine friends mixed in), and all manner of grilled fish. Adding to the festive atmosphere, a motley crew of boozy locals flocks here on weekends. On the quieter southern side of the neighborhood, family-run **Spirito di Vino** is located in a refitted medieval synagogue, with a menu of traditional and ancient Roman specialties—try the *maiale alla mazio,* a favorite pork dish of Julius Caesar's. On the road leading up to the Gianicolo hill, **Antica Pesa (The Old Weigh Station)** is a casually upscale place (and largely undiscovered) with excellent pastas and seafood and a delightful back garden, a former bocce court.

Vatican vittles... Visiting the Vatican can leave you with a powerful hunger, but it can be hard to find restaurants here whose raison d'être *isn't* ripping off unwitting tourists. When they're not cooped up in the Sistine Chapel conclave, visiting cardinals enjoy the heavenly offerings (from vintage Roman to creative international) at the Hotel Columbus's **La Veranda**—the frescoed dining room and beautiful courtyard don't hurt, either. **Da Cesare** is a quiet Tuscan place that contrasts nicely with the crowds at St Peter's. The *prezzo fisso* tasting menus include generous *primi, secondi,* and desserts, and are cheaper than going a la carte. In the medieval Borgo neighborhood, **Velando** serves up affordable gourmet for pilgrims lucky enough to find it. Meat lovers can follow their noses to the scent of sizzling steaks and roasting pork at the **Girarrosto Toscano,** a favorite of carnivores citywide.

Testaccio: Hardware shops and trendy bôites... Working-class Testaccio, just south of the main tourist sights, is one of the most authentic parts of Rome. Testaccio's "strip" is Via Galvani, where numerous eating options, ranging from the traditional to the trendy, mix and mingle with mechanics' shops and grazing goats. One of Rome's top restaurants, **Checchino dal 1887** (see "Local heroes," earlier in this chapter), is at the southern end of the street, across from the old slaughterhouse. At the northern end of Via Galvani, **Da Oio a Casa Mia** keeps it real with no-nonsense *cucina romana* (read: they do a mean fried esophagus and have no time for squeamish tourists). Just around the corner, **Tutti Frutti** is a happening southern Italian spot with tasty *pizzelle* and a young, energetic staff. **Remo** is Testaccio's best and liveliest pizzeria, with rickety tables and plenty of colorful old-timers.

Gone fishin'... Mediterranean fish has a delicacy of flavor that doesn't require any fancy dressing. In Rome, most seafood is prepared in the simplest manner possible, with a squeeze of lemon, a hint of garlic or parsley, and maybe some olive oil. *Ahhh,* pair it with a nice Falanghina and it's heaven—even the seafood-shy can't help but fall in love. Seafood lovers holding platinum cards should head for the Pantheon, where **La Rosetta** (old guard) and **Quinzi e Gabrieli** (more progressive) duke it out for the title of best splurge-worthy fish restaurant in Rome. Run by the people at La Rosetta, nearby **Riccioli Cafe** is part cocktail lounge, part oyster bar, and much more affordable. With an entry that looks like the back room of a fish market and interiors of deep red and blue that recall the paint job on many an Italian fishing boat, **Hosteria del Pesce** is certainly a stylish spot for seafood. The *bis* or *tris di pasta* (small portions of two or three kinds of seafood-based pasta) is a delicious bargain, but beware the 110€ ($138) turbot!—charges for some entrees will bite you like a piranha if you aren't careful to check the weight of the fish. For pure, unadulterated, raw shellfish and crustaceans, head for the bamboo-walled dining room of **Crostaceria Ipanema.** Most fish in Rome doesn't come cheap, but **Osteria der Belli,** in Trastevere, has awesome grilled fish and seafood pastas at bargain prices.

Dishes your Jewish grandma would be proud of... Spend some time in Rome, and you'll learn that there's more to Jewish cuisine than gefilte fish and matzo balls. (However, while most restaurants in the Ghetto adhere to Jewish cooking practices, kosher kitchens are not the norm.) In the shadow of the ruins of the 1st-century B.C. Porticus of Octavia, **Da Giggetto** excites cries of "Jaaared, would you look at those aah-tichokes?" from passersby in the Jewish Ghetto. Giggetto's *carciofi alla giudia* (fried artichokes) and *coda alla vaccinara* (oxtail stew) are indeed some of the best in town, but service can be painfully disorganized. Upscale **Piperno** serves a knockout *fritto misto* (fried fish and vegetables) and a time-tested *trippa,* but it's often packed with as many tourists as locals. Dar Filettaro di Santa Barbara, known to most as **Filetti di Baccalà** after the sign/menu above the door, is a one-trick pony that serves fried and salted codfish to hungry patrons at its indoor/outdoor picnic tables. Just remember to book your bypass surgery before you go.

Food with a view... If you'd rather forsake local flavor for a dazzling view and an astronomical bill, then you'll love rooftop dining in Rome. The greatest gourmet experience in Rome happens to be at the rooftop **La Pergola,** at the Cavalieri Hilton. Chef Heinz Beck's sublime Mediterranean fare consistently gets a three-star Michelin rating, and if the food and wine—chosen by champion sommelier Marco Reitano—don't make you swoon, the view from Monte Mario, over the lights of central Rome, surely will. **Les Etoiles,** perched atop the Hotel Atlante Star, has five-star meals and five-star prices, and an impossibly dramatic view of St. Peter's—the dome looms so close, you feel as if you could reach out and touch it.

Where to go when you're sick of pasta... There's no harm in taking a break from Italian food every now and then. But just remember, international cuisine is *not* Rome's forte. Japanese is your best bet, and sushi fans will flip for **Hamasei,** where the raw preparations and *shabu-shabu* are out of this world. A welcome addition to the Vatican area, **Zen** is a Japanese joint with minimalist, lacquered interiors and a sushi conveyor belt. Scents wafting out of the kitchen of **Thien Kim,** a small Vietnamese restaurant on Via Giulia, tempt passersby on the route between Trastevere and Campo de' Fiori. For samosas, chutneys, and delicious curries, **Maharajah,** near the Forum, has jolly waitstaff attired in traditional Indian garb (and a saucy hostess who will decide your order for you if you hesitate). Tourists frightened by the real Rome seek asylum at the **Hard Rock Cafe,** on Via Veneto.

Eat your greens... **Il Margutta** was the first vegetarian restaurant in Rome and continues to be one of the most popular—largely due to its avant-garde decor (such as Louis XIV chairs bolted to the walls overhead) and health-conscious recipes like pasta with grilled veggies and all sorts of fresh-squeezed juices. (In addition to its original Via Margutta spot, there are two other locations.) Wildly popular at lunch or dinner, **Insalata Ricca** has more than 30 enormous salads, with ingredients like avocado, lobster meat, or buffalo mozzarella. The Largo dei Chiavari flagship is far and away the best of the chain's twelve locations citywide. Vegetarian **Arancia Blu,** in the revitalized student quarter of San Lorenzo, serves a tantalizing assortment of meat-free *primi* and *secondi* like pasta with *pecorino* (sheep's milk cheese) and truffles.

Snacks on the go... For the Type-A tourist who prefers to eat on the run, Vatican-area **Franchi** and Testaccio's **Volpetti** are famous for their cheeses and meats, but they lack one major ingredient for the delicious Italian sandwich panini: bread. So, pick from among their many hot selections, available at lunchtime. Franchi's 1€ ($1.25) *supplì'* (a fried ball of rice, mozzarella, and tomato sauce) is famous citywide. **Frontoni** in Trastevere is known for its generous, made-to-order pizza-bread sandwiches, stuffed with everything from mortadella to grilled zucchini. With its prime location in front of the Trevi Fountain, **L'Antico Forno** could easily fleece its customers; instead, the corner deli/grocer has stayed honest, selling all kinds of fresh, cellophane-wrapped panini (about 2€/$2.50 a piece) to starved sightseers. Otherwise, every single bar in the city has pre-made *tramezzini* (half-sandwiches on white bread)—not the most exciting option, but handy when you just need something in your stomach fast.

Frozen treats... Like a laboratory of gelato-making, **San Crispino** is a white-jacket kind of place where cones are regarded as frivolous and déclassé—this ice cream is served in cups only. Concoctions made of everything from Armagnac (a brandy blend) to standards like *stracciatella* (vanilla with chocolate chips) are considered by some aficionados to be the best in the world. **Blue Ice,** a stroll away from Campo de' Fiori, lacks San Crispino's name recognition but still serves up some of the largest, creamiest scoops of gelato you've ever seen. A veteran of the *centro storico* pedestrian circuit, **Giolitti** is gelato for the old guard, offering flavors made from After Eight chocolate and Grand Marnier. Vatican visitors in the know go to **Pellacchia** for a post-papal frozen treat. For refreshing fruit shakes, Navona-area **Da Quinto** doesn't skimp—3.30€ ($4.15) gets you an entire blender full of whatever fruit you want, plus milk and sugar or honey. If flavored ice is your bag, look for a *grattachecca* kiosk, open from May to September along the Tiber.

Just desserts... When Romans need a birthday cake, they make a beeline for **Vanni Café,** a *pasticceria* and caterer in the *centro storico* revered for its rich cakes, tarts, and *crostate* (a sort of dry cheesecake). For Sicilian-style *dolci,* head to the Galleria Esedra (Repubblica), where you'll find **Dagnino** tucked among faceless discount shops and seedy bars. Cannoli and other Trinacrian treats are all here.

Map 6: Campo De' Fiori & Piazza Navona Dining

Map 7: Spanish Steps & Piazza Del Popolo Dining

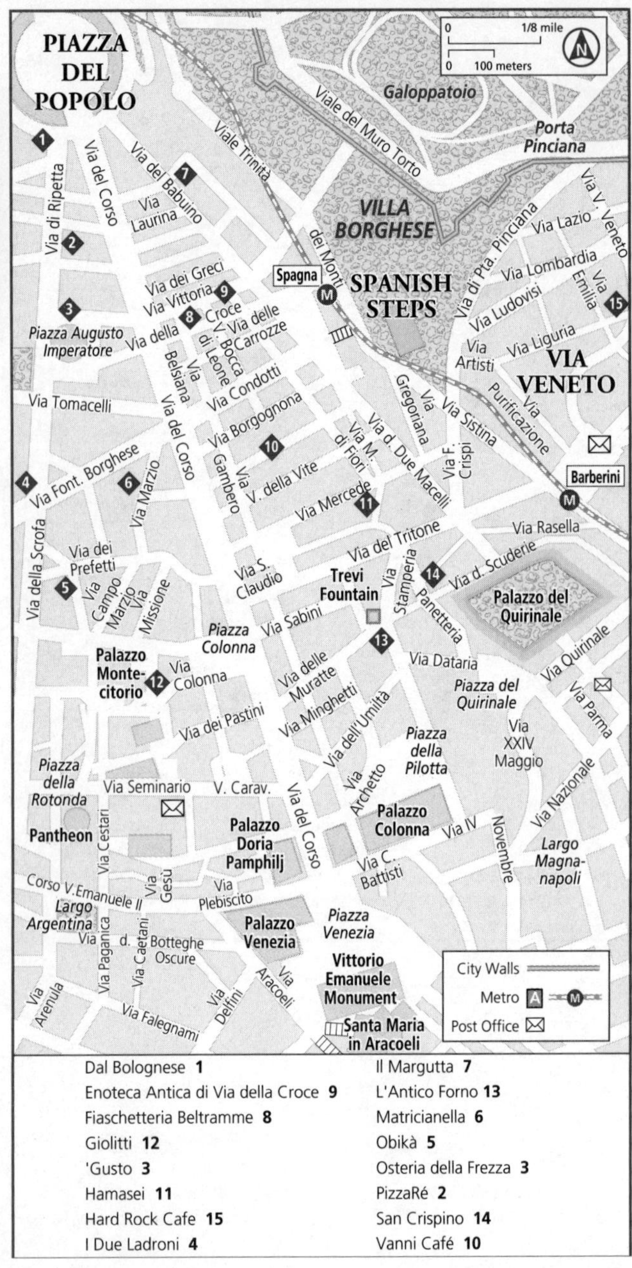

The Index

$$$$$	55€ and up
$$$$	35€–55€
$$$	20€–35€
$$	10€–20€
$	10€ and under

Prices given are per person for entrees only.

Note: 1€ = US$1.25.

The following abbreviations are used for credit cards:

AE	American Express
DC	Diners Club
DISC	Discover
MC	MasterCard
V	Visa

Antica Pesa (p. 56) TRASTEVERE *ROMAN* Dine alongside sophisticated Romans at this largely undiscovered treasure on the way up to the Gianicolo.... *Tel 06/580-9236. Via Garibaldi 18, at Via del Mattonato. Buses 23, 271, or 280. Reservations recommended. AE, DC, MC, V. Dinner Mon–Sat. $$$–$$$$*

See Map 5 on p. 44.

Antico Arco (p. 51) GIANICOLO/WESTERN SUBURBS *CREATIVE ITALIAN* Modern decor and all-around dining pleasure just above Trastevere. Well-known to tourists despite its somewhat remote location.... *Tel 06/581-5274. Piazzale Aurelio 7, at Porta San Pancrazio. Buses 44, 75, or 870. Reservations essential. AE, DC, MC, V. Dinner Mon–Sat. Closed Aug. $$$$*

See Map 5 on p. 44.

Arancia Blu (p. 59) SAN LORENZO *VEGETARIAN* Vegetarian restaurant off the beaten path. Actually a social club, so you'll need to fill out a (free) membership card before dining.... *Tel 06/445-41-05. Via dei Latini 65, at Via dei Sabelli. Buses 11, 71, or 492. No credit cards. Lunch Sun only; dinner daily. $$*

See Map 5 on p. 44.

Blue Ice Gelateria (p. 59) CENTRO STORICO *GELATO* Roman gelato chain with six locations. Also has soy gelato, frozen yogurt, and granita.... *Tel 06/687-61-14. Via dei Baullari 141, at Piazza della Cancelleria. Buses 40, 46, 62, 64, 70, 81, 87, 116, 492, 571, or 628. No credit cards. Open daily. $*

See Map 6 on p. 61.

Caffè delle Arti (p. 53) VILLA BORGHESE *CONTINENTAL* The restaurant and bar attract as many customers as does the adjacent modern art museum. The bar is good for a beer and snacks after a long museum tour, and the terrace really gets going on summer evenings.... *Tel 06/326-51-236. Via Gramsci 73–75, off Viale delle Belle Arti. Tram 3 or 19. AE, DC, MC, V. Lunch daily; dinner Tues–Sun. $–$$$*

See Map 5 on p. 44.

Casa Bleve (p. 55) CENTRO STORICO *WINE BAR* Enoteca with nightly tastings and a generous buffet of salads, cheeses, and meats. Private mini-cellars are rented out to locals.... *Tel 06/686-59-70. www.casableve.it. Via del Teatro Valle 48–49, off Corso Vittorio Emanuele II. Buses 30, 40, 46, 62, 64, 70, 81, 87, 116, 492, 571, or 628. Tram 8. AE, DC, MC, V. Lunch Mon–Sat; dinner Thurs–Sat. $–$$$*

See Map 6 on p. 61.

Celestina (p. 54) PARIOLI *PIZZA/ITALIAN* Mix with celebs and northern Rome's *bella gente* (beautiful people) at this pizzeria with a friendly and vibrant atmosphere.... *Tel 06/807-8242. Viale Parioli 184, near Piazzale della Rimembranza. Buses 52 or 53. AE, DC, MC, V. Lunch and dinner daily. $$*

See Map 5 on p. 44.

Checchino dal 1887 (p. 51) TESTACCIO *ROMAN* Rome's premier offal restaurant, yet paradoxically an elegant dining experience. Appropriately, it's right across from a former abattoir.... *Tel 06/574-63-18. Via di Monte Testaccio 30, at Via Galvani. Metro Piramide. Buses 23, 95, 170, or 280. Tram 3. Reservations essential. AE, DC, MC, V. Dinner Tues–Sat. $$$$–$$$$$*

See Map 5 on p. 44.

Colosseum Party (p. 55) COLOSSEUM *ANCIENT ROMAN/NOVELTY* Gladiator-themed cabaret—cheesy as hell but can be fun if you're in the right mood.... *Tel 06/700-8325. www.colosseumparty.com. Via dei SS Quattro 34–35, between Via dei Querceti and Via S. Stefano Rotondo. Metro Colosseo or San Giovanni. Buses 60, 75, 85, 87, or 175. Tram 3. AE, DC, MC, V. Open daily. $$$*

See Map 5 on p. 44.

Crostaceria Ipanema (p. 57) MONTI *SEAFOOD* Artful towers of raw crustaceans and shellfish in a bamboo-walled dining room.... *Tel 06/482-4758. Via Capocci 26, at Via Panisperna. Metro Cavour. No credit cards. Dinner daily. $$$*

See Map 5 on p. 44.

Crudo (p. 52) CAMPO DE' FIORI *FUSION/RAW* Artsy, garagelike salon with sushi and carpaccio brings a bit of the New York or London scene to Rome.... *Tel 06/683-8989. www.crudoroma.it. Via degli Specchi 6, at Via Monte di Farina. Buses 30, 40, 46, 62, 64, 70, 87, 116, 492, or 571. Tram 8. AE, DC, MC, V.* Aperitivi *and dinner daily. $$–$$$*

See Map 6 on p. 61.

Cul de Sac (p. 54) CENTRO STORICO *WINE BAR* This popular enoteca is a favorite of just about everyone in the city. Remarkably good hors d'oeuvres, *primi* at reasonable prices, and an overwhelming variety of wines by the glass or bottle.... *Tel 06/688-01-094. Piazza Pasquino 73, at Via di San Pantaleo. Buses 40 Express, 62, 64, 70, 81, 87, 492, or 628. MC, V. Lunch Tues–Sun; dinner daily. $$–$$$*

See Map 6 on p. 61.

Da Cesare (p. 56) VATICAN *TUSCAN* Tuscan menus of two courses, dessert, and wine—a lunchtime bargain.... *Tel 06/686-19-12. Via Crescenzio 13, at Via Orazio. Metro Ottaviano. Lunch daily; dinner Mon–Sat. $$–$$$$*

See Map 5 on p. 44.

Da Giggetto (p. 57) JEWISH GHETTO *ROMAN/JEWISH* Well-known trattoria looking out on the ruins of the Portico of Octavia. The artichokes *alla giudia* (flattened, battered, and fried) are some of the best in the neighborhood.... *Tel 06/686-11-05. Via Portico d'Ottavia 21–22, at Via di Sant'Angelo in Pescheria. Buses 23, 271, 280, 780, or H. Tram 8. AE, DISC, MC, V. Lunch and dinner Tues–Sun. $$–$$$*

See Map 6 on p. 61.

Dagnino (p. 60) TERMINI *DESSERTS* Cannoli and other sweet treats from Sicily, plus a daily *tavola calda* ("fast food").... *Tel 06/481-86-60. Via V. E. Orlando 75, at Piazza della Repubblica. Metro Repubblica. MC, V. Mon–Fri 10am–7pm; Sat 10am–1pm. $–$$*

See Map 5 on p. 44.

Dal Bolognese (p. 51) PIAZZA DEL POPOLO *BOLOGNESE* Hearty fare from Bologna, Italy's culinary capital, attracts wealthy tourists. People-watch indoors or outdoors on the bustling Piazza del Popolo.... *Tel 06/361-14-26. Piazza del Popolo 1, at Via Ripetta. Metro Flaminio. Reservations recommended. MC, V. Lunch and dinner Tues–Sun. $$$–$$$$*

See Map 7 on p. 62.

Da Oio a Casa Mia (p. 57) TESTACCIO *ROMAN* Inexpensive, friendly *cucina romana* in authentic Testaccio neighborhood.... *Tel 06/578-26-80. Via Galvani 43–45, at Via Mastro Giorgio. Buses 23, 30, 75, or 280. Tram 3. No credit cards. Lunch and dinner Mon–Sat. $$*

See Map 5 on p. 44.

Da Quinto (p. 60) CENTRO STORICO *GELATO* Enormous smoothies (and other fruit- and veggie-based concoctions) are the main attraction at what used to be just a *gelateria.... Tel 06/686-56-57. Via di Tor Millina 15, at Via dell'Anima. Buses 30, 40, 46, 62, 64, 70, 81, 87, 492, 571, or 628. No credit cards. Daily 10am–1am. Closed in Jan. $*

See Map 6 on p. 61.

Dar Poeta (p. 54) TRASTEVERE *PIZZA* Hugely popular pizzeria with creative toppings, a variety of bruschette and a heavenly Nutella-filled dessert calzone. Get a thick-crust pie for 1€ ($1.25) more by ordering *doppio impasto.... Tel 06/588-05-16. Vicolo del Bologna 45, near Via della Scala. Buses 23, 271, or 280. Reservations taken for 7:30–8:30pm only. DC, MC, V. Dinner daily. $$*

See Map 5 on p. 44.

Enoteca Antica di Via della Croce (p. 55) SPANISH STEPS *WINE BAR* Recommended by all, so a bit touristy, but still cool. Try to grab a stool at the long, wooden bar, where cheese and antipasto plates are available.... *Tel 06/679-08-96. Via della Croce 76b, at Via Bocca di Leone. Metro Spagna. AE, MC, V. Daily 11am–2am. $–$$*

See Map 7 on p. 62.

Enoteca Kottabos (p. 55) COLOSSEUM *WINE BAR* Cavernous spot with wine by the glass, appetizers, and a young, local clientele.... *Tel. 06/7720-1145. www.kottabos.it. Via Celimontana 32, at Via Capo d'Africa. MC, V. Daily 5pm–1am. $–$$*

See Map 5 on p. 44.

Fiaschetteria Beltramme (p. 52) SPANISH STEPS *ROMAN* No phone and slightly grandmotherly interior belie the *Fiascabeltra's* uber-trendy status.... *No phone. www.fiaschetteriabeltramme.com. Via della Croce 39, at Via Belsiana. Metro Spagna. No credit cards. Lunch and dinner Mon–Sat. $$–$$$*

See Map 7 on p. 62.

Filetti di Baccalà (p. 58) CAMPO DE' FIORI *CODFISH/TAKEOUT* Deep-fried, salted codfish and a few other hangover-helper takeout goodies. The picnic tables in a tiny square off the Campo are perfect for discreet people-watching.... *Tel 06/686-40-18. Largo Librari 88, at Via Giubbonari. Buses 30, 40, 46, 62, 64, 70, 87, 116, 492, or 571. No credit cards. Dinner Mon–Sat. Closed Aug. $*

See Map 6 on p. 61.

Franchi (p. 59) VATICAN *DELI* The Gucci of delis near the Vatican crams in a hungry lunch crowd for its delicious hot and cold offerings.... *Tel 06/6874651. www.franchi.it. Via Cola di Rienzo 204, at Via Terenzio. Buses 23, 81, 271, 280, or 492. AE, MC, V. Mon–Sat 9am–7:30pm. $–$$*

See Map 5 on p. 44.

Frontoni (p. 59) TRASTEVERE *DELI* Popular Trastevere deli with yummy made-to-order pizza-bread sandwiches and other hot dishes.... *Tel 06/581-24-36. Viale Trastevere 52. Buses 75, 780, or H. Tram 8. No credit cards. Mon–Sat 10am–11pm, Sun 5–11pm. $*

See Map 5 on p. 44.

Giolitti (p. 60) PANTHEON *GELATO* A Roman institution, the city's oldest combination *gelateria-pasticceria.... Tel 06/679-42-06. www.giolitti.it. Via degli Uffici del Vicario 40, near Via di Campo Marzio. Buses 62, 85, 95, 116, 175, or 492. No credit cards. Daily 8am–2am. $*

See Map 7 on p. 62.

Girarrosto Toscano (p. 56) VATICAN *GRILL/MEATS* The simple pleasures of lamb and beef grilled to perfection, plus can't-go-wrong side dishes like roasted potatoes with rosemary.... *Tel 06/3972-3373. Via Germanico 58–60, at Via Vespasiano. Metro Ottaviano. Buses 23 or 492. Tram 19. Lunch and dinner Tues–Sun. $$$*

See Map 5 on p. 44.

'Gusto (p. 51) PIAZZA DEL POPOLO *ITALIAN* A modern, warehouse-y restaurant, pizzeria, and enoteca with an extensive menu and attached shop selling cookbooks and kitchen stuff.... *Tel 06/322-62-73. www.gusto.it. Piazza Augusto Imperatore 9, off Via Ripetta. Metro Flaminio or Spagna. Bus 913. AE, DC, MC, V. Lunch and dinner Tues–Sun. $$–$$$*

See Map 7 on p. 62.

Hamasei (p. 58) SPANISH STEPS *SUSHI* Japanese clientele (toting real Hermès shopping bags) assures sushi addicts that this is the real "McKoi".... *Tel 06/679-2134. Via della Mercede 35–36, at Via Mario de' Fiori. Reservations recommended. Metro Spagna. Buses 52, 53, 62, 63, 85, 95, 117, or 175. AE, DC, MC, V. Lunch and dinner Tues–Sun. $$$–$$$$*

See Map 7 on p. 62.

Hard Rock Cafe (p. 58) VENETO *AMERICAN* For when you just want to have a big, fat, juicy burger and not feel guilty about it.... *Tel 06/420-30-51. Via Veneto 62, at Via Bissolati. Metro Barberini. Buses 52, 53, 62, 63, 80, 95, 116, 492, or 630. AE, DC, MC, V. Lunch and dinner daily. $$–$$$*

See Map 7 on p. 62.

Hostaria Romanesca (p. 53) CAMPO DE' FIORI *ROMAN* Best bet for no-frills alfresco *cucina romana* on busy Campo de' Fiori.... *Tel 06/686-4024. Campo de' Fiori 40, along east side of square. Buses 40, 62, 64, 70, 87, 116, 492, or 571. No credit cards. Lunch and dinner Tues–Sun. $$–$$$*

See Map 6 on p. 61.

Hosteria del Campidoglio (p. 53) ANCIENT ROME *ITALIAN* Views of the Capitoline and Palatine hills from outdoor tables are beyond stunning; food is not nearly as inspiring.... *Tel 06/678-0250. Via dei Fienili 56, near Via dei Foraggi. Buses 30, 95, or 170. AE, DC, MC, V. Lunch and dinner Tues–Sun. $$–$$$*

See Map 5 on p. 44.

Hosteria del Pesce (p. 57) CAMPO DE' FIORI *SEAFOOD* Hip atmosphere for great seafood. Service is perfunctory, however, and prices on some entrees can be startling.... *Tel 06/686-5617. Via Monserrato 32, at Via Barchetta. Reservations recommended. Buses 23, 116, 271, or 280. AE, DC, MC, V. Dinner Mon–Sat. $$$–$$$$*

See Map 6 on p. 61.

I Due Ladroni (p. 51) PIAZZA DEL POPOLO *ITALIAN* Understated glamour, spot-on traditional cuisine, and frequent celeb sightings at outdoor tables.... *Tel 06/689-6299. Piazza Nicosia 24, near Via di Ripetta. Buses 87, 280, 492, 628, or 913. Reservations recommended. AE, DC, MC, V. Lunch and dinner Mon–Sat. $$$–$$$$*

See Map 7 on p. 62.

Il Bacaro (p. 52) PANTHEON *ITALIAN* Romantic and trendy, with upscale Italian fare and a great wine list.... *Tel 06/6864110. www.ilbacaro.com. Via degli Spagnoli 27, at Via della Vaccarella. Reservations recommended. Buses 30, 70, 87, 116, or 492. AE, DC, MC, V. Lunch and dinner Mon–Sat. $$$–$$$$*

See Map 6 on p. 61.

Il Margutta (p. 59) PIAZZA DEL POPOLO *VEGETARIAN* Rome's premier vegetarian restaurant, now with three locations (also Le Cornacchie on Piazza Rondanini and Al Leoncino on Via del Leoncino); the daily prix-fixe buffet is a bargain. Also open for brunch.... *Tel 06/326-50-577. www.ilmargutta.it. Via Margutta 118, northern end of street. Metro Spagna. AE, MC, V. Lunch and dinner Mon–Sat. $$–$$$*

See Map 7 on p. 62.

Insalata Ricca (p. 59) CAMPO DE' FIORI *SALADS* Wildly popular spot with a wide variety of meal-size salads. Eleven other branches around town don't quite live up to the original.... *Tel 06/688-03-656. www.linsalataricca.it. Largo dei Chiavari 85, at Corso Vittorio Emanuele II. Buses 30, 40, 46, 62, 64, 70, 81, 87, 116, 492, 571, or 628. Tram 8. AE, MC, V. Lunch and dinner daily. $$*

See Map 6 on p. 61.

Isidoro (p. 55) COLOSSEUM *PASTA* Make room in your belly for the *assaggini misti* (pasta sampling menu) at this friendly *osteria* near the Colosseum.... *Tel 06/700-82-66. Via di San Giovanni in Laterano 59–61–63, near Via dei Querceti. Metro Colosseo. Buses 60, 85, 87, 117, 175, 271, or 571. Tram 3. AE, DC, MC, V. Lunch and dinner daily. $$*

See Map 5 on p. 44.

L'Antico Forno (p. 59) TREVI FOUNTAIN *DELI* Reasonably priced deli sandwiches right in front of the Trevi Fountain.... *Tel 06/679-28-66. Via delle Muratte 8. Buses 62, 95, 175, or 492. No credit cards. Daily 8am–8pm. $*

See Map 7 on p. 62.

La Pergola (p. 58) MONTE MARIO *INTERNATIONAL* One of the best meals you'll eat in your life—and priced accordingly. Entrees of fish, beef, and rabbit, and exceptional desserts, on the rooftop terrace of the Cavalieri Hilton.... *Tel 06/350-92-211. Via Cadlolo 101. Reserve at least 1 month in advance. AE, DC, MC, V. Dinner Tues–Sat. Closed part of Jan and Aug. $$$$$*

See Map 5 on p. 44.

La Rosetta (p. 57) PANTHEON *SEAFOOD* Considered the best seafood restaurant in Rome for more than 30 years, thus the sky-high bills. Dishes such as rigatoni with rockfish and tuna carpaccio are standouts.... *Tel 06/686-10-02. www.larosetta.com. Via della Rosetta 8, off Piazza della Rotonda. Reservations essential. Buses 30, 40, 62, 64, 70, 81, 87, 116, 492, 571, or 628. Tram 8. AE, DC, MC, V. Dinner Mon–Sat. $$$$$*

See Map 6 on p. 61.

La Veranda (p. 56) VATICAN *ROMAN* Attached to the Hotel Columbus, this upscale trattoria in the shadow of St Peter's is a favorite of the Vatican press corps and visiting cardinals.... *Tel 06/687-29-73. Borgo S. Spirito 73, off Via della Conciliazione. Reservations recommended. Buses 23, 40, 46, 62, 64, or 271. AE, DC, MC, V. Lunch and dinner daily. $$$*

See Map 5 on p. 44.

Les Etoiles (p. 58) VATICAN *INTERNATIONAL* Impossibly fancy dishes made of such ingredients as truffles, snails, and quails' eggs eaten against the dramatic backdrop of St. Peter's dome.... *Tel 06/687-32-33. Via Vitelleschi 34, at Via della Fossa del Castello. Buses 23, 81, 87, 271, 280, 492. Reservations essential. AE, DC, MC, V. Dinner daily. $$$$$*

See Map 5 on p. 44.

Maccheroni (p. 52) PANTHEON *ITALIAN* A great all-around dining experience, with laid-back atmosphere, simple but perfectly executed dishes, and good value.... *Tel 06/683-07-895. Via delle Coppelle 44, at Via degli Spagnoli. Buses 30, 40, 46, 62, 64, 70, 81, 87, 116, 492, 571, or 628. Tram 8. AE, DC, MC, V. Dinner Tues–Sun. $$–$$$*

See Map 6 on p. 61.

Maharajah (p. 58) COLOSSEUM *INDIAN* Gilt Ganeshes and merry waitstaff from the Subcontinent; curries are deliciously rich, and lunch is a bargain.... *Tel 06/474-7144. www.maharajah.it. Via dei Serpenti 124, at Via Cimarra. Metro Cavour. Buses 60, 71, 85, 87, 175, or 571. AE, DC, MC, V. Lunch and dinner daily. $$–$$$*

See Map 5 on p. 44.

Mamma Che Pizza (p. 54) TRASTEVERE *PIZZA* Top-quality, creative pizza-by-the-slice place in Trastevere offers toppings like *provola* with truffle sauce. It also provides free mineral water.... *Tel 06/580-03-41. Piazza Sonnino 52, at Via della Lungaretta. Buses 23, 271, 280, 780, or H. Tram 8. No credit cards. Daily 11am–11pm. $*

See Map 5 on p. 44.

Matricianella (p. 51) PANTHEON ROMAN Cozy, delicious Roman trattoria established in 1957. A critics' favorite.... *Tel 06/683-2100. Via del Leone 3, at Via di Campo Marzio. Buses 62, 85, 95, 116, 175, or 492. Reservations recommended. AE, DC, MC, V. Lunch and dinner Mon–Sat. $$$*

See Map 7 on p. 62.

Obikà (p. 52) PANTHEON *MOZZARELLA/LIGHT FARE* Unique and buzzy modern space features delicious *mozzarella di bufala*, organic salads, and a wine bar.... *Tel 06/683-2630. Via dei Prefetti, at Piazza Firenze. Buses 70, 87, 116, or 492. AE, MC, V. Daily noon–midnight. $$–$$$*

See Map 7 on p. 62.

Osteria del Gallo (p. 53) PANTHEON *ROMAN* Lovely little trattoria on a quiet alley near Piazza Navona. Extensive menu features unique plates, plus all the standard, heavy Roman fare. The outdoor tables are great for languorous lunching.... *Tel 06/687-37-81. Vicolo di Montevecchio 27, at Via della Pace. Buses 30, 40, 46, 62, 64, 70, 81, 87, 280, 492, or 628. AE, DC, MC, V. Lunch Tues–Sun, dinner Mon–Sat. $$–$$$*

See Map 6 on p. 61.

Osteria della Frezza (p. 51) PIAZZA DEL POPOLO *ROMAN/APERITIVI* Hip offshoot of 'Gusto offers tapas-style munchies, hundreds of cheeses, and top-notch wine by the glass or bottle.... *Tel 06/322-62-73. Via della Frezza 16, at Via Corea. Buses 81, 628, or 913. AE, DC, MC, V.* Aperitivi *and dinner daily. $$–$$$*

See Map 7 on p. 62.

Osteria der Belli (p. 56) TRASTEVERE *SARDINIAN* Lively indoor-outdoor spot serves up Sardinian pasta and seafood dishes in the heart of Trastevere.... *Tel 06/580-37-82. Piazza Sant'Apollonia 9–11, at Via della Lungaretta. Buses 23, 271, 280, 780, or H. Tram 8. AE, DC, MC, V. Lunch and dinner Tues–Sun. $$*

See Map 5 on p. 44.

Pellacchia (p. 60) VATICAN *GELATO* The best gelato in the Vatican area.... *Tel 06/321-08-07. Via Cola di Rienzo 103, at Piazza Cola di Rienzo. Metro Lepanto. Buses 81 or 280. No credit cards. Tues–Sun 10am–10pm (midnight in summer). $*

See Map 5 on p. 44.

Pierluigi (p. 53) CAMPO DE' FIORI *ROMAN* An old standby down the street from Piazza Farnese, this trusty trat with tables inside and out has excellent *soppressata di polipo* (octopus *"salame"*) and *tagliata di manzo* (beef strips on a bed of arugula).... *Tel 06/686-13-02. www.pierluigi.it. Piazza de' Ricci 144, at Via Monserrato. Buses 23, 40, 64, 116, 271, 280, or 571. Lunch and dinner Tues–Sun. $$–$$$*

See Map 6 on p. 61.

Piperno (p. 58) JEWISH GHETTO *ROMAN/JEWISH* One of the Ghetto's most expensive and congenial eateries, serving fried fish, tripe, and other specialties of *cucina ebraica.... Tel 06/688-06-629. Via Monte de' Cenci 9, between Via Arenula and Via del Tempio. Buses 23, 271, 280, 780, or H. Tram 8. Reservations essential. AE, MC, V. Tues–Sun. Closed Aug, Easter, and Christmas. $$$$–$$$$$*

See Map 6 on p. 61.

PizzaRé (p. 54) PIAZZA DEL POPOLO *PIZZA* Monument-weary kids love the thick-crusted Naples-style pizza here. Parents love the air-conditioning.... *Tel 06/321-14-68. Via di Ripetta 14, at Via della Penna. Metro Flaminio. AE, DC, MC, V. Lunch Mon–Sat, dinner daily. $$*

See Map 7 on p. 62.

Pizzeria La Montecarlo (p. 54) PIAZZA NAVONA *PIZZA* A lively pizza joint that's dirt cheap and immensely popular with Roman 20- and 30-somethings. Service is remarkably attentive for how busy it gets.... *Tel 06/686-18-77. Vicolo Savelli 11, at Corso Vittorio Emanuele II. Buses 40, 46, 64, or 571. AE, DC, MC, V. Lunch and dinner Tues–Sun. $$*

See Map 6 on p. 61.

Quinzi e Gabrieli (p. 57) PANTHEON *SEAFOOD* Local VIPs (and other people who can afford it) come to this special spot for the best fish in town.... *Tel 06/687-93-89. Via delle Coppelle 5, at Piazza delle Coppelle. Buses 30, 70, 87, 116, or 492. Reservations essential. AE, DC, MC, V. Dinner Mon–Sat. $$$$$*

See Map 6 on p. 61.

Remo (p. 57) TESTACCIO *PIZZA* Tourists are a rare sight at this jovial, spit-and-sawdust pizza joint in workaday Testaccio.... *Tel 06/574-6270. Piazza Santa Maria Liberatrice 44, at Via R. Gessi. Buses 23, 30, 75, 95, 170, 271, or 280. Tram 3. No credit cards. Dinner Mon–Sat. Closed Aug. $$*

See Map 5 on p. 44.

Riccioli Cafe (p. 57) PANTHEON *OYSTER BAR* Oysters, wine, pizza, and cocktails unite at this sleek restaurant/lounge.... *Tel 06/682-10-313. www.larosetta.com. Piazza delle Coppelle 10A, at Via delle Coppelle. Buses 70, 81, 87, 116, 571, or 628. AE, DC, MC, V.* Aperitivi *and dinner Mon–Sat. Closed Aug. $$–$$$*

See Map 6 on p. 61.

San Crispino (p. 59) TREVI FOUNTAIN *GELATO* The high art of gelato, perfected to a science. Don't even think of ordering your scoop in a cone.... *Tel 06/679-39-24. Via della Panetteria 42, at*

Via del Lavatore. Metro Barberini. Buses 52, 53, 62, 63, 95, 175, or 492. No credit cards. Closed Tues, sometimes Thurs, and 2 weeks in Jan. $

See Map 7 on p. 62.

Santa Lucia (p. 53) PIAZZA NAVONA *NEAPOLITAN* Fashionable alfresco trat with a dream setting—a small, ivy-draped square off Piazza Navona. A favorite of Sophia Loren's and not far from the Roman apartment where she made *Ieri, Oggi, Domani*.... *Tel 06/688-02-427. Largo Febo 12, at Via dell'Anima. Buses 70, 87, 492, or 628. MC, V. Lunch and dinner Wed–Mon. $$$*

See Map 6 on p. 61.

San Teodoro (p. 53) PALATINE *ROMAN/SEAFOOD* Exquisite dishes served in an intimate setting, surrounded by the ruins of the Forum and the Palatine.... *Tel 06/678-09-33. Via dei Fienili 49–51, near Via dei Foraggi. Reservations recommended. Buses 30, 95, or 170. AE, DC, MC, V. Lunch and dinner Mon–Sat. Closed mid-Jan to mid-Feb. $$$*

See Map 5 on p. 44.

Sant'Eustachio (p. 50) CENTRO STORICO *COFFEE BAR* Bar none, the richest, sweetest, best coffee in the city.... *Tel 06/656-13-09. Piazza Sant'Eustachio 82, at Piazza dei Caprettari. Buses 40, 46, 62, 64, 70, 87, 116, 492, 571, or 628. No credit cards. Daily 8:30am–1am. $*

See Map 6 on p. 61.

Spirito di Vino (p. 56) TRASTEVERE *TRADITIONAL ROMAN* Exceptional family-run restaurant located atop a medieval synagogue and a 2nd-century Roman street. Try the mustard-flavored *maiale alla mazio,* an ancient pork recipe that was a favorite of Julius Caesar's.... *Tel 06/589-66-89. Via dei Genovesi 31, at Vicolo dell'Atleta. Buses 23, 271, 280, 780, or H. Tram 8. Reservations recommended. MC, V. Dinner Mon–Sat. Closed Aug. $$$*

See Map 5 on p. 44.

Supperclub (p. 52) PANTHEON *GLOBAL* Dine lying down, among masseurs, lounge music, and white interiors. The full-on trendy European experience.... *Tel 06/688-07-207. www.supperclub.it. Via de' Nari 14, at Via Monterone. Buses 30, 40, 46, 62, 64, 70, 87, 116, 492, or 571. Tram 8. Reservations essential. AE, DC, MC, V. Dinner Tues–Sun. $$$$$*

See Map 6 on p. 61.

Taverna da Tonino (p. 55) COLOSSEUM *ROMAN* Sink your teeth into succulent roast lamb and other hearty *secondi* at this inexpensive Roman trat near the Forum. The no-reservations policy means come early or wait.... *Tel 06/474-53-25. Via Madonna dei Monti 79, at Via dell'Agnello. Metro Cavour. Buses 60, 75, 85, 87, 117, or 175. No credit cards. Lunch and dinner Mon–Sat. $$*

See Map 5 on p. 44.

Taverna del Campo (p. 52) CAMPO DE' FIORI *APERITIVI/SANDWICHES* Great lunch or *aperitivo* spot on Campo de' Fiori. Wine, garlicky pizza-bread sandwiches, and free peanuts.... *Tel 06/687-44-02. Campo de' Fiori 16, at Via dei Baullari. Buses 30, 40, 46, 62, 64, 70, 81, 87, 492, 571, or 628. Tram 8. No credit cards. Tues–Sun 9am–2am. $$*

See Map 6 on p. 61.

Tazza D'Oro (p. 50) PANTHEON *COFFEE BAR* The powerful aroma of coffee from this big bar lures tourists and locals away from the Pantheon..... *Tel 06/678-92-92. Via degli Orfani 84, at Piazza della Rotonda. Buses 30, 40, 46, 62, 64, 70, 87, 116, 492, or 571. No credit cards. Mon–Sat 8am–8pm. $*

See Map 6 on p. 61.

Thien Kim (p. 58) CAMPO DE' FIORI *VIETNAMESE* One of Rome's few reliable options for good-value Asian cuisine, this tasty and tasteful Vietnamese place also happens to be on one of the prettiest streets in town.... *Tel 06/683-07-832. Via Giulia 201, near Ponte Sisto. Buses 23, 116, 271, or 280. AE, DC, MC, V. Dinner Mon–Sat. $$–$$$*

See Map 6 on p. 61.

Trattoria Monti (p. 52) ESQUILINO CENTRAL *ITALIAN* Stylish spot with cuisine from the Marche region, a rarity in Rome. Exceptional pasta, mushrooms, chicken, and rabbit.... *Tel 06/446-65-73. Via di San Vito 13a, at Via Merulana. Metro Vittorio. Bus 714. AE, DC, MC, V. Lunch Tues–Sun; dinner Tues–Sat. $$$*

See Map 5 on p. 44.

Tutti Frutti (p. 57) TESTACCIO *SOUTHERN ITALIAN* Not a smoothie joint, but a unique "food club" in culinarily progressive Testaccio.... *Tel 06/575-79-02. Via Luca della Robbia 3A, at Via Aldo Manuzio. Metro Piramide. Buses 23, 30, 75, 95, 170, or 280. Tram 3. MC, V. Dinner Tues–Sun. Closed Aug. $$–$$$*

See Map 5 on p. 44.

Vanni Café (p. 60) SPANISH STEPS *PASTRY* Sugary cakes, pastries, espresso, and gelato. Catering also available.... *Tel 06/679-18-35. Via Frattina 94, at Via Belsiana. Metro Spagna. No credit cards. Call for open hours. $–$$*

See Map 7 on p. 62.

Velando (p. 56) VATICAN *ITALIAN* A stone's throw from the papal palace, affordable and inventive northern Italian gourmet, but food can be on the heavy side.... *Tel 06/688-09-955. Borgo Vittorio 26, near Viale di Porta Angelica. Buses 23, 40, 46, 62, 64, 271, or 280. AE, DC, MC, V. Lunch and dinner Mon–Sat. $$$*

See Map 5 on p. 44.

Volpetti (p. 59) TESTACCIO *GOURMET GROCERY* Sneaky staff offer free samples of meats and cheeses so divine you'll want to buy all of them, even at $50 per pound.... *Tel 06/574-23-52. Via Marmorata 47, at Via Alessandro Volta. Metro Piramide. Buses 23, 30, 75, or 280. Tram 3. AE, MC, V. Mon–Sat 10am–7:30pm. $–$$*

See Map 5 on p. 44.

Zen (p. 58) VATICAN *SUSHI* Hipper than your average sushi bar, but more a place for those who love raw fish and don't need a lot of trendy decor and people-watching to go with it.... *Tel 06/ 3213420. www.zenworld.it. Via degli Scipioni 243, at Via Marcantonio Colonna. Metro Lepanto. Bus 70 or 280. AE, DC, MC, V. Lunch and dinner Tues–Sun. $$$*

See Map 5 on p. 44.

DIVER

SIONS

3

Map 8: Rome Diversions Orientation

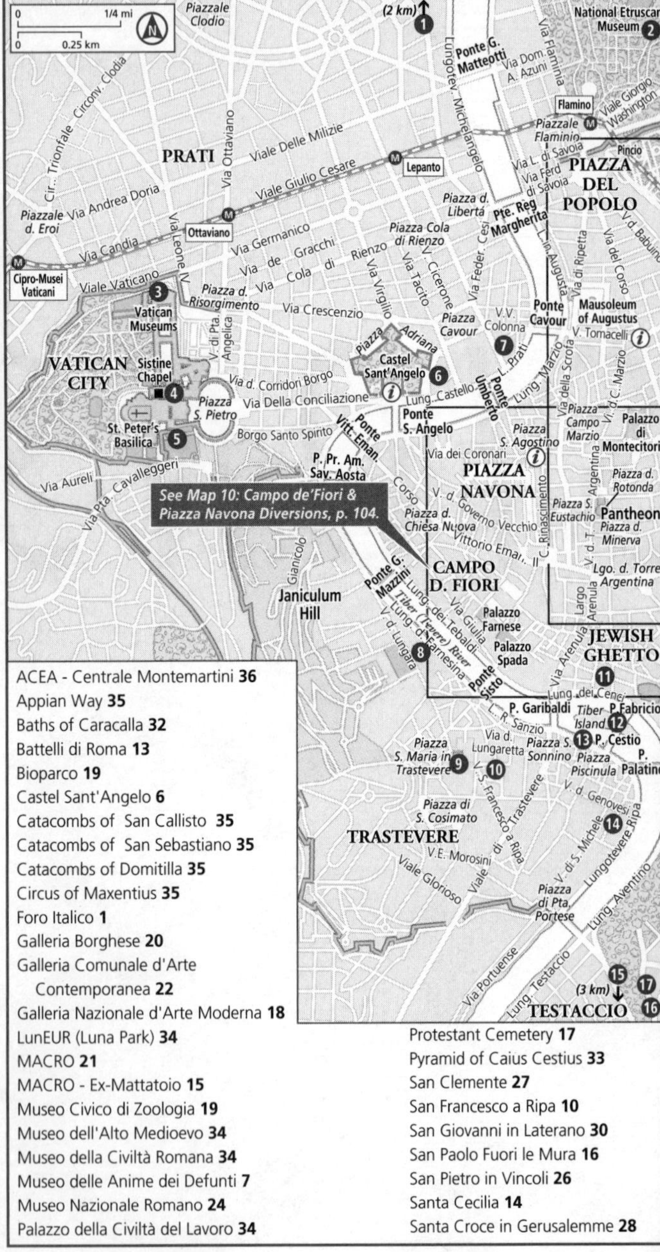

DIVERSIONS

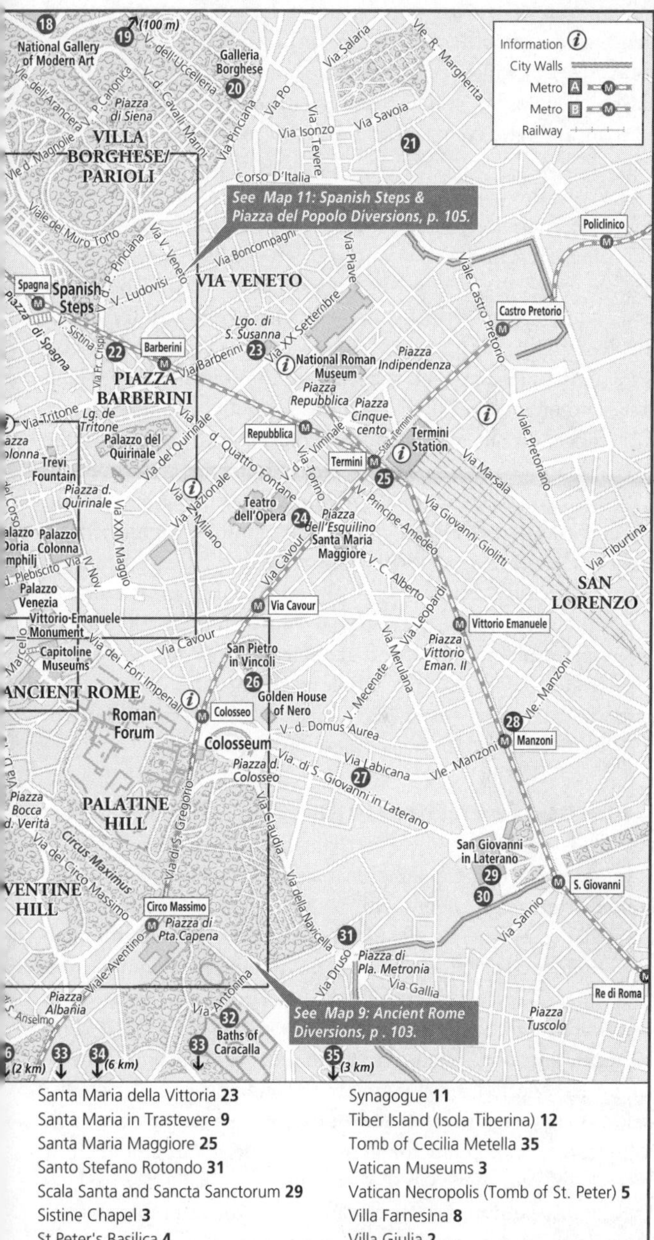

Information
City Walls
Metro A
Metro B
Railway
National Gallery of Modern Art
Galleria Borghese
VILLA BORGHESE/ PARIOLI
Piazza di Siena
Via Salaria
Vle. R. Margherita
Via Po
Via Pinciana
Via Isonzo
Via Tevere
Via Savoia
Corso D'Italia
See Map 11: Spanish Steps & Piazza del Popolo Diversions, p. 105.
Viale del Muro Torto
Via Boncompagni
Via Piave
Policlinico
Spagna
Spanish Steps
VIA VENETO
V. Ludovisi
Via V. Veneto
Viale Castro Pretorio
Castro Pretorio
Lgo. di S. Susanna
Via XX Settembre
Barberini
Via Barberini
National Roman Museum
Piazza Indipendenza
PIAZZA BARBERINI
Piazza Repubblica
Piazza Cinquecento
Repubblica
Termini
Termini Station
Viale Pretoriano
Via Tritone
Lg. de Tritone
Palazzo del Quirinale
Via del Quirinale
Via d. Quattro Fontane
Via Marsala
Trevi Fountain
Piazza d. Quirinale
Via Nazionale
Teatro dell'Opera
Piazza dell'Esquilino
Santa Maria Maggiore
V. Principe Amedeo
Via Giovanni Giolitti
Via Tiburtina
Palazzo Colonna
Via XXIV Maggio
Via Milano
Via Cavour
V. C. Alberto
SAN LORENZO
Palazzo Venezia
Vittorio Emanuele Monument
Vittorio Emanuele
Piazza Vittorio Eman. II
Capitoline Museums
Via dei Fori Imperiali
San Pietro in Vincoli
Via Merulana
Via Leopardi
ANCIENT ROME
Roman Forum
Colosseo
Golden House of Nero
V. d. Domus Aurea
V. Mecenate
Vle. Manzoni
Manzoni
Colosseum
Piazza d. Colosseo
Via Labicana
Via di S. Giovanni in Laterano
PALATINE HILL
Via di S. Gregorio
Via Claudia
Piazza Bocca d. Verità
Circus Maximus
Via del Circo Massimo
San Giovanni in Laterano
S. Giovanni
Via Sannio
AVENTINE HILL
Circo Massimo
Piazza di Pta.Capena
Via della Navicella
Viale Aventino
Piazza di Pla. Metronia
Via Druso
Via Gallia
Re di Roma
Piazza Albania
Via Antonina
See Map 9: Ancient Rome Diversions, p . 103.
Piazza Tuscolo
Baths of Caracalla
(2 km)
(6 km)
(3 km)
(100 m)

Basic Stuff

When it comes to sightseeing, Rome has an aesthetic arsenal that blows every other city in the world—not to mention entire countries—to smithereens. That such a concentration of first-class archaeological and historical sites, architecture, and art can exist in a single, compact urban center is mind-blowing. But that's Rome.

We're the first to trumpet the virtues of the city's ruins, churches, museums, fountains, and topographical features (see our superlative-heavy descriptions below), but don't feel you have to get to all of them—no one ever does. To see Rome, *non basta una vita*—a lifetime is not enough. So, instead of overdoing it with the sightseeing (and spending more time around tourists than locals), pick and choose from our list of sights in this chapter and save plenty of time for aimless wandering and cafe-sitting. What the locals refer to as *la dolce far niente* ("the sweet doing of nothing")—not racing from the Colosseum to St. Peter's and back—is what the Roman experience is all about. Having said that, it's still a good idea to approach sightseeing in a somewhat organized fashion; as in any big city, your time in Rome can easily slip away and you might miss out on some of the sights you were most interested in seeing. But if those 2 hours you'd planned to spend at the catacombs somehow turn into postcard-writing and people-watching at a *centro storico* cafe, don't despair—most likely, that cafe is in the shadow of another historic site or masterpiece of Western art.

Getting Your Bearings

All roads lead to Rome—and then, they lead to confusion. Rome's *centro* is a topographic maelstrom of choppy cobblestoned streets that merge with narrow alleys or lead to irregularly shaped *piazze.* Rare is the Roman street that hits anything at a right angle. Wide and straight thoroughfares are scarce; those that do exist are traffic-choked and best avoided by pedestrians. The eye of the storm in Rome's street "plan" is **Piazza Venezia,** a traffic circle where five busy roads converge, causing a lane-less snarl of intertwining traffic and unclear right-of-way rules. As uncongenial as that sounds, Piazza Venezia does make a good reference point for newcomers—its main architectural feature, the enormous white Vittoriano, is a locally despised but memorable landmark—once you're here, you're pretty close to everything on your sightseeing list.

Just south of Piazza Venezia is the heart of **Ancient Rome,** from the Capitoline Hill to the archaeological areas of the Roman Forum, Palatine, and Imperial Forums. Also to the south, umbrella pine–lined Via dei Fori Imperiali terminates at the **Colosseum,** beyond which rises quiet Celio Hill, with its rustic churches, and the cathedral of San Giovanni in Laterano. Tourist-thronged sights like the **Trevi Fountain** and the **Spanish Steps** lie north and northeast of Piazza Venezia, while **Termini Station** is about 1.6km (1 mile) due east.

Northwest and west of Piazza Venezia is the ***centro storico,*** including the **Pantheon, Piazza Navona, Campo de' Fiori,** and **Ghetto** areas. Occupying the zone within the river Tiber's slightly C-shaped bend, the *centro storico* is the city's mother lode of charm, with dozens of pedestrian squares, countless churches and fountains, and tons of restaurants and bars—this is where you want to hang out when you're not touring monuments and museums. As for the Tiber, the dirty, largely unnoticed river snakes its way through the city from north to south, separating the *centro storico* from the delightful **Trastevere** ("across the Tiber"; pronounced "tras-*teh*-veh-reh") neighborhood and **Vatican City** to the west, and the tony **Prati district** to the north.

On a slope to the east of the Spanish Steps, tree-lined **Via Veneto** is luxury hotel central and certainly pretty, but unless you enjoy the aspirational glamour of sipping overpriced cups of cappuccino at glass-enclosed sidewalk cafes, there's little reason to visit this *La Dolce Vita* street. Via Veneto today is the province of American and German tourists who, in their search for Marcello Mastroianni types, stumble upon the Hard Rock Cafe—and each other—instead.

Spreading out from the top of Via Veneto, the **Villa Borghese** park is a handy "green lung" when all that sightseeing gets to be too much. The **Quirinale** and **Esquiline** areas south and east of here form the "modern" part of central Rome; the main streets (Via Barberini, Via Nazionale, and Via Cavour) feature a conglomeration of government buildings, tacky tourist shops, and smog-stained hotels and apartment houses.

Farther afield, the **Aventine Hill** and **Testaccio** areas lie to the south of the *centro storico* and are overlooked by most tourists. Precisely for that reason, we highly recommend a trip down here, as you'll be rewarded by quiet, leafy luxury on the Aventine and a slice of real workaday Roman life in Testaccio—all at a safe distance from the tourist hordes. The Fascist-era cityscape of **EUR** (Esposizione Universale di Roma; pronounced "*ay*-yur") is about 8km (5 miles) south of central Rome, at the end of Metro Line B. Mussolini's grand project to show off "La Terza Roma" (the Third Rome, after that of the emperors and of the popes), EUR is full of cold, imposing 1930s buildings—a must for fans of architecture and urban planning.

The **Appian Way (Via Appia Antica),** southbound "queen" of Roman roads and home of the catacombs, is the only major tourist sight that isn't walkable from the heart of town. It's only 3.5km (2 miles) from the Colosseum, which may not seem off-putting if you like to walk, but getting there involves a treacherous stretch of narrow road, without any sidewalk, where traffic speeds recklessly.

Guided tours are offered everywhere in Rome and can be a great way to get your bearings while also getting some fascinating historical and artistic commentary. However, the quality and intelligibility of guides vary hugely, and bus tours within central Rome are a complete waste of time (not at all geared toward the Irreverent Guide reader). Walking tours are a much better option; **Enjoy Rome** (Tel 06/4451843; www.enjoyrome.com) and **Context Rome** (formerly known as Scala Reale; Tel 06/482-0911; www.contextrome.com) are well-established agencies and offer a wide range of entertaining and informative itineraries.

Note: The fly-by-night "tour guides" (young Americans, Aussies, and Brits) at the main tourist areas who pose as "architecture students" or similar are operating illegally and often have no clue what they're talking about.

Getting Around

The best and often most efficient way for a newcomer to get around central Rome is on foot; but once you've got your bearings, upgrade to two wheels and a two-stroke engine—the ***motorino*** is by far the most romantic and giddy way to get around. Too many newcomers are terrified by the thought of negotiating the streets of Rome on a Vespa; sure, it takes some daring, but traffic laws and vehicle flow are remarkably forgiving of any mistakes you might make. Just go slowly until you get the hang of it—once you do, it's an unforgettable way to see this gorgeous town. (See the Getting Outside chapter for rental info.)

Public transportation in Rome consists of an extensive but potentially confusing bus network and a dinky subway system

(Metropolitana, or Metro for short). Of the two, I recommend the **bus,** as it will give you the chance to sightsee while getting around. One of the most useful lines for tourists—but definitely not the most scenic—is the 40 Express, which runs from Termini–Via Nazionale–Piazza Venezia–Largo Argentina–Castel Sant'Angelo (near St. Peter's) and back the same way. Bus 64 does the same route, making many more stops, but it is always packed with pickpockets and pervs and best avoided altogether. The **Metro** consists of two lines, A and B, which intersect at Termini Station, on the northeast side of the city center. Having only two lines, the Metro is easy to use and will get you close to major sights like the Colosseum, Vatican, and Spanish Steps, although it skirts the most characteristic parts of the city (Piazza Navona, Pantheon, Campo de' Fiori, and Trastevere), where ancient ruins beneath street level were too dense for city authorities to deal with when they built the Metro in the 1980s. However, plans for a Metro Line C, which would bore right through the archaeologically rich foundations of the *centro storico,* are now underway. When finished, underground stations will have glass panels that showcase the ruins.

If you're pressed for time or are claustrophobic, avoid riding the Metro in the early evening, when it seems every gel-coiffed Roman youth is heading to the Spanish Steps. ***Note:*** Bus stops, trains, and train platforms in general are the gypsies' favorite haunts, so always keep an eye—and a hand—on your bags. (For more on public transport, see the Hotlines chapter.)

Discounts, Passes & Reservations

You can actually see every major sight in Rome—except the Sistine Chapel—for free. (And you can even see the Sistine Chapel—the roof and part of the back wall—for free from Piazza San Pietro; it's those frescoes *inside* that'll cost ya.) When you do feel the need to actually enter monuments and museums, it gets pricey—tickets at most admission-charging sites range from 4€ to 10€ ($5–$13). Almost all student and senior discounts are reserved for E.U. citizens, but Americans can try their luck with ticket booth staff, who might bend the rules if they like you and no supervisors are around. State-owned sites usually have reduced rates for children under 15. A number of sites run by the Archaeological Superintendent also offer joint tickets for other related attractions—20€ ($25) gets you a 7-day pass to the Colosseum, the Palatine, the Baths of Caracalla, the Appian Way's Tomb of Cecilia Metella and Villa of the Quintili, and the four buildings that make up the Museo Nazionale Romano. If you're really lucky, you'll visit Rome during Settimana dei Beni Culturali (Cultural Heritage Week, usually in May), when admission to all publicly owned museums is free. The only major attractions requiring reservations are the Galleria Borghese, the Domus Aurea (Nero's Palace), and the Vatican Necropolis/Tomb of St. Peter. (***Note***: You do *not* need reservations for the rest of the Vatican, including the Sistine Chapel and St Peter's Basilica.) See the Index for booking procedures.

The Lowdown

Must-sees for first-time visitors... The **Colosseum,** with those unforgettable superimposed arches curling around into decadence, is still the most potent demonstration of all that Rome was at the height of the empire. A poignant graveyard of Rome's Golden Age, the **Roman Forum** was the center of the civilized world for over 700 years. The ruins here—of temples, assembly halls, and military monuments—merit multiple visits (and a good tour guide to explain the mess of marble). With its porch of gargantuan granite columns, its original bronze doors and polychrome marble revetment, and its 43m (143-ft.) wide, unsupported dome of poured concrete, the **Pantheon** is the best preserved ancient structure in Rome and one of the world's most impressive architectural achievements. Time-warping ahead to the 16th and 17th centuries, **St. Peter's Basilica** has everything you'd expect from the largest church in Christendom, with ridiculous amounts of gold and marble, and Michelangelo's *Pietà.* Next door, the **Vatican Museums** have amazing ancient sculptures and Renaissance frescoes galore, including those in the Raphael Rooms and the much-hyped, never-disappointing Sistine Chapel.

Rome's most spectacular baroque public spaces—the **Spanish Steps** and **Piazza Navona**—are great places to take a load off and people-watch. During sun-drenched days, both are flooded with lounging tourists and locals (as well as those inevitable byproducts, annoying vendors and buskers). Presiding over the Tiber and *centro storico* like a barrel-chested sentry, **Castel Sant'Angelo** (Hadrian's mausoleum-turned-papal fortress) is a formidable sight, especially in the evening. Legend has it that if you toss—not fire—a coin into the **Trevi Fountain,** you're guaranteed to return to the Eternal City. The Trevi's exaggerated scale and theatricality make it a delight to behold anytime, but the fountain is at its most spellbinding at around, oh, 4am, when all the coin-hurling tourists and roving Casanovas have finally called it a night.

Remains of the day... Romans love to quote the Venerable Bede, who wrote "While the Colosseum stands, Rome shall stand; when the Colosseum falls, Rome shall fall; and when Rome falls, so shall the world." Earthquakes, barbarians, and popes have all done their part to reduce the "Rome Bowl" to its current, half-intact state, but as anyone who's seen it can attest, the **Colosseum** (or *Amphitheatrum Flavium,* A.D. 72–80) is very much still standing. You'll need to use your imagination to reconstruct the monument's interior, but you can walk across a wooden platform over the substructures where the contestants were kept and see the remains of the 32 elevator shafts and trapdoors that brought the gladiators and wild animals to arena level. Still, few locals have ever bothered to go inside the Colosseum—and what's the point, really, now that the gladiators and wild animals are gone? The blood and gore—er, games—were cut off in A.D. 523. More important than the Colosseum historically but a lot more difficult to visualize, the greater **Roman Forum** area was downtown ancient Rome, where commercial, political, and religious activities all took place around a public square. Here, the marble skeletons of the civilization that spanned three continents are at their most haunting after dark, when all the columns and arches are floodlit. For the best view, go to the terraces of the **Capitoline Hill.** Above the Forum valley to the west is the **Palatine,** the lush hill on which wealthy Romans—and later, emperors exclusively—built their palaces. The plebes still don't tend to make it up here, so you can visit the ruins without having to contend with phalanxes of tour groups. From the western edge of the hill (in the ruins of the Domus Flavia), there's a view of the **Circus Maximus** below, ancient Rome's 300,000-spectator-capacity chariot-racing venue. Older than many of Rome's ruins but still perfectly intact, the architecturally astounding **Pantheon** (temple of all the gods) was built by Hadrian about 40 years after the Colosseum's debut. Most of the other monumental ruins in

Rome, including the **Imperial Fora, Trajan's Markets,** the **Area Sacra,** the **Theater of Marcellus,** and the **Porticus of Octavia,** can be seen well enough from the outside. Parts of the **Appian Way (Via Appia Antica),** the superhighway that stretched from Rome all the way to Brindisi on the southern Adriatic coast, are still open to traffic, though public transportation to this famous road is unreliable. (See "Public Transportation," in the Hotlines chapter, for information about the Archeobus, the Appian Way's hop-on, hop-off bus service.) Whether it's a broken stretch of aqueduct under which cars now race indifferently or a graffiti-tagged brick wall that used to belong to a temple, reminders of Rome's ancient history are everywhere, so keep your eyes peeled—even the downstairs McDonald's at Termini station has a sizable chunk of 4th century B.C. Roman walls in its dining area.

How to do the Vatican... First of all, the biggest myth about the Vatican is that you should go at the crack of dawn. Any guidebook that prints such advice is trying to sabotage you, forcing you to contend with the 3,000 passengers from whatever cruise ship decided to make Rome that day's port-of-call. From Easter to late October, go at noon or later; the rest of the year, go in the late morning, as the Vatican Museums close early in the winter. For the average visitor, "seeing the Vatican" is synonymous with getting to the Sistine Chapel, realizing how crowded it is, and then getting the hell out of there. Yes, the **Sistine Chapel** is all it's cracked up to be, but it's a shame to rush past the Vatican's other treasures in your hurry to see those famous frescoes. Before making that beeline to the *Sistina,* don't miss the Greco-Roman sculptural masterpieces *Apollo Belvedere,* the *Laocoön,* and the *Belvedere Torso.* Upstairs the Vatican's Etruscan and Egyptian collections are top-notch—and closed half the time. Near the chapel, a detour to the left leads to the must-see Raphael Rooms, where you can really get up close and personal with the best work of the *other* High Renaissance genius. Your last stop before entering the Sistine Chapel should be the little snack bar just below, where you can get a beer and chill for a minute—it'll make your long-awaited date with Michelangelo's frescoes that much more memorable. Traumatized by crowds inside the museums, many tourists make the mind-boggling mistake of not going inside **St. Peter's Basilica**—when the right-hand door out of the Sistine Chapel leads you straight there! The exterior view of the church, with the dome, is a bit of a cliché, but the interior of St. Peter's has a vastness—not to mention kilotons of marble, bronze, and gold, plus the Pietà—that takes everyone by surprise. In the immense oval of Piazza San Pietro, you can send postcards through the Vatican post office, snap photos of the Swiss Guard, and, if you're lucky, catch a glimpse of His Holiness, the pope himself.

Celebratory columns... Painstakingly sculpted from A.D. 107 to 113 to commemorate the Romans' victory over Dacia (modern-day Romania), the **Column of Trajan** stands 30m (100 ft.) tall, in Trajan's Forum, erect as ever—any phallic resemblance is, of course, coincidental. The spiral relief depicts 2,500 individual figures going about the business of war—bivouacking, catapulting, and hacking each others' heads off. The column's height prohibits a good view of the uppermost reliefs, but plaster casts of

Popes "R" Us

With the death of John Paul II and election of Pope Benedict XVI in April 2005, it seems no trip to Rome is complete without a papal encounter of some kind. To pay your respects to Karol Wojtyla, descend to the grottoes beneath St. Peter's basilica and follow the signs to the Tomba di Giovanni Paolo II. To see an embalmed pope, seek out the nifty glass capsule holding John XXIII, halfway up the right side of the main nave—the "good pope" is still wearing the black slippers he had on when he shuffled off our mortal coil in 1963. For a glimpse of the living pope, show up outside St. Peter's at noon on a Sunday, when Pope Benedict gives the Angelus blessing from his apartment window overlooking the piazza. Smaller papal audiences are held on Wednesday mornings in St. Peter's Square or the modern auditorium just to the south. Don't expect to have any meaningful one-on-one time with Papa Benedetto, however—the gathering is slightly more intimate than a high school graduation ceremony. For tickets, contact the ***Prefettura della Casa Pontifica*** *(Tel 06/698-83-017; fax 06/698-85-863) several weeks in advance. (In a pinch, you can sometimes gain last-minute admission on Tues afternoon by inquiring with the Swiss Guard at the Portone di Bronzo—the big bronze door—located in the colonnade to the right of St. Peter's Basilica.)*

Tourist Traps (& Tourist Don'ts)

Rome's meaningless photo-op par excellence is the ***Bocca della Verità (Mouth of Truth)****, an ancient sewer cover sculpted to look like a face. Legend says that if you've been untruthful, the mouth clamps down and cuts your hand off. If you do queue up for a picture, don't just stand there and smile—you'll get a much less dorky result if you ham it up à la Gregory Peck in* Roman Holiday *and pretend that your arm is being sucked in. Tourists also love to take cheesy photos with the self-described centurioni (locals dressed up in half-assed gladiator costumes of plastic bristle-crested helmets, tin cuirasses, and red socks) in front of the Colosseum. City coach tours operated by outfits like Appian Line, Green Line, and Vastours are a big don't; the "guides" deliver memorized speeches in barely intelligible English, and you'll spend more time picking up other passengers and sitting in traffic than seeing the treasures of Rome. (For general orientation when you're feeling lazy, however, we do endorse the* ***110 Open*** *double-decker bus—see "Public Transportation," in the Hotlines chapter.)*

each scene are on display at the Museo della Civiltà Romana (see below). A knockoff of Trajan's original, the **Column of Marcus Aurelius** recalls Roman military exploits in Germany—or, for film buffs, the opening scene in *Gladiator.*

Hot-tub hedonism... The bathing ritual in ancient times was a big deal. All classes and both sexes could avail themselves of the many low-cost yet luxurious halls of hygiene around the city (and you'll lament the demise of this institution when you find yourself on a hot and stinky bus in July). Rome's thermal complexes had multiple pools of different temperatures, gyms, libraries, and beauty centers. Unfortunately, thoughtless Visigoths severed the city's aqueducts in A.D. 537, and Rome's baths have been dry ever since. In a gorgeous valley of grass and pine trees just south of the Aventine Hill, the 3rd-century-A.D. **Baths of Caracalla** are well worth a visit. Floor mosaics are still intact, massive brick walls still tower overhead, and it doesn't take too much imagination to picture the original splendor here. You can also picnic, nap, lounge in the sun against a fallen granite column, or catch an evening concert here in the summer. Near Termini train station, the Baths of Diocletian were Rome's largest, accommodating up to 3,000 bathers simultaneously. Today, the best-preserved parts of the baths house Michelangelo's Santa Maria degli Angeli church and the **Museo Nazionale Romano,** which has a vast but repetitive store of Etruscan and Roman artifacts.

Egypt-o-mania... It shouldn't take you long to notice that there are a lot of granite spires sticking up in the squares of Rome. In fact, Rome has more obelisks—13 total—than Egypt itself. Nine of these monoliths are actually Egyptian—that is, 3,000+ years old, pillaged from the land of the pharaohs after Rome conquered it in the 1st century B.C. The other four are fakes, cut and carved with hieroglyphics by ancient Roman emperors who wanted to make their subjects think they'd gotten more loot from Egypt than they actually had. Popes in the 16th and 17th centuries had all the obelisks moved from their ancient locations, re-erected in front of churches (surprise, surprise), and crowned with Christian symbols in bronze. The biggest obelisk is at Piazza San Giovanni in Laterano. The most famous one is at the Vatican, brought to Rome by the emperor Caligula (and packed in lentils to keep it from busting its cargo ship apart); the first to be imported (by Augustus in 31 B.C.) is the dramatic centerpiece of Piazza del Popolo. The obelisk at Piazza Montecitorio was once the hand of an ancient Roman sundial. Mussolini revived the ancient practice of stealing tall, thin pieces of granite from Africa when in 1938 he had the 180-ton Axum Stele brought from Ethiopia and placed at the southern end of the Circus Maximus. The Ethiopian government wanted it back, but for years, Italy's cultural ministry waffled. It wasn't until lightning struck and shattered the tip of the stele, in 2003, that superstitious Italy got serious about coming up with a plan to ship it home. In April 2005, thanks to careful engineering and the Herculean efforts of three Russian cargo planes, the Axum Stele had its homecoming.

Michelangelo marks the spot... In *The Innocents Abroad,* Mark Twain comically relates that wherever he went in Rome, his tour guides would repeat the same phrase: "Thees by Michelangelo." They were only stretching the truth a little bit. Though he's associated more with the city of Florence, Mr. Buonarroti was plenty busy in Rome, making his debut in 1499 with the *Pietà* (in St. Peter's, behind bullet-proof glass and difficult to get a really good look at). Michi later moved on to the Sistine

Chapel (1508–12), where he spent more than 4 years getting a backache so that tourists could go in and gawk for 15 minutes. As Michelangelo saw it, sculpture (a subtractive art) was far superior to painting (an additive art) and those ceiling frescoes were one big waste of time. An easy detour from the Colosseum is the church of **San Pietro in Vincoli,** which houses the stern *Moses* statue—*terribilità* was a favorite theme of Michelangelo's. Of course, his most jaw-droppingly awesome sculpture is the *David,* which is at the Accademia in Florence. When he wasn't chipping away at marble, Michelangelo also took on a few architectural projects during his stay in Rome. He laid down the plans for the *cordonata* (a stepped ramp for both humans and horses) leading up to the Capitoline, the most sacred of Rome's seven hills, as well as the black-and-white, star-shaped **Piazza del Campidoglio**—now an icon of the city—at the top. He also designed much of **Palazzo Farnese,** now the French embassy.

A Bernini bonanza... The sinuous, theatrical period of art known as the baroque exploded in Rome in the early 17th century and still flourishes in the tight quarters of the *centro storico.* By far, the most extraordinary exponent of this period was Gian Lorenzo Bernini (1598–1680), a Naples-born golden boy who left his life's work—statues, fountains, and churches—strewn about the city. One of Bernini's most famous works, the Fontana dei Quattro Fiumi, is the centerpiece of Piazza Navona. Commissioned by Pope Innocent X, the **Fontana dei Quattro Fiumi (Four Rivers Fountain)** is a wonderful play of rock, reclining figures, and water, and is best enjoyed in the early morning, before all the junk vendors invade the space. Along with papal patronage came courtesans—that Bernini was well-versed in the body language of love is evident in several of his sculptures around town. Voyeurs should stop in at the church of **Santa Maria della Vittoria** (near Termini), where Bernini's eyebrow-raising *Ecstasy of Santa Teresa* unabashedly blurs the line between religious and sexual rapture. Similarly, Bernini's *Blessed Ludovica Albertoni,* in **San Francesco a Ripa** (in Trastevere), shows the saint clutching her breast and rolling her eyes back in a moment of, *ahem,* spiritual ecstasy. After dark, the beauty of the Bernini-copied angels along Ponte Sant'Angelo, with Castel Sant'Angelo looming magnificent in the background, will make you swoon, too. In traffic-choked Piazza Barberini, named for Bernini's biggest patrons, you can check out the Fontana del Tritone; just across the Via Veneto, the Fontana delle Api (Fountain of the Bees) features the Barberini symbol of bees, found all over Rome. Bernini's best stuff arguably rests in the **Galleria Borghese,** where Cardinal Scipione Borghese gave the young Bernini his big break. In *Apollo and Daphne* and *The Rape of Persephone,* the virtuosity of the sculptures is the ultimate demonstration of what is possible with a hunk of marble, a good set of chisels, and a steady hand. Also here, *David*—a self-portrait of Bernini—winds up to give Goliath a walloping with such realistically knitted brow and pursed lips that you can't help but make the same determined grimace on your own face.

Among gods and emperors... It's been said that for every living resident of imperial Rome, there was a statue. Indeed, faraway-gazing ancient sculpture is as ubiquitous in Rome as somber-eyed paintings of the Madonna and Child are in Tuscany. Frozen in that majestic, self-possessed moment when they ruled the world, Roman emperors, gods, and other ancient celebrities still haunt the city, populating the halls of its museums and lending affable charm to many street corners. Some of the best marble statues were snatched by art-hoarding popes in the 1500s and ended up in the **Vatican Museums.** Check out the Pio-Clementine and Braccio Nuovo wings of the museums for the best line-up, including the *Laocoön,* the *Belvedere Torso,* and the *Augustus of Prima Porta,* with its wonderfully detailed (and nippled) cuirass. More manageable than the Vatican, the exquisite **Capitoline Museums** contain a slew of satyrs, Bacchuses, and expressive emperors, but the most famous pieces are the star bronzes—the 5th-century-B.C. *Capitoline She-Wolf* and the 2nd-century-A.D. *equestrian statue of Marcus Aurelius.* The museums' two buildings, the Palazzo Nuovo and the Palazzo dei Conservatori, are linked by an underground passage that showcases the 78 B.C. *Tabularium* (Archive Hall), which offers dramatic views over the Forum. On the back side of the Palazzo dei Conservatori, the Terrazza Caffarelli snack bar has great views north and west. Not far from here is the Tarpeian

Rock, the famed precipice off which traitors were hurled from Republican times right up through the Renaissance. The overflow from the Capitoline's collection is on display at the **ACEA–Centrale Montemartini,** an old power plant near Testaccio. The unlikely juxtaposition of the marble against the machinery—think Venus in the boiler room—is visually stunning. Traipse around any of the four locations that make up the **Museo Nazionale Romano**—Palazzo Massimo alle Terme, Palazzo Altemps, Terme di Diocleziano, and Crypta Balbi—and you're likely to see enough naked Apollos to last you a lifetime. Lamentably under-visited, the national Etruscan museum at **Villa Giulia** was originally a suburban retreat for 16th-century pope Julius III and now houses a wealth of Etruscan tomb findings, including a 6th-century-B.C. his-and-hers sarcophagus and gold jewelry with astoundingly intricate granulated work.

Holy heavy hitters... Rome's four "patriarchal" basilicas are St. Peter's in the Vatican, Santa Maria Maggiore, St. Paul's Outside the Walls, and St. John Lateran. **Santa Maria Maggiore** is a heavily reworked ancient basilica with dazzling, recently restored 5th-century mosaics and a spectacularly coffered ceiling, supposedly decorated with gold that Columbus brought back from the New World. **San Paolo Fuori le Mura (St. Paul's Outside the Walls)** lies over the tomb of St. Paul, on the Via Ostiense, quite a hike from the *centro* (but if you're on your way to or from EUR or Ostia, the church is an easy stop-off from the Metro). A reconstruction of a 5th-century church that was mostly destroyed by fire in 1823, St. Paul's features *tondi* (round paintings) of all of the popes, and spaces are left for only a few more—it's said that once the spaces run out, the apocalypse is nigh. **San Giovanni in Laterano (St. John Lateran)** is clear on the other side of town from the Vatican, but it is this church, and not St. Peter's, that is the cathedral of Rome and mother church of the world. The first Christian church ever built in Rome stood on this spot (today's basilica is a baroque building), and every pope from the 4th through the 14th centuries lived in the adjoining Lateran Palace. Two other pilgrimage sites near San Giovanni are also worth noting. The **Scala Santa,** or "Holy Stairs," are said to be the steps that Christ ascended in Pontius Pilate's house during his trial. No feet are allowed to touch the Scala Santa, and true pilgrims are expected to get on their knees in order to climb the 28 marble steps (long since fitted with wooden planks). Also in the building that houses the Scala Santa is the mysterious-sounding **"Holy of Holies" (Sancta Sanctorum),** with frescoes by Cimabue—once the popes' private chapel, it's now open to anyone willing to pay 3€ ($3.75). **Santa Croce in Gerusalemme** isn't one of the "Big Four," but it's home to some A-list Christian relics, including some splintery pieces of the True Cross, a nail, two thorns from the Crown of Thorns, and St. Thomas's doubting finger. The first Roman church dedicated to Mary was **Santa Maria in Trastevere,** on the charming piazza of the same name in Rome's Village-y "left bank."

Fine-art freebies... The advent of the euro has sure made that old Europe-on-a-shoestring concept obsolete, but in Rome, some of the greatest masterpieces of Western art can be enjoyed for free. Rome's *centro storico* churches are packed with works by Michelangelo, Raphael, Caravaggio, and Bernini, just to name a few. If you're a fan of *trompe l'oeil* design, go to **Sant'Ignazio,** where Andrea Pozzo designed a flat-roofed church with a ceiling that appears to curve upwards into a dome. Stand on the inlaid yellow marble disc halfway up the nave for the best effect. Another Jesuit church not far from here is the **Gesù,** with over-the-top baroque stuccoes by Pozzo and illusionistic decoration throughout. The homely exterior of **Santa Maria del Popolo** belies a treasure trove inside: Raphael's ornate Chigi Chapel is tucked away in the back, while two of Caravaggio's finest works—*Crucifixion of St. Peter* and *Conversion of St. Paul*—are in the Cerasi Chapel. Three more Caravaggios—some of his best, and best-lit, works in the city—are his *Life of St. Matthew* series, in **San Luigi dei Francesi,** near the Pantheon. Nearby, Caravaggio's *Madonna of the Pilgrims* is in Sant'Agostino. Raphael's *Sybil* frescoes, in **Santa Maria della Pace** (near Piazza Navona), were restored in 2000.

Private collections for public viewing... Quite a few aristocratic families still live in some of Rome's *palazzi,* or at least keep their art collections in them. The largest private collection is the **Galleria Doria Pamphilj,** with works by Titian, Caravaggio, Correggio, Velázquez, and Dutch and Flemish masters, and a free audio guide (available in many languages, including English) narrated by the living Doria Pamphilj princes themselves, who freely opine about the paintings they love or hate. The painting collection at the **Galleria Spada** can't quite compete, but the star here is the visually deceptive Borromini corridor—it's only 9m (30 ft.) long but it looks like it's 30m (100 ft.). Cardinal Scipione Borghese, who founded the splendid **Galleria Borghese,** packed so many Caravaggios and Berninis (plus the odd Titian and Raphael upstairs) into his collection that you have to make a reservation to see them. Palazzo Barberini, the former home of the baroque's best patron, Pope Urban VIII, has the standard array of 16th- and 17th-century masters, the highlight being Raphael's bare-breasted *Fornarina* (supposedly a portrait of his mistress, a baker's daughter). Only three rooms at the **Villa Farnesina** are open to the public, but Raphael's unique *Triumph of Galatea* is worth the price of admission.

Architecture Romans love to hate... Tourists snap away at it just as much as they do at the Colosseum, but locals could do without the **Vittoriano,** the garish heap of white marble that squats at the southern side of Piazza Venezia. Often referred to as the "wedding cake," the "typewriter," or even "the dentures," the grandiose monument to Italy's first king is a neoclassical confection of festoons, equestrian statues, and winged victories, completely out of proportion with and tone-deaf to the harmony of the rest of Rome's ocher-toned buildings. The Vittoriano is on such an exaggerated scale that in 1911, when it was inaugurated, a banquet for 20 was held inside the stomach of the bronze horse at the center of the monument. Nevertheless, the Vittoriano's terraces offer stunning views. On the west side of Piazza Venezia, the 15th-century **Palazzo Venezia** was Mussolini's headquarters during the Fascist regime, where he made his rousing speeches from the balcony in the middle of the main facade. *Il Duce* also razed everything between here and the Colosseum to create Via dell'Impero (now Via dei Fori Imperiali), a work of rhetorical genius that gave him and his listeners a gun-barrel view of all that Rome was and all that he promised it would be again under Fascism. Another equally ridiculed structure is the neo-baroque Palazzo di Giustizia (nicknamed the *Palazzaccio,* "awful, offensive palace"), an oversize court building on the banks of the Tiber that began sinking under its own hulking weight in the 1970s. Not yet a century old and already falling apart? In Rome, that ain't gonna cut it.

A river runs through it... The **Isola Tiberina (Tiber Island)** will get you as close as you'll probably want to get to the dirty Tiber. Connected to the Ghetto by the **Ponte Fabricio,** Rome's oldest bridge still in use, and the younger **Ponte Cestio** on the Trastevere side, the island is the site of a hospital, a church, and a medieval tower. Isola Tiberina is rustic and pretty but not especially exciting—except when the odd local lunatic decides to dive off one of the bridges—but it is a great spot to soak up some rays. Take the stairs down to the travertine esplanade for views across the river to Trastevere. The ship-shaped island was in fact sculpted with the prow of a ship in ancient times—some of this is preserved off the port bow. While you're down there, you can also get a closer look at the **Ponte Rotto,** one of Rome's earliest bridges, now broken, and an island unto itself. Inaugurated in 2003, the **Battelli di Roma** riverboat service has two types of craft—*di turismo* and *di linea*—that ply the waterway between Tiber Island and the Foro Italico. No, the Tiber is not the Seine, but on a sunny day it's a nice river on which to unwind and rest your feet, and the younger set can keep busy monitoring the waters for nutrias (plus-size water rodents) and unlikely refuse (scooters). The riverboat makes hourly stops along the banks below several bridges in the heart of town.

Going medieval... Filled as it was with hard times—Goths, plagues, having to go to church instead of the Colosseum—the medieval period is one era that Rome has mostly managed to make disappear from its architectural record. An exception to this rule is **Castel Sant'Angelo,** a veritable hamburger of history. Rome's castle started out as the squat, cylindrical mausoleum of the emperor Hadrian. Later, it was fortified to defend the papal strongbox against barbarian hordes. In troubled times, the pope could scurry across the *Passetto,* a crenellated corridor connecting the

Vatican to the castle. The latest additions were made in the Renaissance, when lavish apartments were added to the uppermost terraces—if the popes had to spend months here waiting out sacks and sieges, they were gonna do it in style. The Borgo neighborhood, between the Castel Sant'Angelo and the Vatican, still retains its medieval layout and feel to some extent. **Santa Maria Sopra Minerva,** built in the 13th century, is the best (and only) Gothic church in Rome.

Visiting the Jewish Ghetto... Passing by church after church, you would hardly know that Rome is home to the largest Jewish community in Italy and the oldest in Europe, period. About 16,000 Jews still live in Rome, many in the original Ghetto area (around Via del Portico d'Ottavia) that was established by papal bulls in the 16th century. For a small entrance fee, you can visit the handsome, 20th-century **Synagogue** and a smallish museum that houses priceless *parokhets* (decorative curtains that hang within holy arks), old photos, and other valuable items. And while Rome's Christian catacombs get all the publicity, the ancient Jews also buried their dead in underground tunnels along the Via Appia—see "The X-Files," below, for more on the Jewish catacombs.

My Feet Hurt

Wandering aimlessly is by far the best way to see Rome, but those cobbles do a number on your tootsies after a few hours. Don't worry, it happens to the best of us. To give your feet a rest and see the city, go for a ride on tram 3, which gives you views of the Villa Borghese, the Colosseum, the Circus Maximus, and the Aventine Hill. Bus 271 goes from St Paul's Outside the Walls to Piramide, the Colosseum, and the Theater of Marcellus; along the river to the Vatican; and up to the Fascist-era Foro Italico. (See also ***Battelli di Roma*** *on p. 95. Feeling lazy after dinner but don't want to go back to your hotel yet? Have a taxi take you for a panoramic drive past the Colosseum and other major monuments—these sights take on a whole new, breathtaking beauty when they're floodlit.*

The city's top views... Rome's rooftops max out at about six stories, so you don't have to climb too high to get a good view of everything. The most romantic viewing spot is the west-facing **Pincio,** just above Piazza del Popolo and a short stroll from the top of the Spanish Steps. Right smack in the middle of things, the

Vittoriano provides almost 360-degree views of the city from its upper terraces. Not nearly as comprehensive a panorama, but a hell of a lot more dramatic, the **Capitoline Hill**'s southern face offers heart-stopping views over the Forum. Seeing it in the evening, with a little wine in you? Even better. The other Roman lookout point par excellence (neck and neck with the Pincio for top make-out spot) is the Janiculum Hill above Trastevere, a long, tree-filled ridge with views of the *centro storico* and points east. The Aventine Hill's Orange Garden provides low-key viewing pleasure over the Tiber and points north. Also on the Aventine, seek out the keyhole in the bronze door of the headquarters of the **Order of the Knights of Malta** for a perfectly framed view of St. Peter's. **Castel Sant'Angelo**'s *Terrazza dell'Angelo* will bring you even closer to St. Peter's and the popes' fortified corridor—just don't pull a Tosca and do a swan dive into the river below. The highest point in Rome is the dome of St. Peter's itself, but here, you're pretty far west of most things a tourist wants to see. Pay 5€ ($6.25) for the elevator halfway up, then walk about 250 steps to the top. (If you want to be a bad-ass and forgo the lift, you will have to climb about 45 stories and still have to fork over 4€/$5.)

What lies beneath (or, why the subway system sucks)... Only 35% of ancient Rome has been excavated, and an entire other city of roads, homes, and places of worship is buried under modern-day Rome. No one knows for certain the extent of what's beneath the surface. The phenomenal underground cities that comprise the Christian **Catacombs of San Callisto,** the **Catacombs of San Sebastiano,** and the **Catacombs of Domitilla** contain miles of musty tunnels whose soft tufa walls are gouged out with tens of thousands of burial niches, including crypts of popes and a few bones. The infamous fire of A.D. 64 cleared enough land for Nero to build his enormous **Domus Aurea (Golden House)** on the Oppian Hill, behind the Colosseum. Now underground, almost 150 frescoed and stuccoed rooms of the whimsical palace are open to the public, including the famed octagonal dining room. Perhaps the best example of Rome's lasagna-like archaeological strata is the basilica of **San Clemente.** Here, a 12th-century church sits on top of a 4th-century church, which sits on top of a

1st-century-A.D. Christian meeting place, which sits on top of a 1st-century-B.C. Mithraic cult chamber.

Literary itineraries... The big names of the Romantic Movement—Lord Byron, Percy Bysshe Shelley, and John Keats—all lodged at the **Keats-Shelley House,** at the bottom of the Spanish Steps. On exhibit are some personal effects, body parts (!), and original manuscripts. True literary pilgrims should also head to the lovely **Protestant Cemetery,** where both Keats and Shelley are buried. Goethe wrote much of his *Italian Journey* travelogue in his apartment on Via del Corso. The **Casa di Goethe** features exhibits on the life and times of the German author. American author Henry James set many of his novels (*Roderick Hudson, The Portrait of a Lady*) in Rome, and Nathaniel Hawthorne's mystery, *The Marble Faun,* was inspired by a sculpture in the Capitoline Museums. For fans of more modern bestsellers, Dan Brown's *Angels and Demons* will whisk you from the Vatican to the travertine quarries of Tivoli.

The X-Files... Would-be Indiana Joneses should familiarize themselves immediately with **Ripartizione** X (Tel 06/671-03-819; fax 06/689-21-15), the cryptically named division of the city heritage department that oversees archaeological sites—like the Area Sacra at Largo Argentina, Ludus Magnus (gladiators' barracks), Jewish catacombs, Excubitorium (ancient fire station), Aqua Virgo aqueduct, and underground basilica at Porta Maggiore—that are normally closed to the public. You'll also need to contact Ripartizione X for access to the *mithraea* under the Circus Maximus, under Santa Prisca on the Aventine, and under the Baths of Caracalla. (A *mithraeum* is a subterranean chamber where adherents of the Persian cult of Mithras met for rituals and bloodletting.) The gears of Roman bureaucracy grind slowly, so fax your request in as soon as possible, indicating what sites you want to see and when.

Tombs of the rich and famous... Dozens of popes, including John Paul II, are entombed in the crypt under St. Peter's Basilica, but the tomb of St. Peter himself lies even lower than crypt-level in the **Vatican Necropolis. Castel Sant'Angelo** owes its round shape and its massive bulk to the 2nd-century-A.D. **Mausoleum of Hadrian,** upon which the medieval fortress was built. Along the river just south of Piazza del Popolo, the **Mausoleum of Augustus** was the resting place of Rome's first emperor. Mussolini dreamed of having his own remains deposited here—hence the Fascist look of the piazza around it—but history had a change of plans. (Adjacent is another Augustan monument, the 9 B.C. **Ara Pacis.** Its controversial new enclosure, designed by American architect Richard Meier, has been likened to "a gas station in Texas" by some harsh critics.) The **Tomb of Cecilia Metella** (30 B.C.) is the most picturesque landmark on the old Appian Way—one of the best views of it is from the middle of the **Circus of Maxentius,** an ancient chariot racetrack nearby. A real gem, and perhaps the most tranquil spot in all of central Rome, is the **Protestant Cemetery,** where non-Catholics like Keats and Shelley and Communists like Antonio Gramsci rest in peace amid docile cats and pretty greenery. Right next door, looking as absurd today as it must have when it was built, is the spiky white marble **Pyramid of Caius Cestius,** tomb of a 1st-century-B.C. Roman magistrate (not open to the public). The burial spots of some of Italy's great artists are in Rome as well: Raphael's tomb is in the **Pantheon,** Fra Angelico's grave is at **Santa Maria Sopra Minerva,** and the modest gravestone for Gian Lorenzo Bernini is at **Santa Maria Maggiore.**

Morbid Rome... From gladiators to martyrs to barbarians, Rome has certainly seen her share of death and gore over the years. If you can fit in only one macabre attraction, by all means make it the **Crypt of the Capuchin Monks,** beneath the church of Santa Maria della Concezione. Here you will find the skeletal remains of some 4,000 Capuchin monks affixed to walls in elaborate patterns or fashioned into chandeliers, all of which makes for some bizarrely beautiful "body art." Each chapel has a theme—pelvises, skulls, and so on—and a few feature monks, still in their cassocks and desiccated skin, who stare back at you quizzically. An uplifting plaque in the last chapel reminds you that you, too, "will be what we are now." Less morbid but still pretty freaky is the tiny **Museo delle Anime dei Defunti,** which has Bibles, pieces of cloth, and other items "touched" by souls waiting to enter heaven (significant scorch marks are the proof). While it's not certain that

St. Peter was indeed incarcerated here, many prisoners of Caesar's Rome, with formidable names like Vercingetorix, were tortured and executed in the dark, dank **Mamertine Prison** above the Roman Forum. Relic-hunters can view St. Thomas's finger at **Santa Croce in Gerusalemme,** the suspiciously small head of St. Agnes preserved in a glass case at Sant'Agnese in Agone, or the very gridiron on which St. Lawrence was barbecued at San Lorenzo in Lucina. The otherwise lovely church of **Santa Cecilia** houses a sculpture of the martyr, in which gash marks across her neck—from a failed decapitation attempt—are rendered in fine detail. For a pictorial who's-who in grisly martyrdoms, seek out the frescoes at **Santo Stefano Rotondo,** on the rustic Celio.

Roma moderna... In their rush to see ancient Rome, many tourists completely overlook the city's modern and contemporary art offerings. (And they're not all wrong—it's not as if we're overflowing with Pollocks and Warhols here.) First and foremost is the **Galleria Nazionale d'Arte Moderna e Contemporanea,** the high palace of modern art at the top of the Villa Borghese. The collection is heavy on Modigliani and De Chirico, with the odd van Gogh and Klimt to break up the monotony. The attached cafe looks out onto the park and is great for a post-museum glass of wine. The city's modern art gallery, the **Galleria Comunale d'Arte Moderna e Contemporanea,** is smaller and features much of the same. Meanwhile, a more ambitious municipal modern art space, **MACRO (Museo D'Arte Contemporannea Roma),** recycles the old Peroni brewery to make room for about 4,000 works of contemporary Italian art. MACRO at the Ex-Mattatoio is an exhibition space at Testaccio's defunct slaughterhouse. The most exciting new cultural space, however, is the Auditorium–Parco della Musica (see the Entertainment chapter) designed by architect Renzo Piano. The complex, with three beetle-shaped concert halls and special exhibition spaces, has given a welcome breath of modern air to northern Rome.

Hip 'hoods off the beaten path... The neighborhoods of **Testaccio** and **San Lorenzo** are the current hot hangouts of hip young Roman things. Populated by young families, retirees, and struggling *artisti,* Testaccio has a wonderfully authentic, working-class Roman feel by day, but by night the area is club central. Bars, lounges, discos, and livestock pens (!) surround Monte Testaccio ("mountain made of pottery"), where ancient Romans dumped their empty *amphorae* for hundreds of years. East of Termini station, San Lorenzo has a left-wing chip on its shoulder and has long been home base for Rome's Communists and anarchists, not coincidentally a result of its proximity to the campus of Rome's La Sapienza University. Visually speaking, the area is ugly, with few fancy public spaces and charmless architecture; but its tattoo parlors, cheap pizza joints, college-town personality, and a smattering of stylish restaurants work in San Lorenzo's favor.

Fascist Rome... A complete U-turn from radical San Lorenzo is EUR (Esposizione Universale di Roma), Mussolini's fantasyland, replete with imposing Fascist architecture. The few tourists who make the trip out here visit the **Museo della Civiltà Romana,** which features scaled-down versions of some of imperial Rome's most adored monuments; or the **Museo dell'Alto Medioevo,** crammed full of artifacts from the Middle Ages—a time when people worked hard. Also cutting a sharp image in EUR is the **Palazzo della Civiltà del Lavoro,** known locally as the "square Colosseum." Another Fascist-era set of buildings is the **Foro Italico,** a huge sports complex along the river north of central Rome. Still here is a huge marble obelisk with MVSSOLINI DVX inscribed on it vertically. Adjacent to the Stadio Olimpico, Rome's professional soccer venue, is the entertaining Stadio dei Marmi, rimmed with dozens of ridiculous-looking, muscle-bound marble studs clutching various sports apparatus. As you walk around this area, don't forget to look down—the black-and-white mosaics depict the glories of the cult of athleticism, along with rhetorical DVCE DVCE DVCE panels here and there.

Kid stuff... Children with even an ounce of imagination *ooh* and *aah* when confronted with such fascinating sites as the Colosseum, but that doesn't mean they're gonna want to waste their pent-up energy spending hours at ruins or all day in a museum. At wide-open spaces like **Villa Borghese,** you can rent bikes, boats, or in-line skates, or kick around the soccer ball with local kids. Also tucked away on this swath of parkland is the zoo, today known as the **Bioparco,** which is slowly revamping the cramped quarters where it keeps its animals, and the **Museo Civico di Zoologia (Museum of Zoology),** which features a 15m (50-ft.) long whale skeleton as well as a scary reproduction of a bear cave. **LunEUR** (also called Luna Park) is a hokey little amusement park in EUR; it's no Six Flags, but Roman kids make do. For a cruise on the Tiber, the **Battelli di Roma** riverboats offer a bare-bones, shuttle-style service for 1€ ($1.25), or fancier, narrated cruises—some with food and drink—for 10€ ($13) and up. Sights along the journey include the mighty Castel Sant'Angelo—and the equally mighty Tiber nutrias (enormous aquatic rodents).

Map 9: Ancient Rome Diversions

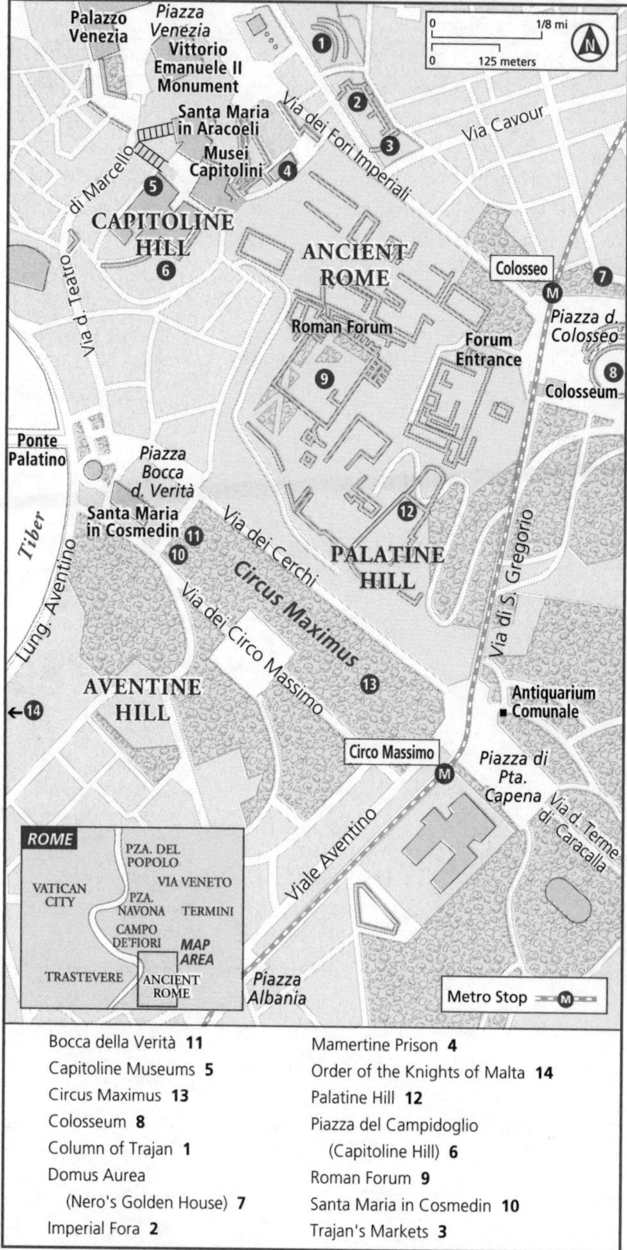

Bocca della Verità **11**
Capitoline Museums **5**
Circus Maximus **13**
Colosseum **8**
Column of Trajan **1**
Domus Aurea
(Nero's Golden House) **7**
Imperial Fora **2**
Mamertine Prison **4**
Order of the Knights of Malta **14**
Palatine Hill **12**
Piazza del Campidoglio
(Capitoline Hill) **6**
Roman Forum **9**
Santa Maria in Cosmedin **10**
Trajan's Markets **3**

Map 10: Campo De' Fiori & Piazza Navona Diversions

Map 11: Spanish Steps & Piazza Del Popolo Diversions

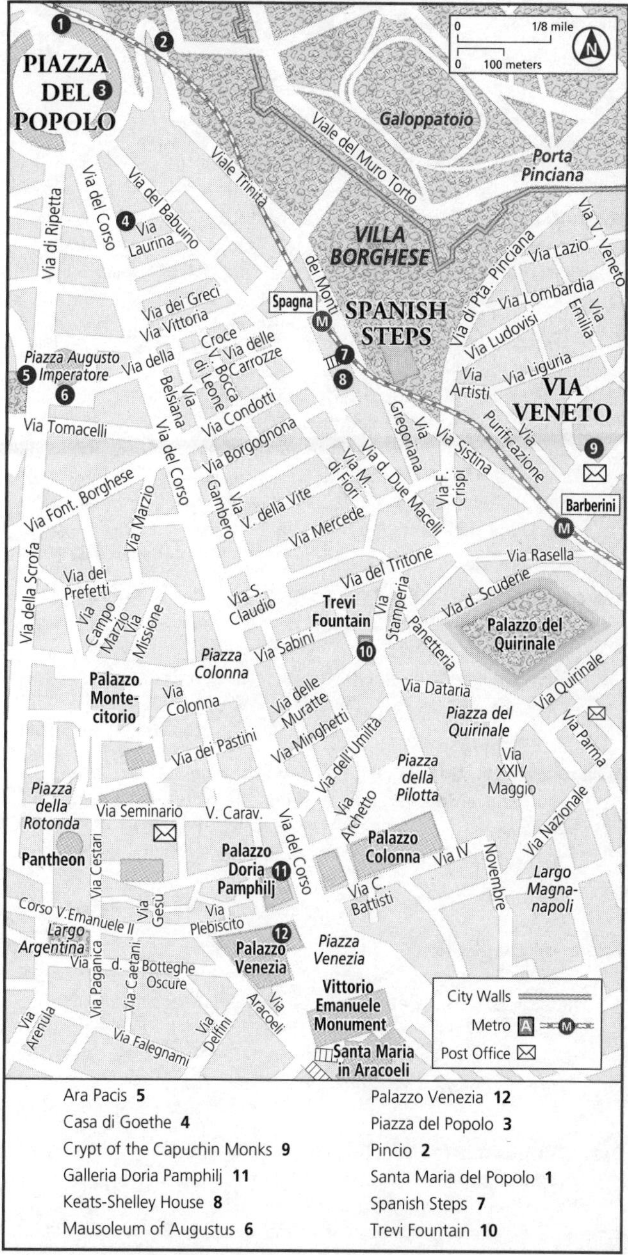

Ara Pacis **5**	Palazzo Venezia **12**
Casa di Goethe **4**	Piazza del Popolo **3**
Crypt of the Capuchin Monks **9**	Pincio **2**
Galleria Doria Pamphilj **11**	Santa Maria del Popolo **1**
Keats-Shelley House **8**	Spanish Steps **7**
Mausoleum of Augustus **6**	Trevi Fountain **10**

The Index

ACEA–Centrale Montemartini (p. 92) OSTIENSE A decommissioned power station, housing the impressive marble leftovers from the Capitoline Museums.... *Tel 06/574-80-30. Via Ostiense 106, near Piazza del Gazometro. Metro Piramide. Buses 23 or 271. Tues–Sun 9:30am–7pm. Admission 4.20€ ($5.25).*

See Map 8 on p. 78.

Appian Way (p. 82) SOUTHERN SUBURBS The queen of roads, built in 312 B.C. Umbrella pines, farms, pagan tombs, and Christian catacombs.... *For information, contact Parco Regionale Dell'Appia Antica. Tel 06/512-63-14. Fax 06/518-83-879. www.parcoappiaantica.org. Via Appia Antica 42. Bus 118. Free admission to the park and churches.*

See Map 8 on p. 78.

Ara Pacis (p. 99) PIAZZA DEL POPOLO Augustan "altar of peace," with art-historically important, delicate marble friezes. Closed since 1999 for restoration, due to reopen in its new Richard Meier–designed pavilion.... *www.arapacisaugustae.it. Lungotevere in Augusta, at Piazza Augusto Imperatore.*

See Map 11 on p. 105.

Area Sacra (p. 86) PANTHEON/GHETTO Below street level, cat-filled ruins of four temples and the site of Caesar's assassination.... *No phone. Largo di Torre Argentina. Buses 30, 40, 46, 62, 64, 70, 87, 492, or 571. Tram 8. By appointment only; see "The X-Files," earlier in this chapter, for details.*

See Map 10 on p. 104.

Baths of Caracalla (p. 88) AVENTINE Wander through towering brick walls or relax in the grass at Rome's best-preserved and most picturesque baths.... *Tel 06/575-86-26. Viale delle Terme di Caracalla 52. Metro Circo Massimo. Buses 60, 75, 118, 175, or 628. Tram 3. Tues–Sun 9am–sunset; Mon 9am–2pm. Closed Jan 1, May 1, and Dec 25. Admission 5€ ($6.25).*

See Map 8 on p. 78.

Battelli di Roma (p. 95) TRASTEVERE/CAMPO DE' FIORI Rome's riverboat service stops under Ponte Cestio, Ponte Sisto, and Ponte Sant'Angelo, and travels north to the Foro Italico. Not always scenic, but a break for your feet and fun for the kids.... *Tel 06/693-80-264. www.battellidiroma.it. Tickets 1€ ($1.25) for* *shuttle service; 10€–50€ ($13–$63) for guided, wine-tasting, or dinner cruises.*

See Map 8 on p. 78.

Bioparco (p. 102) VILLA BORGHESE More depressing than the eco-friendlier zoos elsewhere but slowly cleaning up its act.... *Tel 06/360-82-11. www.bioparco.it Via del Giardino Zoologico 1, at Via Ulisse Aldrovandi. Buses 52 or 53. Trams 3 or 19. Daily 9:30am–5pm. Admission 8.50€ ($11) adults, 6.50€ ($8.15) children 4–12, free for children under 4.*

See Map 8 on p. 78.

Bocca della Verità (p. 88) ANCIENT ROME Ancient sewer cover turned tourist attraction and lie detector.... *Tel 06/678-14-19. Piazza della Bocca della Verità 18. Buses 30 or 170. Daily 9am–1pm and 2:30–6pm (until 5pm Nov–March). Free admission.*

See Map 9 on p. 103.

Capitoline Museums (p. 91) ANCIENT ROME Two Michelangelo-designed *palazzi* with a vast collection of classical busts, statues, and Renaissance paintings. Home of the equestrian statue of Marcus Aurelius, the giant marble finger of Constantine, and the bronze She-Wolf.... *Tel 06/671-02-071. www.museicapitolini.org. Piazza del Campidoglio 1. Buses 30, 40, 46, 62, 64, 70, 87, 170, or H. Tues–Sun 9am–7pm; public holidays 9am–1pm. Closed Jan 1, May 1, and Dec 25. Admission 7.80€ ($9.75).*

See Map 9 on p. 103.

Casa di Goethe (p. 98) PIAZZA DEL POPOLO Former apartment of the German author displays sketches and paintings from his times, as well as some personal mementos.... *Tel 06/326-50-412. www.casadigoethe.it. Via del Corso 18–20, at Via della Fontanella. Metro Flaminio. Tues–Sun 10am–6pm. Admission 3€ ($3.75).*

See Map 11 on p. 105.

Castel Sant'Angelo (p. 84) VATICAN Medieval fortress built atop Hadrian's cylindrical mausoleum.... *Tel 06/687-50-36. Lungotevere Castello 50. Buses 23, 40, 46, 62, 64, 271, 280, or 571. Tues–Sun 9am–7pm. Closed public holidays. Admission 5€ ($6.25).*

See Map 8 on p. 78.

Catacombs of Domitilla (p. 97) APPIAN WAY/SOUTHERN SUBURBS Appia Antica–area catacombs with some important wall frescoes.... *Tel 06/511-03-42. Via delle Sette Chiese 282, off Via Ardeatina. Bus 118. Wed–Mon year-round 8:30am–noon; April–Sept 2:30–5:30pm; Oct–March 2:30–5pm. Closed Jan. Admission 5€ ($6.25).*

See Map 8 on p. 78.

Catacombs of San Callisto (p. 97) APPIAN WAY/SOUTHERN SUBURBS The largest of Rome's catacombs, and the most impressive of those open to the public. Beautifully kept gardens aboveground.... *Tel 06/513-01-580. www.catacombe.roma.it. Via Appia Antica 110–126, at Via Ardeatina. Bus 118. Thurs–Tues year-round 8:30am–noon; April–Sept 2:30–5:30pm; Oct–March 2:30–5pm. Closed Feb. Admission 5€ ($6.25).*

See Map 8 on p. 78.

Catacombs of San Sebastiano (p. 97) APPIAN WAY/SOUTHERN SUBURBS Mass burial site for Christians; adjoining *piazzuola* has interesting pagan tombs.... *Tel 06/788-70-35. Via Appia Antica 136, at Vicolo della Basilica. Bus 118. Mon–Sat year-round 9am–noon; May–Sept 2:30–6:30pm; Oct–April 2:30–5:30pm. Closed Nov. Admission 5€ ($6.25).*

See Map 8 on p. 78.

Circus and Villa of Maxentius (p. 99) APPIAN WAY/SOUTHERN SUBURBS Ruins of a 4th century A.D. emperor's villa/chariot racetrack complex on the Appian Way.... *Tel 06/780-13-24. Via Appia Antica 153, at Via di San Sebastiano. Tues–Sun 9am to 1 hr. before sunset. Admission 2.60€ ($3.25).*

See Map 8 on p. 78.

Circus Maximus (p. 85) ANCIENT ROME Venue for ancient chariot races and modern-day dog walks.... *No phone. Via del Circo Massimo. Metro Circo Massimo. Buses 60, 75, 175, or 628. Tram 3. Free admission.*

See Map 9 on p. 103.

Colosseum (p. 81) ANCIENT ROME Former fighting ground of gladiators and enduring emblem of imperial Rome.... *Tel 06/700-42-61. Piazza del Colosseo. Metro Colosseo. Buses 60, 75, 85, 87, 117, or 175. Daily 9am to 1 hr. before sunset. Closed Jan 1, May 1, and Dec 25. Admission 8€–10€ ($10–-$13) (ticket also good for admission at the Palatine Hill).*

See Map 9 on p. 103.

Column of Marcus Aurelius (p. 88) VIA DEL CORSO Marcus Aurelius's self-congratulatory tribute to his military prowess.... *No telephone. Piazza Colonna, at Via del Corso. Buses 62, 85, 95, 116, or 492.*

See Map 10 on p. 104.

Column of Trajan (p. 87) ANCIENT ROME Huge marble column with play-by-play recap of Trajan's campaigns in Dacia (Romania).... *No phone. Via dei Fori Imperiali, at Via Alessandrina. Buses 40, 60, 62, 64, 70, 85, 87, 117, 170, 175, 492, or H.*

See Map 9 on p. 103.

Crypt of the Capuchin Monks (p. 99) VENETO Above-ground crypt featuring numerous skulls. Hands-down the creepiest sight in Rome.... *Tel 06/488-27-48. Santa Maria della Concezione. Via Veneto 27, at Via San Nicola da Tolentino. Metro Barberini. Buses 52, 53, 62, 80, 95, 116, 175, or 492. Daily 7am–noon and*

3:45–7:30pm; crypt Fri–Wed 9am–noon and 3–6pm. Donation expected.

See Map 11 on p. 105.

Domus Aurea (p. 97) ANCIENT ROME The underground ruins of crazy emperor Nero's "Golden House," which once occupied a third of the city. Whimsical architecture and "grotesque" frescoes.... *Tel 06/399-67-700. Via Labicana 136, at Via della Domus Aurea. Metro Colosseo. Buses 60, 75, 85, 87, or 117. Tram 3. Wed–Mon 9am–7:45pm. Reservations required; book 1 week in advance. Admission 6.50€ ($8.15).*

See Map 9 on p. 103.

Fontana dei Quattro Fiumi (p. 90) PIAZZA NAVONA Bernini's signature fountain (completed in 1651), representing four rivers for four continents: the Danube, the Ganges, the Nile, and the Plata. Its "Egyptian" obelisk is actually a Roman fake and once stood on the Appian Way.... *No telephone. Piazza Navona. Buses 30 Express, 40, 62, 64, 70, 81, 87, 492, or 628. Free admission.*

See Map 10 on p. 104.

Foro Italico (p. 101) NORTHERN SUBURBS Massive sports complex on the river north of the city center, Mussolini's paean to the cult of athleticism. Check out hilarious Fascist-era sculptures and mosaics, and *Serie A* soccer games at the Stadio Olimpico.... *No telephone. Largo de Bosis, at Lungotevere Maresciallo Cadorna. Buses 32, 271, or 280. Tram 2. Free admission.*

See Map 8 on p. 78.

Galleria Borghese (p. 91) VILLA BORGHESE The Borghese family art collection is one of the richest and most manageable museums in the city, featuring Bernini's sublime sculptures of *Apollo and Daphne, The Rape of Persephone,* and *David,* as well as an impressive flush of Caravaggios.... *Tel 06/328-10. www.galleriaborghese.it. Piazzale Scipione Borghese 5, near Via Pinciana. Buses 52, 53, 116, or 910. Trams 3 or 19. Tues–Sun 9am–7pm. Closed public holidays. Reservations required; try to book 1 week in advance. Admission 8.50€ ($11).*

See Map 8 on p. 78.

Galleria Comunale d'Arte Moderna e Contemporanea (p. 100) VENETO Rome's municipal museum for modern art.... *Tel 06/47-42-84-89-09. Via F. Crispi 24. Metro Barberini. Buses 52, 53, 61, 62, 63, 71, 95, 175, 492, or 630. Tues–Sat 9am–7pm; Sun 9am–1pm. Admission 5€ ($6.25).*

See Map 8 on p. 78.

Galleria Doria Pamphilj (p. 94) PIAZZA VENEZIA One of the finest private art collections in Rome. Caravaggio, Titian, Raphael, and Velázquez are represented.... *Tel 06/679-73-23. www.doriapamphilj.it. Piazza del Collegio Romano 2, at Via del Corso.*

Buses 30, 40, 60, 62, 64, 70, 85, 87, 95, 117, 170, 175, 492, or 628. Fri–Wed 10am–5pm. Admission 8€ ($10).

See Map 11 on p. 105.

Galleria Nazionale d'Arte Moderna e Contemporanea (p. 100) VILLA BORGHESE Imposing *palazzo* in Villa Borghese, with Italy's largest collection of modern art.... *Tel 06/322-41-52. www.gnam.arti.beniculturali.it. Viale delle Belle Arti 131. Buses 490 or 495. Trams 3 or 19. Tues–Sun 8:30am–7:30pm. Admission 6.50€ ($8.15).*

See Map 8 on p. 78.

Galleria Spada (p. 94) CAMPO DE' FIORI The Titians and Guercinos are fine, but the *pièce de résistance* here is Borromini's illusionistic corridor.... *Tel 06/687-48-96. www.galleriaborghese.it/spada/en/einfo.htm. Piazza Capo di Ferro 3, at Via dei Balestrari. Buses 23, 271, or 280. Tram 8. Tues–Sun 8:30am–7:30pm. Admission 5€ ($6.25).*

See Map 10 on p. 104.

Gesù (p. 93) PIAZZA VENEZIA Rome's first Jesuit church; fantastic nave and dome, each frescoed by baroque artist Il Baciccia.... *Tel 06/678-63-41. Piazza del Gesù, at Via del Plebiscito. Buses 30, 40, 62, 64, 70, 81, 87, 492, or 571. Daily 7am–12:30pm and 4–7:15pm. Free admission.*

See Map 10 on p. 104.

Imperial Fora (p. 86) ANCIENT ROME Across Via dei Fori Imperiali from the main Forum, the *fora* of Augustus, Nerva, and Trajan were public squares built to accommodate the Roman population boom—and the egos of the emperors.... *Tel 06/679-77-86. www.capitolium.org (great info on the life and times of ancient Romans). Via dei Fori Imperiali. Metro Colosseo. Buses 60, 75, 84, 85, 87, 117, 175, or 571. Open to guided visits booked with the Imperial Forum Visitors' Center.*

See Map 9 on p. 103.

Isola Tiberina (p. 95) GHETTO/TRASTEVERE Building on an ancient Roman myth, early city architects constructed a travertine platform around the island so that it would resemble a ship. Port and starboard, fore and aft, the "decks" today are great for sunning. Long associated with healing, Isola Tiberina has its own hospital and small church.... *No telephone. Buses 23, 63, 271, 280, 780, or H. Tram 8. Free admission.*

See Map 8 on p. 78.

Keats-Shelley House (p. 98) SPANISH STEPS Shrine to English Romantic poets who lived in Italy.... *Tel 06/678-42-35. www.keats-shelley-house.org. Piazza di Spagna 26. Metro Spagna. Bus 117. Mon–Fri 9am–1pm and 3–6pm; Sat 11am–2pm and 4–6pm. Closed public holidays and 10 days in Aug. Admission 3€ ($3.75).*

See Map 11 on p. 105.

LunEUR (Luna Park) (p. 102) EUR Dinky amusement park in Rome's EUR suburbs has a loop-de-loop roller coaster and bumper boats. A good laugh for kids of all ages.... *Tel 06/591-44-01. www.luneur.it. Via delle Tre Fontane (EUR). Metro Magliana, Palasport, or EUR Fermi. Buses 706, 707, 714, 717, 765, or 771. Mid-June through mid-Sept Mon–Thurs 4pm–1am, Fri–Sat 4pm–2am, Sun 10am–1am; mid-Sept through mid-June Mon–Thurs 3–9pm, Fri–Sat 3pm–2am, Sun 10am–11pm. Free admission. Individual attractions priced separately.*

See Map 8 on p. 78.

MACRO (p. 100) EASTERN SUBURBS/TESTACCIO In the former Peroni brewery, the city's premier space for contemporary art exhibitions. Satellite location, the Mattatoio, is the brilliantly converted former city slaughterhouse... *Tel 06/884-49-30. www.macro.roma.museum. Via Reggio Emilia 84, at Via Alessandria. Mattatoio: Piazza O. Giustiniani 4. Buses 36, 60, 62, 63, 490, or 495. Tues–Sun 9am–7pm. Admission 4€ ($5).*

See Map 8 on p. 78.

Mamertine Prison (p. 100) ANCIENT ROME Torture and execution chamber for Rome's most formidable enemies from the Republic through the Empire. Legend says that St. Peter was imprisoned here.... *Tel 06/679-29-02. Clivo Argentario 1, at Via del Tulliano. Buses 60, 75, 85, 87, 117, 175, or 571. April–Sept daily 9am–noon and 2:30–6pm; Oct–March daily 9am–noon and 2–5pm. Donation expected.*

See Map 9 on p. 103.

Mausoleum of Augustus (p. 99) PIAZZA DEL POPOLO Cylindrical tomb of Rome's first emperor, now derelict and overgrown with weeds in an otherwise fancy part of town.... *No telephone. Piazza Augusto Imperatore. Metro Flaminio. Buses 224 or 913. Open by appointment only; see "The X-Files," earlier in this chapter, for details.*

See Map 11 on p. 105.

Mausoleum of Hadrian See Castel Sant'Angelo.

Museo Civico di Zoologia (p. 102) VILLA BORGHESE Natural-history museum with exhibits of indigenous flora and fauna and an enormous whale skeleton.... *Tel 06/321-65-86. www2.comune.roma.it/museozoologia. Via Ulisse Aldrovandi 18, at Via S. Mercadante. Buses 52, 53, or 910. Trams 3 or 19. Tues–Sun 9am–5pm. Admission 4.50€ ($5.65) adults, 2.50€ ($3.15) children 8–15, free for children under 8.*

See Map 8 on p. 78.

Museo della Civiltà Romana (p. 101) EUR Home to the immense and fascinating 1:250 model of Rome in the 4th century A.D.; other highlights are small-scale and full-scale models of ancient

Roman buildings and monuments.... *Tel 06/592-60-41. www.museidiroma.com/civilta.html. Piazza Giovanni Agnelli 10, off Via Cristoforo Colombo. Metro EUR Palasport or EUR Fermi. Tues–Sat 9am–7pm; Sun 9am–1pm. Admission 6.20€ ($7.75).*

See Map 8 on p. 78.

Museo dell'Alto Medioevo (p. 101) EUR Art and relics from medieval Rome.... *Tel 06/54-22-81-99. Viale Lincoln 3, off Via Cristoforo Colombo. Metro EUR Marconi. Tues–Sat 9am–2pm; Sun 9am–1pm. Admission 4€ ($5).*

See Map 8 on p. 78.

Museo delle Anime dei Defunti (p. 99) VATICAN Two display cases' worth of money, clothing, and Bibles "burned" by the fingers of souls in purgatory.... *Tel 06/680-65-17. Sacro Cuore church, Lungotevere Prati 12, near Via Ulpiani. Metro Lepanto. Buses 49, 70, 87, or 280. Daily 7–11am and 4:30–7pm. Free admission.*

See Map 8 on p. 78.

Museo Nazionale Romano (p. 89) TERMINI Mind-boggling collection of Etruscan and Roman artifacts, including stone inscriptions, vase fragments, everyday tools, marble busts, frescoes, and mosaics. So vast, it's housed in four separate buildings: Palazzo Massimo (Largo di Villa Peretti 1; Metro Termini); Palazzo Altemps (Piazza San Apollinare 44; buses 70, 87, or 492 to Via Zanardelli/Piazza Cinque Lune); Baths of Diocletian (Viale Enrico de Nicola 79; Metro Repubblica); and Crypta Balbi (Via delle Botteghe Oscure 31; buses 30, 40, 62, 64, 70, 87, or 492, or tram 8 to Largo Argentina).... *Tel 06/399-67-700. Tues–Sun 9am–7pm. Admission 6€ ($7.50) at each location.*

See Map 8 on p. 78.

Order of the Knights of Malta (p. 97) AVENTINE Bronze keyhole offers perfectly framed view of St. Peter's, 2 miles away.... *No telephone. Piazza dei Cavalieri di Malta, off Via di Santa Sabina. Metro Circo Massimo. Buses 30, 95, or 175. Tram 3.*

See Map 9 on p. 103.

Palatine Hill (p. 85) ANCIENT ROME Archaeological park contains the ruins of imperial palaces, the elusive Hut of Romulus, and lots of greenery.... *Tel 06/699-01-10. Entrance on Via di San Gregorio or via the Forum. Metro Colosseo. Buses 60, 75, 85, 87, 117, 175, or 571. Daily 9am to 1 hr. before sunset. Admission 8€–10€ ($10–$13); ticket also good for admission at the Colosseum.*

See Map 9 on p. 103.

Palazzo della Civiltà del Lavoro (p. 101) EUR The Fascist version of the Colosseum (the "square Colosseum" or the "*Colosseo quadrato*") and the imposing anchor of the EUR enclave.... *No telephone. Viale della Civiltà del Lavoro, off Via Cristoforo Colombo. Metro EUR Palasport. Not open to the public.*

See Map 8 on p. 78.

Palazzo Farnese (p. 90) CAMPO DE' FIORI Gorgeous Renaissance palace designed in part by Michelangelo, now the French embassy.... *No telephone for the public. Piazza Farnese. Buses 23, 30, 40, 46, 62, 64, 87, 115, 116, 271, or 280. Tram 8. Not open to the public.*

See Map 10 on p. 104.

Palazzo Venezia (p. 94) PIAZZA VENEZIA Built in 1455, became Mussolini's headquarters in 1929 (he gave rousing speeches from its balcony). Museum has unrelated decorative art and temporary exhibitions.... *Tel 06/679-8865. Via del Plebiscito 118, at Piazza Venezia. Buses 30, 40, 62, 64, 70, 85, 87, 95, 170, 175, 492, or 571. Tues–Sat 9am–7:30pm. Admission 4€ ($5).*

See Map 10 on p. 104.

Pantheon (p. 81) A marvel of engineering, the A.D. 125 temple of all gods is the best-preserved ancient Roman building in the world, period. Rain falls through the *oculus* in the dome.... *Tel 06/ 6830-0230. Piazza della Rotonda. Buses 30, 40, 62, 64, 70, 87, 116, 492, or 571. Mon–Sun 9am–7pm; public holidays 9am–1pm. Closed Jan 1, May 1, and Dec 25. Free admission.*

See Map 10 on p. 104.

Piazza del Campidoglio (Capitoline Hill) (p. 90) ANCIENT ROME Glorious and mighty civic space, designed by Michelangelo; a copy of the equestrian statue of Marcus Aurelius stands in the middle of the square.... *No telephone. Piazza del Campidoglio. Buses 30, 40, 46, 62, 64, 70, 87, 170, or H. Free admission.*

See Map 9 on p. 103.

Pincio (p. 96) VILLA BORGHESE Romantic stone parapets and great views over domes and rooftops to the Vatican.... *No telephone. Piazzale Napoleone. Metro Flaminio. Buses 117 or 119. Free admission.*

See Map 11 on p. 105.

Ponte Cestio (p. 95) TIBER ISLAND Built in the 1st century B.C., this bridge was restored in A.D. 370.... *No telephone. Ponte Cestio, at Lungotevere degli Anguillara. Buses 23, 271, 280, or 780.*

See Map 8 on p. 78.

Ponte Fabricio (p. 95) TIBER ISLAND Rome's oldest bridge, built in 62 B.C., and still used today as a footbridge. During the Middle Ages, two powerful families controlled its use by erecting a toll tower, still standing.... *No telephone. Ponte Fabricio, at Lungotevere dei Cenci. Buses 23, 271, 280, or 780.*

See Map 8 on p. 78.

Ponte Rotto (p. 95) TIBER ISLAND/AVENTINE The "broken bridge," which fell in 1588. Best viewed from Isola Tiberina.... *No telephone. Below Ponte Palatino. Buses 23, 271, 280, or 780. No access.*

Ponte Sisto TRASTEVERE Pedestrian bridge linking Trastevere with Campo de' Fiori. Popular squat of drunken beggars.... *No telephone. Ponte Sisto, between Lungotevere dei Vallati/dei Tebaldi and Piazza Trilussa. Buses 23, 115, 116, 271, or 280.*

See Map 10 on p. 104.

Porticus of Octavia (p. 86) GHETTO A monumental gateway to an ancient temple precinct, now engulfed by the Ghetto.... *No telephone. Via del Portico d'Ottavia, at Largo 16 Ottobre. Buses 23, 271, 280, or 780. Tram 8. Daily 9am to 1 hr. before sunset. Free admission.*

See Map 10 on p. 104.

Protestant Cemetery (p. 98) TESTACCIO The peaceful Cimitero Acattolico is the final resting place of Keats, Shelley, Gramsci, and other non-Catholics.... *Tel 06/574-19-00. Via Caio Cestio 6, near Piazzale Ostiense. Metro Piramide. Buses 23, 30, 60, or 95. Tram 3. Tues–Sun April–Sept 9am–6pm; Oct–March 9am–5pm. Last admission 30 min. before closing. Donation expected.*

See Map 8 on p. 78.

Pyramid of Caius Cestius (p. 99) TESTACCIO Egypt-inspired tomb of a wealthy Roman who died in 12 B.C.... *No telephone. Piazzale Ostiense. Metro Piramide. Buses 23, 30, 60, or 95. Tram 3. Not open to the public.*

See Map 8 on p. 78.

Roman Forum (p. 84) ANCIENT ROME Marble skeletons of downtown ancient Rome; this was the center of the world for the 700 years that Rome ruled it. The ruins are at their most dramatic in the early morning, at dusk, or after dark.... *Tel 06/699-01-10. Via dei Fori Imperiali (entrances at Largo Romolo e Remo and by the Arch of Titus). Metro Colosseo. Buses 60, 75, 84, 85, 87, 117, 175, 271, or 571. Daily 9am to 1 hr. before sunset. Closed Jan 1, May 1, and Dec 25. Free admission.*

See Map 9 on p. 103.

San Clemente (p. 97) ANCIENT ROME/SAN GIOVANNI Multiple layers at this church demonstrate Rome's checkered architectural history.... *Tel 06/704-51-018. Via di San Giovanni in Laterano, at Piazzale San Clemente. Metro Colosseo. Buses 85, 87, 117, or 571. Tram 3. Mon–Sat year-round 9am–12:30pm; April–Sept 3:30–6:30pm; Oct–March 3:30–6pm; Sun year-round 10am–12:30pm and 3:30–6:30pm. Free admission to church; 3€ ($3.75) for excavations.*

See Map 8 on p. 78.

San Francesco a Ripa (p. 90) TRASTEVERE A hospice when St. Francis of Assisi visited Rome in 1219, this modest church still contains his crucifix and stone pillow, as well as Bernini's racy *Beata Ludovica Albertoni*.... *Tel 06/581-90-20. Piazza San*

Francesco d'Assisi 88, near Via di Porta Portese. Buses 23, 280, or 780. Tram 8. Daily 7:30am–noon and 4–7pm. Free admission.

See Map 8 on p. 78.

San Giovanni in Laterano (p. 92) SAN GIOVANNI The cathedral of Rome is a baroque church with an ancient history. Before the papacy moved to France in 1309, this and the adjoining Lateran Palace, not the Vatican, were the main church and residence of the pope.... *Tel 06/77-20-79-91. Piazza di San Giovanni in Laterano 4. Metro San Giovanni. Buses 85, 87, 117, or 571. Tram 3. April–Sept daily 7am–7pm; Oct–March daily 7am–6pm. Free admission to church; 2€ ($2.50) for cloister.*

See Map 8 on p. 78.

San Luigi dei Francesi (p. 93) PANTHEON The church of French expats in Rome, most remarkable for its Caravaggio *Life of St. Matthew* masterpieces, located in the fifth chapel on the left.... *Tel 06/688-271. Piazza San Luigi dei Francesi, at Via del Salvatore. Buses 30, 70, 81, 87, 116, or 492. Daily 8am–12:30pm; Fri–Wed 3:30–7pm. Free admission.*

See Map 10 on p. 104.

San Paolo Fuori le Mura (p. 92) OSTIENSE Huge pilgrimage church, rebuilt on the site of a 4th-century basilica destroyed by fire in the 1800s.... *Tel 06/541-03-41. Viale di San Paolo, at Via Ostiense. Metro San Paolo. Buses 23 or 271. Daily 7:30am–6:40pm (last admission 15 min. before closing). Free admission.*

See Map 8 on p. 78.

San Pietro in Vincoli (p. 90) ANCIENT ROME "St. Peter in Chains" features the shackles that supposedly held St. Peter captive in Mamertine Prison, as well as Michelangelo's imposing *Moses*.... *Tel 06/488-28-65. Piazza di San Pietro in Vincoli 4a, off Via Cavour. Metro Colosseo. Buses 60, 75, 84, 85, 87, 117, 175, or 571. Year-round daily 7am–12:30pm; April–Sept daily 3:30–7pm; Oct–March daily 3:30–6pm. Free admission.*

See Map 8 on p. 78.

Santa Cecilia (p. 100) TRASTEVERE Cavallini frescoes and a morbid sculpture of Santa Cecilia—her neck is slashed—are the highlights of this pretty church.... *Tel 06/581-90-20. Piazza Santa Cecilia, off Via di Santa Cecilia. Buses 23, 280, or 780. Tram 8. Daily 7:30am–noon and 4–7pm. Free admission.*

See Map 8 on p. 78.

Santa Croce in Gerusalemme (p. 93) SAN GIOVANNI/ESQUILINO Big-time relics from the actual Passion of the Christ—three pieces of the cross, a nail, and two thorns—are kept in a display case in a chapel to the left of the altar. Also be on the lookout for a finger, said to be the very one doubting St. Thomas stuck into Christ's wound.... *Tel 06/701-47-69. www.basilicasanta croce.it. Piazza di Santa Croce in Gerusalemme 12. Metro Vittorio. Bus 649. Tram 3. Daily 6am–12:30pm and 3:30–7pm. Free admission.*

See Map 8 on p. 78.

Santa Maria della Pace (p. 93) PIAZZA NAVONA Graceful little neoclassical church near chic cafes, home to Raphael's *Sybil* frescoes.... *Tel 06/686-11-56. Vicolo del Arco della Pace 5, at Via della Pace. Buses 70, 81, 87, 116, or 492. Tues–Sat 10am–noon and 4–6pm; Sun 9–11am. Free admission.*

See Map 10 on p. 104.

Santa Maria della Vittoria (p. 90) QUIRINALE/TERMINI The Cornaro Chapel houses Bernini's ostensibly spiritual, unmistakably sexual *Ecstasy of St. Teresa*.... *Tel 06/482-61-90. Via XX Settembre 17, at Largo Santa Susanna. Metro Repubblica. Buses 60, 62, or 492. Daily 6:30am–noon and 4:30–6pm. Free admission.*

See Map 8 on p. 78.

Santa Maria del Popolo (p. 93) PIAZZA DEL POPOLO Home to Caravaggio's *Martyrdom of St. Peter* and *Conversion of St. Paul;* the Chigi Chapel features sculpture by Bernini.... *Tel 06/361-08-36. Piazza del Popolo 12. Metro Flaminio. Buses 117 or 119. Mon–Sat 7am–noon and 4–7pm; Sun 8am–2pm and 4:30–7:30pm. Free admission.*

See Map 11 on p. 105.

Santa Maria in Cosmedin ANCIENT ROME The most important Greek church in Rome. Site of the Mouth of the Truth and Byzantine mosaics.... *Tel 06/678-14-19. Piazza della Bocca della Verità 18. Buses 23, 30, 170, 271, or 280. Daily 9am–1pm and 2:30–6pm (until 5pm Nov–March). Free admission.*

See Map 9 on p. 103.

Santa Maria in Trastevere (p. 93) TRASTEVERE Large medieval basilica whose facade and apse glisten with polychrome and gold 12th-century mosaics. Mosaics above the altar are by Cavallini.... *Tel 06/581-94-43. Piazza Santa Maria, in Trastevere. Buses 23, 271, 280, or 780. Tram 8. Daily 7:30am–8pm. Free admission.*

See Map 8 on p. 78.

Santa Maria Maggiore (p. 92) TERMINI/ESQUILINO One of Rome's four patriarchal basilicas, Santa Maria Maggiore contains a dazzling series of 5th-century biblical mosaics on its triumphal arch.... *Tel 06/48-31-95. Piazza di Santa Maria Maggiore. Metro Termini or Cavour. Bus 70. Daily 7am–7pm (last admission 15 min. before closing). Free admission.*

See Map 8 on p. 78.

Santa Maria Sopra Minerva (p. 96) PANTHEON Rome's only Gothic-style church has blue, peaked vaults awash in a starry sky motif, the tombs of St. Catherine of Siena and Fra Angelico, and a bad Michelangelo *(Christ Carrying the Cross)*.... *Tel 06/679-39-26. Piazza della Minerva 42. Buses 30, 40, 46, 62, 64, 70, 81, 87, 116, 492, or 571. Daily 7am–noon and 4–7pm; cloister Mon–Sat 8:30am–1pm and 4–7pm. Free admission.*

See Map 10 on p. 104.

Sant'Ignazio (p. 93) PANTHEON Andrea Pozzo's "dome" is one of the finest examples of *trompe l'oeil* in the city.... *Tel 06/679-44-06. Piazza di Sant'Ignazio, near the Pantheon. Buses 30, 40, 46, 62, 64, 70, 87, 116, 492, or 571. Daily 7:30am–12:30pm and 4–7:15pm. Free admission.*

See Map 10 on p. 104.

Santo Stefano Rotondo (p. 100) SAN GIOVANNI/COLOSSEUM Haunting, round church with gruesome frescoes of martyrdoms.... *Tel 06/421-191. Via di Santo Stefano Rotondo 7, at Via della Navicella. Bus 81. Year-round Tues–Sat 9am–1pm; April–Oct Mon–Sat 3:30–6pm; Nov–March Mon–Sat 2–4pm. Free admission.*

See Map 8 on p. 78.

Scala Santa and Sancta Sanctorum (p. 92 and p. 93) SAN GIOVANNI Taken from Jerusalem in the 4th century, the Holy Stairs (Scala Santa) are climbed by good pilgrims on their knees. At the top, the "Holy of Holies" has a bench from the Last Supper and Cimabue frescoes.... *Tel 06/70-49-44-89. Piazza di San Giovanni in Laterano 14. Metro San Giovanni. Buses 85, 87, or 571. Tram 3. Daily 6:30–11:50am and 3:30–6:45pm. Free admission for Scala Santa; 3€ ($3.75) for Sancta Sanctorum.*

See Map 8 on p. 78.

Sistine Chapel (p. 86) VATICAN Built for Pope Sixtus IV in the 1470s and frescoed over the next 50 years by Italy's Renaissance masters, from Botticelli to Michelangelo, who did the famous *Creation* on the ceiling from 1508–12 and the *Last Judgement* on the altar wall from 1535–41. Also the site of papal elections.... *For details, see "Vatican Museums," below.*

See Map 8 on p. 78.

Spanish Steps (Scalinata di Spagna) (p. 81) The gracious sweep of travertine steps leads from Piazza di Spagna up to Trinità dei Monti. Called "Spanish" because the Spanish embassy to the Vatican is located opposite; actually designed by a Frenchman, De Sanctis, and built by Italians.... *No telephone. Piazza di Spagna. Metro Spagna. Buses 117 or 119.*

See Map 11 on p. 105.

St. Peter's Basilica (p. 84) VATICAN The largest church in Christendom and tallest building in Rome, with a museum-like collection of sculptural masterpieces, including Michelangelo's *Pietà* and Bernini's *baldacchino*.... *Tel 06/698-84-466 or 06/698-84-866. Piazza San Pietro. Metro Ottaviano. Buses 23, 40, 46, 62, or 64. Tram 19. Daily 7am–7pm; treasury April–Sept 9am–6:30pm, Oct–March 9am–5:30pm; Vatican grottoes April–Sept 7am–6pm, Oct–March 7am–5pm; dome April–Sept 8am–6pm, Oct–March 8am–5pm. Free admission to basilica and grottoes (crypt); treasury 3€ ($3.75); dome 4€ ($5) if you walk, 5€ ($6.25) if you take the lift halfway up.*

See Map 8 on p. 78.

Synagogue (p. 96) GHETTO Admission includes a tour of the on-site museum containing important relics from Rome's long-standing Jewish community.... *Tel 06/68-40-06-61. www.museoebraico.roma.it. Lungotevere dei Cenci, at Via del Tempio. Buses 23, 271, 280, or 780. Tram 8. Mon–Thurs 9am–5pm; Fri 9am–2pm; Sun 9:30am–12:30pm. Closed public holidays. Admission 6€ ($7.50).*

See Map 8 on p. 78.

Theater of Marcellus (p. 86) GHETTO 13 B.C. theater reborn as Renaissance palace, still inhabited.... *Tel 06/481-48-00. Via del Teatro di Marcello. Buses 23, 30, 170, 271, 280, or 780. Tram 8. Exterior daily 9am to 1 hr. before sunset. Free admission to exterior.*

See Map 10 on p. 104.

Tomb of Cecilia Metella (p. 99) APPIAN WAY/SOUTHERN SUBURBS The landmark round mausoleum featured in romantic depictions of the Roman countryside.... *Tel 06/780-24-65. Via Appia Antica 161, at Via di Cecilia Metella. Bus 118. Tues–Sun 9am to 1 hr. before sunset. Closed public holidays. Admission 2€ ($2.50).*

See Map 8 on p. 78.

Trajan's Markets (p. 86) ANCIENT ROME Ruins of a three-story ancient shopping center.... *Tel 06/679-00-48. Via IV Novembre, at Via Magnanapoli. Buses 40, 60, 64, 70, 75, or 170. Tues–Sun 9am–7pm (last admission 1 hr. before closing). Admission 6.20€ ($7.75).*

See Map 9 on p. 103.

Trevi Fountain (Fontana di Trevi) (p. 81) TREVI Rome's most over-the-top and inviting fountain. Truly awesome and crowd-free from 2 to 7am.... *No telephone. Fontana di Trevi. Buses 52, 53, 62, 95, 116, 175, or 492.*

See Map 11 on p. 105.

Vatican Museums (p. 84) Former papal palaces containing some of the most priceless works of art in the world. The Greco-Roman sculpture collection, the Gallery of the Maps, the Raphael Rooms, and the Sistine Chapel are not to be missed when in Rome.... *Tel 06/698-83-333. http://mv.vatican.va. Città del Vaticano. Metro Ottaviano. Nov–Feb Mon–Sat 8:45am–1:45pm;*

March–Oct Mon–Sat 8:45am–4:45pm; last Sun of month 8:45am–1:45pm (last admission 1 hr 25 min before closing). Closed Jan 1 and 6; Feb 11; March 19; Easter and Easter Monday; May 1, 5, and 26; June 29; Aug 15; Nov 1; Dec 8, 25, and 26. Admission 12€ ($15) adults, 8€ ($10) students. Free on last Sun of month.

See Map 8 on p. 78.

Vatican Necropolis (Tomb of St Peter) (p. 98) Catacomb-like excavations under the massive St Peter's basilica give even non-Catholics the chills.... *Tel 06/698-85-318. Fax 06/698-85-518. uff.scavi@fabricsp.va. Città del Vaticano, along south wall of St Peter's. Metro Ottaviano. Mon–Sat by appointment only. Fax or e-mail request at least 1 month in advance. Admission 9€ ($11).*

See Map 8 on p. 78.

Villa Borghese (p. 81) Rome's most central park, with lawns and umbrella pines, museums, a zoo, a lake, and great views from the Pincio gardens. Bikes, rowboats, and in-line skates available for rent.... *www.villaborghese.it. See individual reviews for Bioparco, Galleria Borghese, Museo Nazionale dell'Arte Moderna e Contemporanea, and Villa Giulia. See also the Getting Outside chapter. Free admission to park.*

See Map 11 on p. 105.

Villa Farnesina (p. 94) TRASTEVERE Former Farnese family villa, home to Raphael's lush, "undersea" *Triumph of Galatea* fresco.... *Tel 06/688-01-767. Via della Lungara 230, near Via dei Riari. Buses 23, 115, 271, or 280. Tues–Fri 9am–1pm; Mon and Sat 9am–4pm. Admission 4.50€ ($5.65).*

See Map 8 on p. 78.

Villa Giulia (p. 92) VILLA BORGHESE Home of the excellent, under-visited National Etruscan Museum. Highlights are the Marriage Sarcophagus and cases of exquisite gold jewelry.... *Tel 06/322-65-71. Piazzale di Villa Giulia 9, at Viale delle Belle Arti. Buses 52, 490, or 495. Trams 2, 3, or 19. Tues–Sat 9am–7pm; Sun 9am–1pm. Admission 4€ ($5).*

See Map 8 on p. 78.

Vittoriano (p. 94) PIAZZA VENEZIA Rome's largest monument, locally reviled as "the typewriter".... *Tel 06/699-17-18. Piazza Venezia. Buses 30, 40, 60, 62, 64, 70, 85, 87, 95, 117, 170, 175, 492, or 628. Tues–Sun 10am–4pm. Free admission to exterior and climb to upper terraces.*

See Map 10 on p. 104.

GETTING

OUTSIDE

4

Basic Stuff

For all its traffic and urban chaos, Rome is amazingly well endowed with *pulmoni verdi* ("green lungs"); in fact, there's more parkland per square kilometer here than in any other large city in Europe. To the south of Piazza Venezia, the narrow, cobblestoned alleys of the *centro storico* give way to Rome's wide-open archaeological areas, with their broad swathes of grass and umbrella pines. Planted in the Fascist era to accentuate the monumentality of ancient Rome, these sexy, signature trees stand in proud ranks all over town, cutting an especially fine figure on the high ridge above the Circus Maximus and along the boulevards leading to the Colosseum. Elsewhere in town, the villas that once belonged to Rome's nobility—sprawling estates that verge on wilderness—are now public parks where you can walk or jog on groomed paths, make out on romantic benches, or picnic on the grass. If, on the other hand, you want to leave the urban grind completely, there are plenty of fun and rewarding day trips you can take, whether it's a romp through Etruscan tombs, a visit to a charming hill town, or a dip in the Mediterranean.

The Lowdown

City parks and green spaces... Villa Borghese (Metro Spagna) is Rome's best known and most central park, bordered on the west by the Pincio Gardens and on the south by the Aurelian Walls and Via Veneto. With a circumference of about 6km (4 miles), the grounds include an artificial lake with rowboats, broad avenues and narrower paths, a pathetic zoo, a few museums, and acres of grass shaded by umbrella pines and cedars of Lebanon. Villa Borghese is at its best on uncrowded weekdays; on weekends, the park teems with tourists, families, and lovers, and can be anything but relaxing. At the **Circus Maximus** (Metro Circo Massimo), the storied venue for ancient Rome's chariot races, the packed dirt of the sunken track area sees its share of (mostly foreign) walkers and joggers, and its grassier, flatter north end makes a decent pitch for impromptu soccer matches. Locals recline and smoke joints on the grassy slopes where the stadium seating used to be, but the real drug here is the view of the Palatine hill ruins presiding imperially over the opposite side of the track. With giant shade trees, paved trails, and a playground, **Villa Celimontana** (buses 60, 75, 81, or 175; tram 3), on the Celio hill south of the Colosseum, provides welcome relief after traipsing through the ruins of ancient Rome. Also in the vicinity is the **Colle Oppio** park (Metro Colosseo); parts of it are graffiti tagged and derelict, but the area near the entrance to the **Domus Aurea** (Nero's palace) is well kept and a pleasant place to relax. The beloved **Gianicolo** (Janiculum hill; bus 870) is the panoramic ridge above Trastevere, just south of the Vatican. Dotted with grassy areas and sycamore trees, the gorgeous lookout spot is populated by balloon-toting tots during the day and steamy-windowed cars by night. If you're near the Gianicolo around noon, brace yourself—each day, at noon sharp, the cannon on the hill by the Garibaldi monument is fired. Listen carefully for the splash in the river a few seconds later—nah, just kidding, it's a blank shot, but you'll jump a mile if you're caught unaware. Just west of the Gianicolo is **Villa Doria Pamphilj** (buses 44, 75, or 870), Rome's largest park, also known as the Giardino del Belrespiro ("garden of good breathing"). Its 182 hectares (455 acres) include formal gardens, patterned flower beds, and man-made grottoes, but the vast majority of the space is rolling meadows and dense woods, with well-kept trails throughout. Northeast of the city center, well off the beaten tourist track, **Villa Ada** (buses 52, 53, 63, or 310; trams 3 or 19) is the public park of choice for affluent Pariolini. Once the private hunting ground of the House of Savoy (the Italian royal family), Villa Ada is now home to the Italian bureau of the World Wildlife Fund. The vegetation here is thick, with lots of huge pines, cypresses, holm oaks, and palm trees.

Where to work out... While Italy has a strong athletic tradition, Romans tend to stay in shape by gesticulating, smoking, and kick-starting their scooters rather than actually breaking a sweat. Visitors determined to get in a workout or two while in Rome are probably kidding themselves, but you do have a few options beyond squats and push-ups in the hotel room. Joggers can hit the ancient chariot track at the **Circus Maximus.** This is kind of amateur turf, though; just south of here, the shady green belt opposite the **Baths of Caracalla** (Metro Circo Massimo) attracts a more fleet-footed crowd. **Villa Borghese** has a handsome network of groomed paths that wind around statues, neoclassical temples, and man-made ponds, making for a lovely jog on a weekday morning. Go on Saturday or Sunday, though, and you'll have to contend with teetering inline skaters, reckless tricycles, and an amusing pageant of see-and-be-seen pseudo-athletes in Prada workout gear. Alternatively, the rolling hills of **Villa Pamphilj** have plenty of wooded trails for walkers and runners, as well as exercise stations along the way. Marathoners may want to consider timing their trip to coincide with the **Maratona di Roma** (www.maratonadiroma.it), held every year in late March. Rome's 26-miler zigzags past many of the city's most famous sights, from St. Peter's to the Foro Italico to the finish line at the Colosseum. For amateurs, the 5K **Stracittadina** fun run is held on the same day. Another 5K run, the hugely popular **Susan G. Komen Race for the Cure** (www.komen.org), takes place every year on a Sunday in late May in the heart of Rome's green archaeological zone, raising money to fight breast cancer. **Roman Sports Center** (Tel 06/320-16-67), under Villa Borghese, is the best-equipped and most central large gym in the city and accepts day members (Metro Spagna, then a long series of moving walkways; rates from 30€/$38 per day). Yogis who can't kick the habit can contact **Context Rome** (Tel 06/482-0911 in Italy; 888/467-1986 from the U.S.; info@contextrome.com) for a private instructor.

Free wheelin'... I won't sugarcoat it: Motorscooters really do fly at you like bats out of hell in Rome. While some people find this off-putting, I say, if you can't beat 'em, join 'em. For the image-conscious scooter-renter, **RomaRent,** Vicolo dei Bovari 7a (Tel 06/689-6555; buses 40, 62, 64, 87, 116, or 492), near Campo de' Fiori, has a stylish fleet of orange Vespas. (*Motorini* at other rental outfits tend to be dorkier models, with the agency's name and phone number embarrassingly emblazoned all over the chassis.) Bicycling can be a fun way to see the city, but rough patches of cobblestones and the crush of Rome's weekday traffic can make for a stressful ride. If you are dead-set on pedaling yourself around town, stick to the parks as much as possible or ride on weekends, when traffic is much lighter. Alternatively, sign up for **Enjoy Rome**'s 3-hour bike tour, offered March to October (Tel 06/445-1843; 25€/$31). You can rent both bikes and scooters at Villa Borghese from **I Bike Rome** (Tel 06/322-52-40), a mobile kiosk on the west side of the park, near Viale delle Magnolie. **Collati,** Via del Pellegrino 82 (Tel 06/688-01-084; buses 40, 62, 64, or 116), is a small, bikes-only rental shop near Campo de' Fiori. **Francesco Tranchina,** Via Cavour

80a (Tel 06/481-58-669; csdovt@tin.it), runs a comprehensive rental shop near Termini station; old-school gearless bicycles, new-fangled scooters, and souped-up motorcycles are all available for hire. A bike rental should run you about 3€ ($3.75) per hour or 15€ ($19) per day, while most scooter rentals start at 40€ ($50) per day—depending on the model and engine size. Most scooter rentals require a cash or credit card deposit of 250€ ($313) or so. (You'll find me lobbying for scooters throughout this book, but the little rascals are not without their hazards: Watch out for cobblestones jutting up at weird angles and don't drive in the rain, when the cobbles get perilously slippery. If you do have an *incidente,* remember that emergency care is free at Italian hospitals.)

Giddy-up... Horse-drawn carriage tours of Rome are bumpy, smelly, and overpriced (100€/$125 gets you an hour). For a much more memorable and unique equestrian experience, trot 5km (3 miles) south of the center to the **Cavalieri dell'Appia Antica** (Tel 06/780-12-14; reservations required), where even novices can go for pleasant hour-long excursions among the ruins and lush greenery of the Appian Way for 15€ ($19) per person.

Poolside... Rome in July and August can be torrid, and summer visitors who try to do too much sightseeing will quickly hit thermal breakdown. Addled by the heat, some jump into the Trevi Fountain (which is fun, but illegal), or worse yet, the Tiber (which is just plain nasty). To cool off in a hurry, we suggest you find the nearest hotel pool—just be prepared to hand over some serious cash for the privilege of using the not-very-luxurious facilities. The **Cavalieri Hilton, Grand Hotel del Gianicolo, Exedra, Radisson–SAS,** and **Parco dei Principi** hotels (see the Accommodations chapter) all offer free pool privileges to hotel guests, but fees for nonguests range from 25€ to 45€ ($31–$56) per day for adults and 15€ to 25€ ($19–$31) per day for kids under 12. As for public pools, EUR's Olympic-size **Piscina delle Rose,** Viale America 20 (Tel 06/592-67-17; Metro EUR Palasport), has rates from 10€ to 12€ ($13–$15) per person per day—and you pay only 5€ ($6.25) if you get there after 5pm. Another pool is the **Oasi della Pace,** Via degli Eugenii 2 (Tel 06/718-45-50), a basic facility located off the Via Appia Antica. Rates here are 8€ ($10) on weekdays, 10€

($13) on weekends. All pools require that you wear a bathing cap, sold for 5€ ($6.25) or so on-site.

Get outta town!... There are so many delightful day trips to take from Rome that it's hard to pick just one. About 30km (18 miles) east of Rome, **Tivoli** is a classic day trip, with its two UNESCO World Heritage sites, **Villa d'Este** and **Villa Adriana (Hadrian's Villa).** The steeply terraced gardens of the 16th century Villa d'Este (Tel 0774/31-20-70) are world-famous for their astounding orgy of fountains, from gushing gargoyles to inviting grottoes with waterfalls. Five kilometers (3 miles) down the hill from Villa d'Este and Tivoli proper are the vast and delightful remains of **Hadrian's Villa** (Tel 0774/53-02-03), whose ingenious architecture and landscape design features are totally unique in the Roman world. Highlights of the 2nd century A.D. emperor's summer playground include the **Canopus,** a faux Egyptian canal with sunbathing marble crocodiles and an elegant arcade supported by caryatids, and the **Maritime Theater,** an elaborate island "living room" and circular lap pool once equipped with an artificial current. (To get to Tivoli, take a COTRAL bus to Tivoli/Villa Adriana from Metro Ponte Mammolo; about 1 hr.)

Even closer (and easier to get to) than Tivoli is Rome's ancient port city, **Ostia Antica** (Tel 06/563-52-830; take the Ostia–Lido train from Piramide/Porta San Paolo station; about 30 min.). The extensive ruins at this once-booming town offer a fascinating look at daily life in ancient Rome—especially interesting are the Corporations Square, with its great mosaics; apartment blocks; cafes; baths; and the perennial-favorite ancient latrine. About an hour's bus ride northwest of Rome is the fantastic Etruscan necropolis at **Cerveteri,** Necropoli della Banditaccia (Tel 06/994-00-01; take a COTRAL bus from Metro Lepanto)—a totally Indiana Jones-ish, junglelike environment where you can climb all over and explore the cavernous innards of hundreds of 2,500-year-old *tumuli* (giant mound-shaped burial chambers). Other ideas for day trips are **Lake Bracciano** (Roma-Nord from Flaminio/Metro Line A to Saxa Rubra, then COTRAL bus to Bracciano/Anguillara), where you can visit a castle and go for a swim; **Orvieto** (train from Roma Termini, about 1 hr.)—perched high atop a spur of red tufa, this Umbrian town has picturesque medieval architecture and an exquisite *duomo;* and **Palestrina,** a medieval town just southeast of Rome (take a COTRAL bus to Palestrina from Metro Ponte Mammolo; about 1 hr.). There, you'll find the impressive Roman ruins of the 1st century B.C. hillside sanctuary of **Fortuna Primigenia.**

Where's the beach?... **Ostia** is no pearl of the Mediterranean, but it's the easiest seashore to reach from the city center—and, locals claim, its dark sand expedites tanning. To get there, take the Ostia Lido train from Piramide/ Porta San Paolo station to Ostia Centro, Stella Polare, or Cristoforo Colombo (about 40 min.). From any of these stops, it's a short walk to the water, which is chock-a-block with beach clubs, about 10€ ($13) per day. The **Kursaal** beach club, Lungomare L. Catulo 38 (Tel 06/5647-0977), Ostia's most revered, also has a salt-water pool with a high dive. For access to Ostia's free beaches, take a bus from Cristoforo Colombo to the Spiaggia Libera di Castelporziano (locally known as *"i cancelli"*), where there are pretty dunes but few facilities—just a couple of snack huts here and there. About 20km (12 miles) up the coast, **Fregene** is most locals' favorite beach, and while Romans act as if Fregene is a million times nicer than Ostia, it ain't exactly paradise. Unfortunately, Fregene's high concentration of super-bronzed poseurs means that there's a permanent film of coconut oil on the water's surface. Beaches are wider and sandier, however, and there are number of good seafood restaurants—the spaghetti with clams at beachfront **Il Mastino,** Via Silvi Marina 19 (Tel 06/66560966; lunch daily), is to die for. (To get to Fregene, take a COTRAL bus from Metro Lepanto, at least 1 hr., more on weekends.) If you get an early start and want to make a full day of going to the beach, pretty **Sperlonga,** with its whitewashed town above, really feels like an escape. Here you can also visit Tiberius's Grotto (Tel 0771/54-80-28), an ancient dining room built on an island inside a seaside cave. (From Roma-Termini, take a Naples-bound *diretto* train to Fondi, then catch the local bus to Sperlonga, about 1½ hr.)

SHOP

PING

5

Map 12: Rome Shopping Orientation

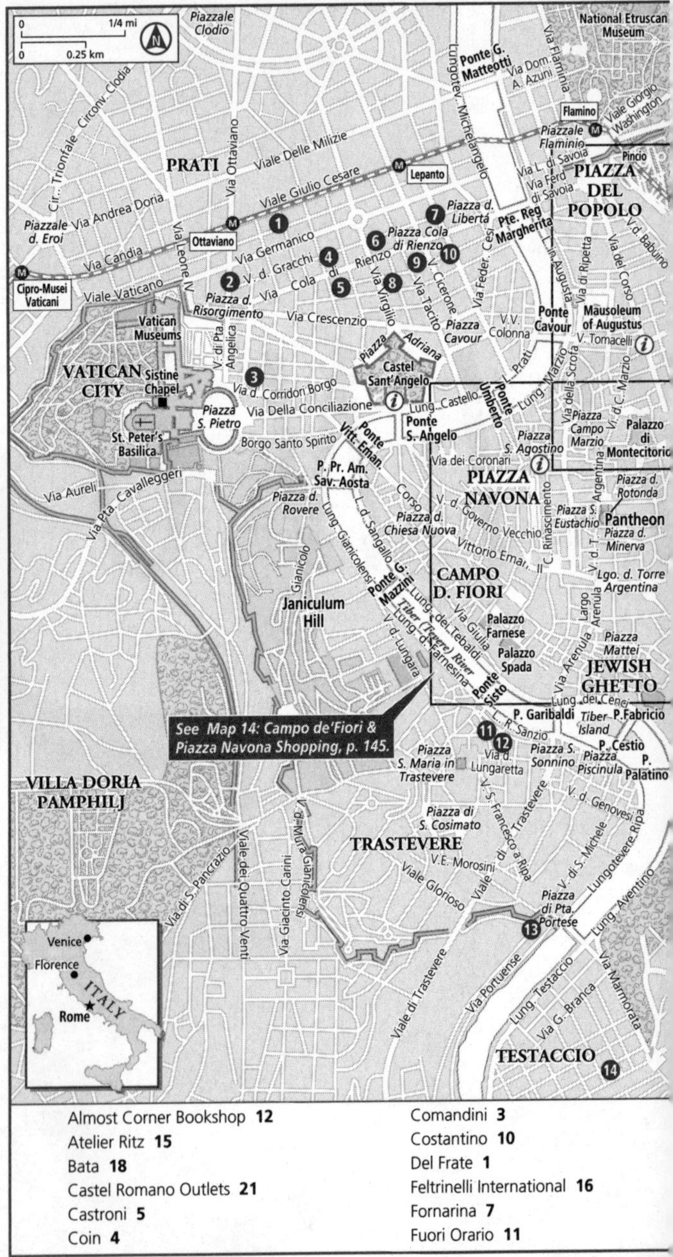

SHOPPING

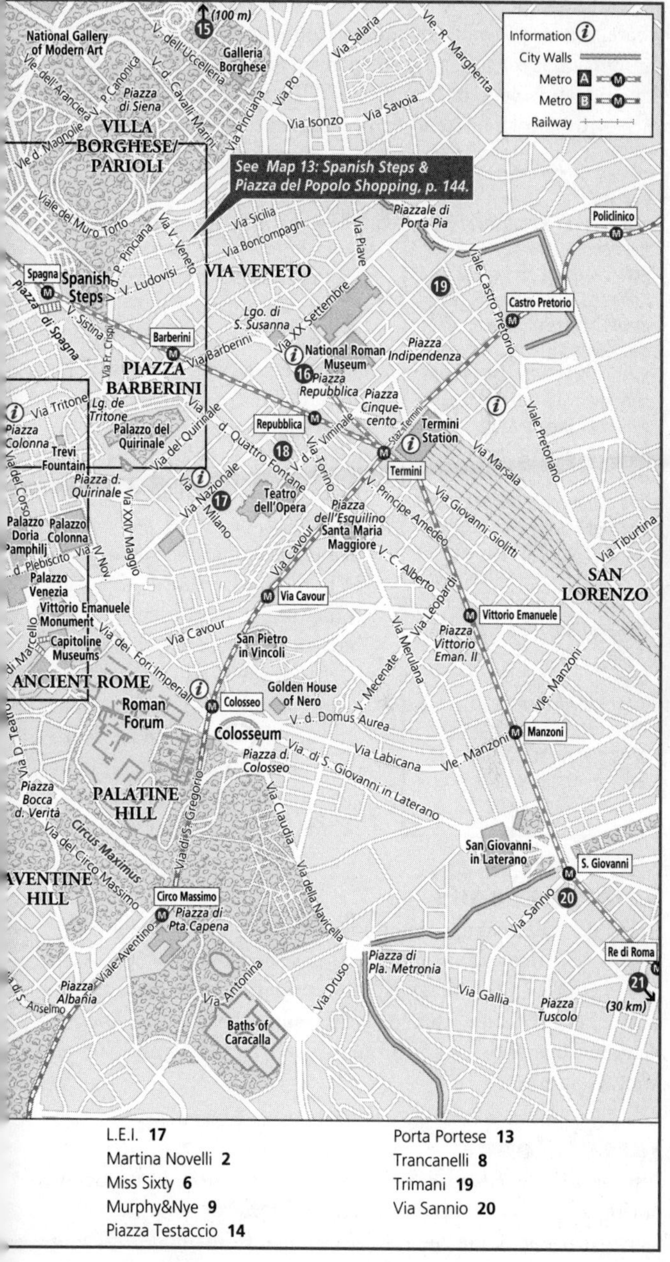

L.E.I. **17**
Martina Novelli **2**
Miss Sixty **6**
Murphy&Nye **9**
Piazza Testaccio **14**
Porta Portese **13**
Trancanelli **8**
Trimani **19**
Via Sannio **20**

Basic Stuff

Yes, fashionable people are all over, and boutiques are everywhere, but if you want to shop in Rome, it takes a lot of sifting through junk (or just a lot of money) to get to the good stuff. Anyone who's been to Florence or Milan will notice the difference—Roman shops tend to be cramped, sales "assistants" are anything but helpful, and unless you're looking at the high-end designer stuff (which Rome does quite well), you're better off in upmarket northern Italy. Make no mistake, with some determination (and our guidance, of course), you'll still be able to run up a Visa bill that'll have the creditors calling in no time, whether you're purchasing Frette linens, a vintage motorcycle jacket, a wheel of parmigiano, or liquor made by monks. Whereas you can collect all those items in the space of 2 blocks in Florence, in Rome you'll simply need to cover a lot more ground. At independent stores, always purchase with care, as only the high-end boutiques and chains have ever heard of refunds and exchanges.

Sizing

Women with a little meat on their bones may have a tough time shopping for clothes in Rome, as most women's garments are sized 38 to 46 (U.S. equivalent of 0–10). Likewise, men's clothes are cut smaller here than in the U.S.—Italian guys fully live up to their reputation for wearing their shirts nice and snug. The smallest and cheapest boutiques often don't let you try on tops, for fear that you'll get makeup or—gasp—deodorant on them. What's more, many of their tees and tanks are taglia unica ("only size"—which is really just an elitist and lazy way of saying "small"). Sasquatch-sized feet are out of luck at most stores, as Italian shoes only go up to a women's 9 and men's 12.

Sales Seasons

Italy's end-of-season sale periods (Feb and July) are a shopper's utopia, as prices all over town are slashed by anywhere from 40% to 70%. In this magical, intoxicating time, you can all too easily be convinced that a $750 yellow snakeskin clutch—marked down from $1,500, mind you—is a deal you'd be an idiot to pass up.

Target Zones

Just west of the Spanish Steps, on Via Condotti and its neighboring streets (Via Borgognona, Via Mario de' Fiori, and Via Bocca di Leone), are the only acceptable Roman addresses for the hotshots of Italian and international fashion, where the boutique names are straight out of the front matter of *Vogue*—Armani, Gucci, Valentino, Fendi, Prada, Hermes, Versace, and Dolce & Gabbana. Moving further west, to more plebeian environs, you'll find **Via del Corso,** the congested street running north-south down the middle of the *centro storico.* Hundreds of shops selling trendy fashions at fairly reasonable prices bring the Roman equivalent of the bridge-and-tunnel crowd here in droves, and it can be a nightmare on weekends. Some great stores and great bargains are on **Via Nazionale,** between Piazza Venezia and Termini, but the grimy, traffic-choked street is hardly a congenial place to shop and stroll. Less tacky than Via del Corso and Via Nazionale and less exclusive than the Spanish Steps, **Via Cola di Rienzo,** near the Vatican, is an excellent middle ground, with a good range of clothing and shoe shops, and two of the best food shops in the city. In the real heart of the *centro storico,* **Via del Governo Vecchio** and the streets south and east of **Campo de' Fiori** have their fair share of vintage shops and hip boutiques sandwiched between motorcycle mechanics and branch offices of the Communist Refoundation Party.

Hours of Business

Stores in Rome open at 10 or 10:30am, close for about 2 hours for lunch around 1:30pm, then reopen from about 3:30 until 7:30pm (and usually until 8pm in the summer). Chain stores and some entrepreneurial boutiques keep "*orario* nonstop," meaning that they stay open all day with no lunch break. (This doesn't mean they stay open 24/7, however.) Sundays and Mondays are when most shop owners take *riposo,* closing for part or all of the day. Die-hard shoppers will be happy to learn that Sunday is not totally sacred in Rome; many boutiques, especially those on Via del Corso, keep afternoon hours. Summer weekends *are* sacred, however, and from June to September, smaller shops are closed on Saturday afternoons, when Romans hit the beach. Many boutiques shut down completely for all or part of August—another reason why that torrid month is a horrible time to come to Rome.

Sales Tax

Look for shops that display the TAX FREE FOR TOURISTS sticker. If you purchase goods worth more than 155€ ($194) in one of these stores, you are entitled to receive a VAT—or IVA, in Italian—refund of the 12% to 35% tax you paid (already included in the price on the tag) when purchasing the item or items. The cashier should give you a VAT refund form that you will need to show—along with your purchases—to customs officials upon your departure from Rome (or your last European port). Note that items that are noticeably worn or have been bought used are not eligible for this rebate. For more on taxes, see the Hotlines chapter.

The Lowdown

Designer decadence... For some, no trip to Rome is complete without ringing up a ghastly charge on your credit card at one of the city's designer boutiques. Most newcomers to the world of high fashion come away with accessories only, as most of the actual clothes (a) cost 3,000€ ($3,750), or (b) look ridiculous on anyone who's not a scowling Ukrainian model. But if you do want in on the action, all the usual suspects of the international fashion elite, from Armani to Zegna, keep high-profile boutiques along Via Condotti and the other small streets (Via Bocca di Leone, Via Borgognona, Via Mario de' Fiori, and Via Babuino) between the Spanish Steps and Via del Corso. Fortunately, they tend to be less snobby toward browsers and less pushy toward buyers than the same stores in New York or Milan. Opposite each other on Via Condotti, polished **Prada** and glamorous **Gucci** are great for splurging on shoes and handbags. Hotshot designer **Roberto Cavalli,** long a fixture in Italian *alta moda* but only recently risen to international prominence, has a boutique on Via Borgognona; his unabashedly sexy, curve-celebrating styles have made loyal customers of such stars as Jessica Simpson and Beyonce. Colorful zigzags are the signature of **Missoni**'s chic knitwear—pick up a scarf or sweater at their Piazza di Spagna boutique. **Alberta Ferretti** helped bring the now-ubiquitous boho-chic look into the mainstream with her breezy, ethnic-tinged clothing. Pucker-lipped couturier **Valentino** has a pretentious, red-carpeted boutique on Via Condotti; another location on Via del Babuino features the lower-priced Valentino Red line. Rome-based **Fendi** recently opened a magnificent new flagship and showroom at Largo Goldoni (the western end of Via Condotti); while the clothes seldom translate into the real world, the accessories—especially 2005's Spy bag and the venerable *baguette*—are always covet-worthy. The collections at

Dolce & Gabbana can range from punk-rocker chic to goddess couture, but the fit of the clothes, especially trousers, is always great—growing up in Sicily, the duo clearly learned that real women have curves. If you'd rather shop for a lot of labels at the same time, check out the *alta moda* emporiums **Gente, Eleonora, Degli Effetti,** and **Nuyorica,** which carry designers like Marni, Chloe, and Balenciaga that don't have their own Roman store. Of course, most people in Rome can't afford the 300€ ($375) T-shirts on Via Condotti, and fortunately, a huge number of mass retailers are hyper-attuned to the latest trends, dishing up the latest looks at a fraction of the price and quality—see "*Molto* fashion," below. For secondhand designer goods, see "Lord of the fleas," later in this chapter.

***Molto* fashion...** For obvious reasons, shoppers in Italy set their sights on fashion, and if you're someone who calls jeans and a T-shirt an "outfit," well, step aside. Like their language and their art, Italian fashion is full of flourishes, and the uninitiated will require daring hutzpah and massive quantities of accessories to look the part of the Roman trendster. Tourists not ready to tackle the full-on local look—or who fear being ridiculed for their purchases upon return to the U.S.—can stick to the safe territory of Benetton and **Stefanel.** These national chains are more or less the Italian versions of Gap and Banana Republic, only hipper (and they don't have their own branded line of home scents). Cheaper still, **Sportstaff** specializes in stretchy monochromatic separates for work or going out (but not for sport). For that boho-cheap, I-just-made-a-blazer-out-of-Grandma's-drapes look, check out **Ethic.** Dresses, sweaters, and skirts in funky fabrics that pill easily are the hot items here. Leaping ahead in quality and price, cutting-edge **Pinko** may seem pricey, but the

Outlet Bound

You'll need to rent a car or hitchhike to get there, but Rome's ***Castel Romano Outlets,*** *an attractive outdoor mall about 24km (15 miles) southeast of the center, are well worth the trip. With big guns like Dolce & Gabbana, Frette, La Perla, and Versace all represented, you can make off with factory overruns, seconds, and irregulars from the best labels in fashion, lingerie, and linens for a fraction of what you'd pay at their boutiques near the Spanish Steps.*

well-cut pants and even the skimpy tops are built to last. **Sole** near Campo de' Fiori has a fab selection of sassy clothes, outerwear, and accessories from up-and-coming Italian designers. Should you be invited by a local prince (they do exist) to dinner at the family *palazzo,* **L.E.I.,** on grimy Via Nazionale, is where you should go to get a dress.

Suggestions for Souvenir Shoppers

Need a gift for someone back home or just something to remember your trip by? Try department stores ***COIN*** *or* ***La Rinascente*** *for a wide selection of affordable, quality Italian fashion accessories; a less expensive but less well-made assortment is at the* ***Via Sannio*** *street market. Soccer fans will appreciate the official club merchandise at the A.S. Roma Store, and anyone with a working set of taste buds will enjoy the packaged gourmet food items at haute delis* ***Castroni,*** *Franchi, and Volpetti. (Wine, available everywhere, is a classic souvenir of Italy, but it's bulky and heavy, and you're only allowed to bring two bottles back to the U.S.)* ***Franco Maria Ricci*** *publishes impossibly gorgeous coffee table books on Italian art, architecture, and fashion. Elegant kitchen and tabletop items, both traditional and modern, can be found at* ***Modigliani.*** *For collectors of kitsch, Rome abounds with papal bric-a-brac and miniature plaster Colosseums. Everyday items are the cheapest souvenir of all and can be as much fun as real "gifts"–pay a visit to the nearest supermercato or profumeria for a packet of mass-market risotto mix or a tube of Italian toothpaste.*

One-stop shopping... Occupying a five-floor *palazzo* on Via del Corso, **La Rinascente** is the closest thing Italy has to a classy department store. It's no Saks—heck, it ain't even Bloomingdale's—but despite its dated look, the store actually has some great merchandise, with an especially strong assortment of bags, belts, scarves, hats, and gloves on the ground floor. La Rinascente is also open every night of the week, including Sunday, until 10pm—unheard-of in Italy. **Coin,** which operates stores near the Vatican and San Giovanni, features great-looking (and well-priced) handbags and other accessories—many produced under the store's own label, Koan—and a forgettable array of Italian, French, and American clothing. The 1999 overhaul of the once-seedy Termini train station saw the introduction of a snazzy subterranean shopping concourse, with clothing chains like Etam and Benetton, as well as a tanning salon—de rigueur, of course, in any mall. In 2003, the 18th-century Galleria Colonna, just off Via del Corso, was opened as a smallish shopping mall and redubbed **Galleria Alberto Sordi,** for a dearly departed Roman comic actor.

Shoes, glorious shoes... Clothes shopping in Rome, quite frankly, can be beat, but you can't touch the shoes. Sensible styles (like rounded toes and flats) have entered the mix, but women in Rome still love what makes them look sexy, which means pointed toes and stiletto heels. A word to the uninitiated: The cobblestones of Rome are fraught with heel-snaring cracks, and while Italian women can navigate this terrain with painless nonchalance, newcomers with narrow heels will likely teeter unglamorously. (But when you're sitting down—boy, do you look good.) **Martina Novelli,** a tiny shop near the Vatican, packs in a tantalizing range of cutting-edge styles, from super-sexy heels to comfy moccasins. For that lusty medieval wench look, **Cesare Paciotti**'s women's shoes are expensive and sexy with a capital S, all adorned with the designer's trademark dagger charm. **Loco,** near Campo de' Fiori, has some of the most outré shoes in the city (for men and women), but look past the Hobbit booties, and there are quite a few wearable couture styles from names like Les Tropeziennes and Ixos. A chic newcomer in the same 'hood, **Campo de' Fiori 52** has a small but refined selection of funky yet elegant designs, including Viktor & Rolf and Robert Clergerie's Espace line. Also nearby, Posto Italiano is a local's secret weapon for the latest looks in a variety of colors at merciful prices. Via del Corso's Peroni has great shoes from upper-range designers like Giancarlo Paoli and Gianna Meliani as well its own lower-priced house label. Vatican-area **Trancanelli** has an expertly edited selection of all the best men's and women's styles for every occasion, from sneakers to stilettos. Men's shoes aren't much wilder in Italy than what you'll find back home—just a touch more fashion-forward, and made with better leather. Roman men usually wear sneakers—not the meant-for-athletic-activity kind, but the latest trendy designs from Onitsuka Tiger and Adidas. Every conservative, style-conscious Roman male has a pair of Hogans; these and other Italo-preppy shoes can be found at **Davide Cenci** or **Mario Lucchesi.** For easy loafers and men's dress shoes, look no further than **Bruno Magli.** Affordable knockoffs of all the current looks in footwear are prevalent throughout the city—for the best range of styles for men and women, the national chain **Bata** is like a higher quality and more stylish Payless Shoe Source (and a bit more expensive: Most pairs are priced 50€–70€/$63–$88).

The well-dressed fellow... Roman men primp and preen just as much as the women do (and they unabashedly look each other up and down, just as the women do), so trade in those Gap jeans already. Pick up classic ties, sober suits, or even something in suede at **Brioni,** safe in the knowledge that these are the guys behind James Bond's wardrobe in every 007 film. **Ermenegildo Zegna**—another big-timer on the menswear scene—also has sharp-looking suits, casual shirts and pants, and accessories. When politicians need to dress the part, they stop by **Davide Cenci,** a popular place for custom-made men's shirts and suits just down the street from the Palazzo Montecitorio (Italy's Chamber of Deputies). Unable to spend time getting measured? You can save time and quite a bit of money at **David Saddler,** an off-the-rack clothier with a large selection of dress shirts, casual pants, and belts. For sportier stuff, check out **Prototype,** on Via dei Giubbonari, which has trendy, printed T-shirts and every possible permutation of Converse high-tops under the sun. Spilled wine on your only pair of khakis and need to replace them in a hurry? **Brooks** (no relation to the Brothers) should do the trick.

Sassy and sporty... Roman teenagers (and their middle-aged parents who refuse to dress their age) get their retail fix at one of the myriad techno-blaring storefronts on the northern, pedestrianized half of Via del Corso. Aided by its always cheeky window displays, Italian urbanwear behemoth **Diesel** sells jeans and edgy sportswear with a high-tech slant. **Onyx** specializes in colorful tracksuits and flimsy accessories for brash junior high schoolers who think they're the next Britney Spears. The clothing at **Fornarina** is made for the under-20 set, but the colorful sandals and pumps can be worn by women, too. **Energie** has sporty clothing, footwear, and backpacks from popular youth brands like Kappa and Killah. A similar selection, plus some slightly more formal apparel, is at **Jam Store,** in the new Galleria Alberto Sordi mall. Great for jeans and sassy party clothes with a retro look, **Miss Sixty** has stores on Via del Corso as well as the quieter Via Cola di Rienzo, near the Vatican. Roman 20- to 50-somethings love to dress as if they're in training for the next America's Cup, and a casual range of nautical-inspired technical-looking gear can be found at **Murphy&Nye.**

Something about leather... Be it a jacket, a handbag, a belt, or a pair of gloves, there's nothing like coming home from Italy with the smell of tanned cowhide in your suitcase. If you love leather, your first stop should be **Bottega Veneta** (pronounced "*ven*-eh-ta"), temple of luxury accessories and home to the buttery soft, signature *intrecciato* woven leather. Your second stop, since you can't afford anything at Bottega Veneta, should be **Furla,** where modern and moderately priced handbags and accessories abound. One of the best purchases you can make in Italy, of course, is a hot-looking leather jacket. **Fuori Orario,** in Trastevere, has its own line of well-priced bombers, trenches, and motorcycle jackets, in bright colors as well as sensible beige, camel, and black, for men and women. **Sermoneta,** on Piazza di Spagna, has an astounding selection of reasonably priced women's gloves. *Pelletterie* (leather shops) abound in Rome, but some are cheesy tourist traps—always be sure to inspect garments and accessories for quality of workmanship.

The 24-Hour Accessory

Sunglasses are worn night and day in Rome, so you'd better get yourself outfitted fast—go big and go bold. Pretty much any boutique—designer or budget-oriented—has its own line of shades, but your best source is often the ottica, a ubiquitous shop that sells a wide range of sunglasses, so you can try on multiple looks from different makers at your leisure. (Ottiche also have prescription glasses, contact lenses and solutions, and sometimes camera equipment.) Love those new Dior shades that everyone's wearing but don't want to shell out $200 for 'em? Check out the local street stalls and you'll probably find a much more affordable imitation. So what if the cheap plastic lenses don't protect your peepers from searing UV rays? It's fashion, baby!

Shopping for the bambini... Italy has one of the lowest birth rates in Europe, which means that those little ones who do manage do join the fray are in for some serious spoiling. **Città del Sole**'s magical array of creative toys and construction sets will make you wish you were 8 again, too. At the north end of Piazza Navona is the stuffed-animal and collectibles emporium **Al Sogno,** wildly popular with children and Dungeons and Dragons geeks alike.

A feast of food markets... Some Romans have been lured away by the convenience of supermarkets—but most citizens still do their grocery shopping in the local *alimentari* (deli), butcher shops, and produce markets. Big vats of Cerignola and other oil-cured olives, sacks of dry herbs, and ripe fruits and vegetables by the crateful are just a few of the finds at **Campo de' Fiori,** a daily (except Sun) market that's liable to make first-time foodie visitors faint. It's gotten touristy in recent years, and the junk stalls hawking aprons bearing likenesses of Michelangelo's *David* now almost outnumber the produce stands. Still, everyone, from local chefs to pilgrims, rubs elbows in the Campo, eager to get their hands on some choice artichokes or an *etto* (just short of a 1/4 lb.) or two of the finest porcini mushrooms. The most authentic Roman market in the city is still at **Piazza Testaccio,** an indoor bazaar where colorful locals—but very few tourists—pick up the best Roman produce (Mon–Sat 6am–2pm) for less than elsewhere. Before you get too carried away at the food markets, remember that fruit and veg will be confiscated by customs if you try to bring it home with you.

Edibles to go... Wine, balsamic vinegar, olive oil, decorative pasta, and other packaged goods are all great things to buy in Italy. **Castroni,** a Roman *alimentari* with several branches around the city, is a one-stop shop for Italian coffee, sweets, pasta, and liqueurs. It's also where many expat locals go to get American comfort foods, like Bisquick. The main offerings at gourmet delis Franchi and Volpetti (see the Dining chapter for both) are cheeses and cold cuts, but you can't travel with those; what you can pick up for foodie friends back home are packets of dried *funghi porcini* or jars of truffled olive pâté. After downing a shot of some of the best espresso in the city, pick up a package of ground coffee or chocolate-covered espresso beans from **Bar Sant'Eustachio** (see the Dining chapter).

Fine wines... Oenophiles shouldn't miss **Trimani.** Despite its sleek look, this enoteca was founded in 1821 and is Rome's most venerable wine vendor, with approximately 3,000 vintages in stock from every region in Italy. Smart tourists who discover the Tridente area's road-less-traveled—Via Ripetta—will be rewarded with **Buccone.** Every kind of red and white wine under the Italian sun, including some pricey vintages of Brunello, lines its shelves. **Mr. Wine,** the favorite enoteca of parliamentarians (it's across the street from Italy's *parlamento*), stocks an equally large range of both moderately priced and expensive wines. On Piazza Cavour, near Castel Sant'Angelo, **Costantini** has a fabulous Art Nouveau vine motif wrought-iron storefront and attached tasting room, Il Simposio. Also near the Vatican, friendly **Del Frate** is the preferred wine seller of the wealthy residents of Prati.

Lords of the fleas... Noisy crowds, some altogether unsavory characters, and plenty of junk are what you'll encounter at Rome's popular Sunday flea market at **Porta Portese,** along the river in the southern part of Trastevere. There's a bit of everything here, new and old, live and inanimate—massive bins of clothes, racks of CDs, antique furniture, Reagan-era used appliances, carnivorous plants, and goldfish. Early birds (as in, the 7am crowd) stand the best chance of getting their hands on the truly fantastic vintage stuff, which is well hidden among miles of vendors hawking lame approximations of retro bric-a-brac. A warning to those who've been out late Saturday night: Porta Portese is not recommended if you have a hangover. Agoraphobes who'd rather avoid the chaos of Porta Portese can browse the more tranquil stalls of the market at **Via Sannio** (Mon–Sat), near San Giovanni, where leather jackets, belts, unofficial soccer jerseys, and the latest trendy accessories can be found. A parking garage off the Via Veneto houses the **Underground,** a monthly market full of the usual schlock, as well as jewelry, flatware, and doorknobs. The **Mercato delle Stampe,** between the Pantheon and Piazza del Popolo, has a charming selection of antiquarian books (in Italian, English, French, and other languages), back issues of magazines, and art prints. Looking for a vintage Pucci scarf or a classic motorcycle jacket? The **Atelier Ritz** is a twice-monthly market where rich Romans unload everything from last season's Gucci bags to Valentino suits to Chanel jewelry.

Antiques and collectibles... Antiques hounds should make a beeline for Via dei Coronari, Rome's main artery for *antiquariato*. The jumbled assortment of marbles at **Marmi Line** includes some remarkably faithful copies of Roman portrait busts, fountains, and a whole lot of pointless "accent pieces" that might have been lifted from the set of *All My Children*. **W Apolloni,** specializing in silver and 17th-century furniture, is one of Rome's best-known antiques stores. If you're looking for collectibles from the 20th century or Art Deco furnishings, seek out **Comics Bazar.** Of course, if you have a good eye for antiques and are willing to battle crowds, your best bet may be to head for one of the flea markets like **Porta Portese** (see above).

Book it, baby... Maybe you need a trashy novel to offset all the heavy culture Rome throws at you, or maybe you feel like boning up on your *Inferno*—whatever your pleasure, the city has English-language booksellers for all tastes. The Roman flagship of Italian bookstore chain **Feltrinelli** is a multimedia megastore that occupies an entire *palazzo* on Largo Argentina. Opened in 2003, the store carries mostly Italian-language books, but there's a decent-sized international section, with some specialized books in

Work That Deal: The Fine Art of Italian Negotiation

Unless you want to be written off as a sucker foreigner, you'd better learn how to haggle prices at Rome's flea markets and antiques shops. Typical of markets and secondhand outlets worldwide, marked prices for many items here are at least 50% above what the vendor actually expects to receive. Counter with a lower offer or ask for a sconto *(discount), and you may just get a deal. If the vendor won't budge on something you know is worth much less, feel free to cock your head forward, smirk, and do the* che sono, scemo? *(what am I, a fool?) hand gesture: Bring fingers to thumb, palms pointing upward, then wag the hand back and forth (toward you, then away from you—you've seen this in myriad mafia movies). The gesture can be done with one hand, or—for greater efficacy—with both. (If the deal goes sour, turn back and repeat the gesture to the offending vendor as you're walking away, just so it's clear you're not a fool.) Of course, haggling can't be done everywhere. The prices in retail stores are usually fixed* (prezzo fisso) *and are often indicated as such with handmade signs near the register. At independent boutiques, however, it's reasonable to ask for a small discount if you're paying in cash.*

English about Roman tourism, as well as CD listening stations and a cafe where readings are sometimes held. **Feltrinelli International,** near Piazza della Repubblica, has a much larger selection of foreign-language titles. For a university-quality array of books on Italian art and architecture (as well as physics and horticulture), head for **Anglo-American Book,** near the Spanish Steps, which also has plenty of paperback "vacation novels" from which to choose. Every nook and cranny of the tiny English-language **Almost Corner Bookshop,** in Trastevere, is crammed with all genres of literature, from ancient erotica anthologies to Mussolini biographies. They also stock bestsellers, but the expat lit snobs who run the place will treat you like a second-class citizen if all you buy is *Angels and Demons.*

Vatican chic... The Rodeo Drive of religious articles is Via de' Cestari, a small street near the Pantheon with nearly a dozen shops selling everything you need to hold your own liturgical services, whether you're in the market for a new embroidered cassock or a jewel-encrusted communion goblet. Cardinals go to **Ghezzi** for robes and socks in more colors than there are in Tom Ridge's terrorism alert chart. **De Ritis** has made-to-order vestments and casual wear for priests, as well as a line of haute habits and sleepwear for the fashion-conscious lady of the cloth. Despite its understated storefront, **Gammarelli** is no stranger to flashy ceremonial garb—the family has been the personal tailor to the pope for over a century. Pilgrims near the Vatican should peruse the wares of **Comandini,** where Shroud-of-Turin holograms, lighters with the likenesses of famous saints, or Padre Pio playing cards are just a few of the classy items on offer.

Map 13: Spanish Steps & Piazza Del Popolo Shopping

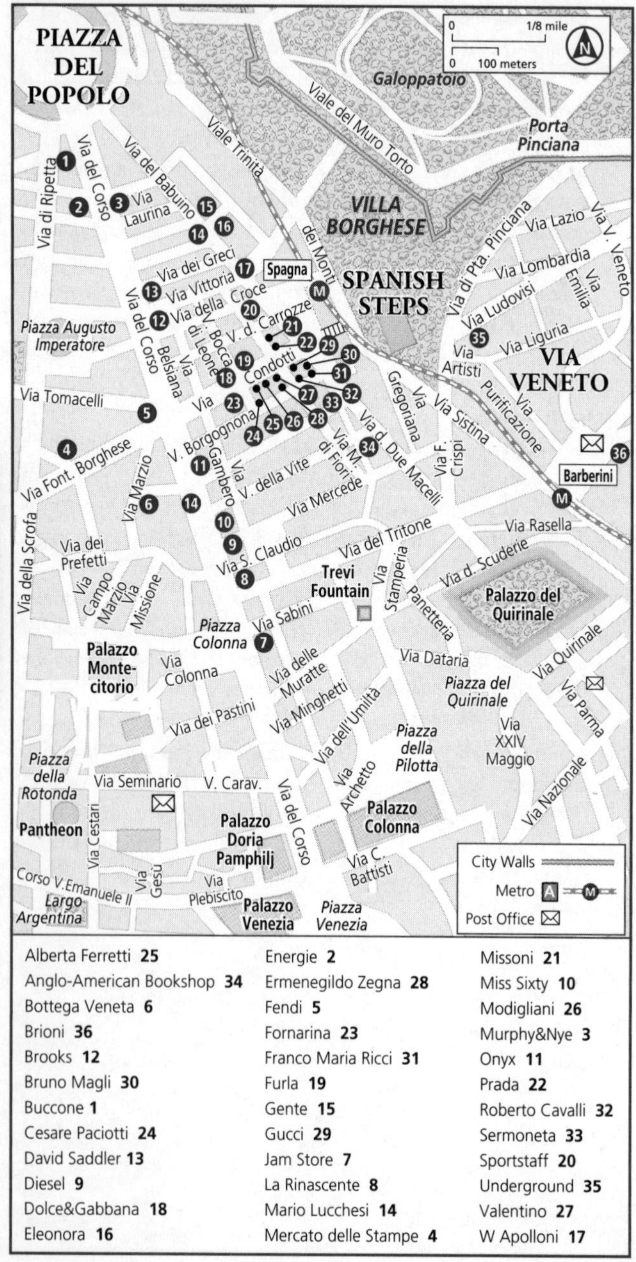

Alberta Ferretti **25**
Anglo-American Bookshop **34**
Bottega Veneta **6**
Brioni **36**
Brooks **12**
Bruno Magli **30**
Buccone **1**
Cesare Paciotti **24**
David Saddler **13**
Diesel **9**
Dolce&Gabbana **18**
Eleonora **16**
Energie **2**
Ermenegildo Zegna **28**
Fendi **5**
Fornarina **23**
Franco Maria Ricci **31**
Furla **19**
Gente **15**
Gucci **29**
Jam Store **7**
La Rinascente **8**
Mario Lucchesi **14**
Mercato delle Stampe **4**
Missoni **21**
Miss Sixty **10**
Modigliani **26**
Murphy&Nye **3**
Onyx **11**
Prada **22**
Roberto Cavalli **32**
Sermoneta **33**
Sportstaff **20**
Underground **35**
Valentino **27**
W Apolloni **17**

Map 14: Campo De' Fiori & Piazza Navona Shopping

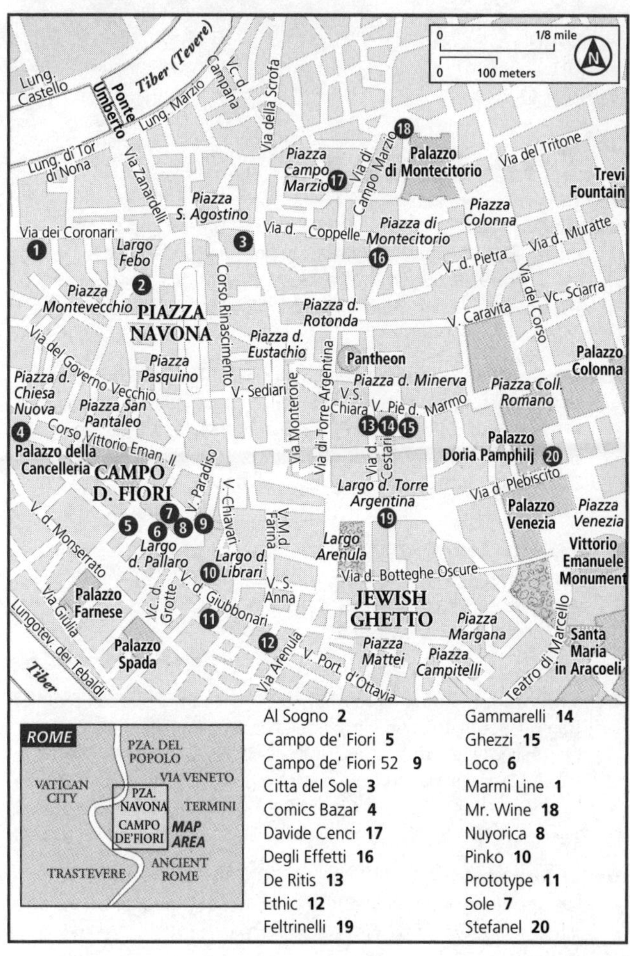

The Index

Alberta Ferretti (p. 134) SPANISH STEPS Breezy and graceful *alta moda*. The designer's Philosophy line is also available here.... *Tel 06/699-11-60. www.albertaferretti.com. Via Condotti 34, at Via Bocca di Leone. Metro Spagna. Mon–Sat 10am–7:30pm.*

See Map 13 on p. 144.

Almost Corner Bookshop (p. 143) TRASTEVERE Tiny English bookstore has an impressive array of fiction, poetry, history, and art books.... *Tel 06/583-6942. Via del Moro 45, at Vicolo de' Renzi. Buses 23, 271, or 280. Tram 8. Mon–Sat 10am–1:30pm, 3:30–8pm; Sun 11am–1:30pm, 3:30–8pm.*

See Map 12 on p. 130.

Al Sogno (p. 140) PIAZZA NAVONA A world of plush stuffed animals, arranged in inventive layouts.... *Tel 06/686-41-98. www.alsogno.com. Piazza Navona 53. Buses 30, 40, 46, 62, 64, 70, 81, 87, 116, or 492. Mon–Sat 10am–7:30pm.*

See Map 14 on p. 145.

Anglo-American Book (p. 143) SPANISH STEPS The premier Roman outlet for scholarly books in English; also has lighter, bestseller-type stuff.... *Tel 06/679-5222. www.aab.it. Via della Vite 102, at Via Mario de' Fiori. Metro Spagna. Mon 3:30–7:30pm; Tues–Sat 10am–7:30pm. Closed for 2 weeks in the middle of Aug.*

See Map 13 on p. 144.

Atelier Ritz (p. 141) PARIOLI/VILLA BORGHESE Monthly flea market featuring cast-off clothing and accessories from Rome's elite.... *Tel 06/807-81-89. Via Frescobaldi 5 (Hotel Parco dei Principi). Buses 52, 53, or 910. Tram 3. Every other Sun only 10am–8pm.*

See Map 12 on p. 130.

Bata (p. 138) VIA NAZIONALE Inexpensive shoes for fashion-conscious men and women.... *Tel 06/482-45-29. www.bata.com. Via Nazionale 88a, at Via Depretis. Buses 40, 60, 64, 70, 170, or H. Mon–Sat 10am–7:30pm.*

See Map 12 on p. 130.

Bottega Veneta (p. 139) SPANISH STEPS Leather goods and accessories for those who demand the very best.... *Tel 06/ 6821-0024. www.bottegaveneta.com. Piazza San Lorenzo in Lucina 9. Buses 62, 85, 95, 116, or 492. Mon–Sat 10am–7:30pm.*

See Map 13 on p. 144.

Brioni (p. 138) PIAZZA BARBERINI Classic suits, shirts, and accessories for men, plus expert tailoring.... *Tel 06/484-517. www. brioni.it. Via Barberini 79, at Piazza Barberini. Metro Barberini. Mon–Sat 10am–7:30pm.*

See Map 13 on p. 144.

Brooks (p. 138) SPANISH STEPS Casual wear for the guy who forgot to pack his Gap T-shirt.... *Via del Corso: Tel 06/361-43-72; www.brooks-ltd.it; Via del Corso 86, at Via Vittoria; Metro Spagna; Mon–Sat 10am–7:30pm. Via Cola di Rienzo: Tel 06/324-1894; Via Cola di Rienzo 241; buses 23, 81, or 492; tram 19 to Piazza Risorgimento/Via Cola di Rienzo; Mon–Sat 10am–7:30pm. Via dei Giubbonari: Tel 06/6830-7087; Via dei Giubbonari 69; buses 40, 62, 70, 87, 116, or 492 to Campo de' Fiori; Mon–Sat 10am–1:30pm, 3:30–8pm.*

See Map 13 on p. 144.

Bruno Magli (p. 137) SPANISH STEPS Loafers and dress shoes for Italian playboys.... *Tel 06/6920-2264. www.brunomagli.it. Via Condotti 6, at Piazza di Spagna. Metro Spagna. Mon–Sat 10am–7:30pm.*

See Map 13 on p. 144.

Buccone (p. 141) PIAZZA DEL POPOLO Packed to the ceiling with wine from every region, extra-virgin olive oil, balsamic vinegar, and packaged foodstuffs.... *Tel 06/361-21-54. Via di Ripetta 19–20, at Piazza del Popolo. Metro Flaminio. Mon–Sat 10am–8pm; Sun 11am–7pm.*

See Map 13 on p. 144.

Campo de' Fiori (p. 133) CENTRO STORICO Famous produce market in the heart of the *centro storico*.... *No telephone. Piazza Campo de' Fiori. Buses 30, 40, 46, 62, 64, 70, 87, 492, or 571. Tram 8. Mon–Sat roughly 6am–2pm.*

See Map 14 on p. 145.

Campo de' Fiori 52 (p. 137) CAMPO DE' FIORI Small but sophisticated selection of shoes and clothing for women.... *Tel 06/ 687-5775. Piazza del Paradiso 72, at Via del Biscione. Buses 30, 40, 46, 62, 64, 70, 87, 492, or 571. Tram 8. Mon–Sat 10am–7:30pm.*

See Map 14 on p. 145.

Castel Romano Outlets (p. 135) OUTSIDE ROME Suburban outlet center opened in 2003, a bit of everything, from North Sails to

Versace.... *Tel 06/5050050. Via Ponte di Piscina Cupa. Need own transportation. Daily 10am–7:30pm.*

See Map 12 on p. 130.

Castroni (p. 140) VATICAN Gourmet store with Italian goodies and hard-to-find international food items. A Roman institution.... Via Cola di Rienzo: *Tel 06/687-43-83; www.castronigroup.it; Via Cola di Rienzo 196–198 (at Via Terenzio). Via Ottaviano: Tel 06/3972-3279; Via Ottaviano 55, at Via Germanico. Metro Ottaviano. Mon–Sat 8am–7:30pm.*

See Map 12 on p. 130.

Cesare Paciotti (p. 137) SPANISH STEPS Women's shoes with full-throttle sex appeal.... *Tel 06/679-6245. www.cesare-paciotti.com. Via Bocca di Leone 92, at Via Borgognona. Metro Spagna. Mon–Sat 10am–7:30pm.*

See Map 13 on p. 144.

Città del Sole (p. 140) PANTHEON A wonderland of creative toys for kids of all ages.... *Tel 06/687-54-04. www.cittadelsole.it. Via della Scrofa 65. Buses 30, 70, 87, 116, or 492. Mon–Sat 10am–7:30pm; Sun 10am–1pm, 3:30–7pm.*

See Map 14 on p. 145.

Coin (p. 136) VATICAN AND SAN GIOVANNI Italy's biggest department-store chain. Good finds in the jewelry and accessories departments, but clothes are frumpissimo.... *Via Cola di Rienzo: Tel 06/3600-4298; www.coin.it; Via Cola di Rienzo 173; Metro Ottaviano. Piazzale Appio: Tel 06/708-00-20; Piazzale Appio 7; Metro San Giovanni. Mon–Sat 9:30am–8pm.*

See Map 12 on p. 130.

Comandini (p. 143) VATICAN Kitschy papal souvenirs and gifts.... *Tel 06/687-50-79. www.comandini.it. Borgo Pio 151. Metro Ottaviano. Mon–Sat 10am–8pm.*

See Map 12 on p. 130.

Comics Bazar (p. 142) CAMPO DE' FIORI Bawdy furniture from the 1700s, collectibles from the 1940s, and lots of other stuff from the years in between.... *Tel 06/688-02-923. Via dei Banchi Vecchi 127. Buses 23, 40, 46, 62, 64, 116, 271, 280, or 571. Tues–Sat 10am–1pm; Mon–Sat 3:30–7:30pm.*

See Map 14 on p. 145.

Costantini (p. 141) VATICAN Wine emporium and tasting bar near Castel Sant'Angelo.... *Tel 06/320-3575. www.pierocostantini.it. Piazza Cavour 16. Buses 70, 87, 280, or 492. Tues–Sat 9am–1pm; Mon–Sat 4:30–8pm.*

See Map 12 on p. 130.

Davide Cenci (p. 138) PANTHEON Made-to-order outfitter of men's shirts and suits since 1926. Women's shop has Pucci, Polo, and other classics.... *Tel 06/699-06-81. www.davidecenci.com. Via*

Campo Marzio 1–7. Buses 62, 85, 95, 116, or 492. Mon–Sat 10am–7:30pm.

See Map 14 on p. 145.

David Saddler (p. 138) SPANISH STEPS Menswear chain with an especially nice selection of reasonably priced shirts; many larger sizes.... *Tel 06/871-98-819. www.david-saddler.com. Via del Corso 103. Buses 62, 85, 95, 116, 175, or 492. Mon–Sat 10am–7:30pm.*

See Map 13 on p. 144.

Degli Effetti (p. 135) PANTHEON Hip boutique stocks clothes, bags, and shoes from Miu Miu, Jil Sander, and others.... *Tel 06/679-02-02. Piazza Capranica 93–94. Buses 62, 85, 95, 116, 175, or 492. Mon–Sat 10am–1:30pm, 3:30–7:30pm.*

See Map 14 on p. 145.

Del Frate (p. 141) VATICAN Friendly wine shop favored by the wealthy residents of Prati.... *Tel 06/323-6497. Via degli Scipioni 118. Metro Ottaviano. Mon–Sat 9:30am–2pm, 4–8pm.*

See Map 12 on p. 130.

De Ritis (p. 143) PANTHEON Loads of liturgical items. But expect surly glances if you're not a man or woman of the cloth.... *Tel 06/686-58-43. Via de' Cestari 48. Buses 30, 40, 46, 62, 64, 70, 87, 116, or 492. Mon–Fri 10am–1:30pm, 3:30–7pm.*

See Map 14 on p. 145.

Diesel (p. 138) SPANISH STEPS Jeans, street wear, and cheeky window displays.... *Tel 06/678-66-41. www.diesel.com. Via del Corso 185. Buses 62, 85, 95, 116, 175, or 492. Mon–Sat 10am–7:30pm.*

See Map 13 on p. 144.

Dolce & Gabbana (p. 135) SPANISH STEPS Sexy couture from the Sicilian duo.... *Tel 06/678-29-90. www.dolcegabbana.com. Via Condotti 51–52. Metro Spagna. Mon–Sat 10am–7:30pm.*

See Map 13 on p. 144.

Eleonora (p. 135) SPANISH STEPS Cutting-edge boutique with coffee bar and the latest fashions from under-the-radar designers like Alexander McQueen and John Galliano.... *Tel 06/679-31-73. www.eleonoraboutique.it. Via del Babuino 97. Metro Spagna. Mon–Sat 10am–7:30pm.*

See Map 13 on p. 144.

Energie (p. 138) PIAZZA DEL POPOLO Assorted urban street wear for teenage girls and boys.... *Tel 06/687-12-58. Via del Corso 408–409. Metro Flaminio. Buses 62, 85, 95, 116, 119, or 492. Mon–Sat 10am–8pm; Sun 10am–1:30pm, 3:30–8pm.*

See Map 13 on p. 144.

Ermenegildo Zegna (p. 138) SPANISH STEPS Master men's couture tailor. Easy urban suits to elegant tuxedos, plus a wide range of ties, belts, and casual wear.... *Tel 06/678-91-43. www.zegna.com. Via Borgognona 7E. Metro Spagna. Mon–Sat 10am–7:30pm.*

See Map 13 on p. 144.

Ethic (p. 135) CAMPO DE' FIORI Funky, inexpensive duds that look like vintage.... *Tel 06/68-30-10-63. www.ethic.it. Piazza Benedetto Cairoli 11–12. Buses 30, 40, 46, 62, 64, 70, 87, 492, or 571. Tram 8. Mon–Sat 10am–8pm; Sun noon–7pm.*

See Map 14 on p. 145.

Feltrinelli (p. 142) PANTHEON Megastore for books, CDs, and DVDs in the heart of the *centro storico*.... *Tel 06/6866-3001. www.lafeltrinelli.it. Largo di Torre Argentina 11. Buses 30, 40, 62, 64, 70, 87, or 492. Tram 8. Mon–Thurs 9am–9pm; Fri–Sat 9am–11pm; Sun 10am–2pm, 4–8pm.*

See Map 14 on p. 145.

Feltrinelli International (p. 143) REPUBBLICA Polyglot branch of the national bookstore chain has a vast array of titles in English, Spanish, French, and German, as well as other languages.... *Tel 06/482-7878. www.lafeltrinelli.it. Via V. E. Orlando 84–86, off Piazza della Repubblica. Metro Repubblica. Mon–Sat 9am–8pm; Sun 10am–1:30pm, 4–8pm. Closed Sun in Aug.*

See Map 12 on p. 130.

Fendi (p. 134) SPANISH STEPS In its smashing new world headquarters, now and forever the "it" brand for Rome's ladies who power-lunch.... *Tel 06/679-76-41. www.fendi.com. Largo Goldoni. Metro Spagna. Mon–Sat 10am–7:30pm.*

See Map 13 on p. 144.

Fornarina (p. 138) SPANISH STEPS/VATICAN Teen clothing label with cute shoes for women, too.... *Via Condotti: Tel 06/679-0862; www.fornarina.com; Via Condotti 36; Metro Spagna. Via Cola di Rienzo: Tel 800/050-366 (within Italy only); Via Cola di Rienzo 117; Metro Ottaviano; Buses 23, 70, 81, 280, or 492. Mon–Sat 10am–7:30pm.*

See Map 12 on p. 130.
See Map 13 on p. 144.

Franco Maria Ricci (p. 136) SPANISH STEPS Publisher of exquisite, old-fashioned-looking coffee table books on art and architecture.... *Tel 06/679-3466. Via Borgognona 4D, at Piazza di Spagna. Metro Spagna. Mon 3–7:30pm; Tues–Sat 10am–1:30pm, 3:30–7:30pm.*

See Map 13 on p. 144.

Fuori Orario (p. 139) TRASTEVERE Colorful, affordable leather jackets, plus funky Euro wear.... *Tel 06/581-71-81. Via del Moro 29.*

Buses 23, 115, 271, or 280. Tram 8. Mon 4–7:30pm; Tues–Sat 10am–1:30pm, 4–7:30pm.

See Map 12 on p. 130.

Furla (p. 139) SPANISH STEPS Ladylike handbags and accessories with clean design.... *Via del Corso: Tel 06/36003619; www.furla.com; Via del Corso 481; Metro Spagna. Piazza di Spagna: Tel 06/69200363; Piazza di Spagna 22. Via Dei Condotti: Tel 06/6791973; Via Dei Condotti 55–56. Branches all over. Mon–Sat 10am–8pm.*

See Map 13 on p. 144.

Gammarelli (p. 143) PANTHEON Religious outfitter, known to many as the "pope's tailor".... *No telephone. Via di Santa Chiara 34, at Via dei Cestari. Buses 30, 40, 46, 62, 64, 70, 87, 116, 492, or 571. Mon–Fri 10am–1:30pm, 3:30–7pm.*

See Map 14 on p. 145.

Gente (p. 135) SPANISH STEPS From denim to dresses, an up-to-date selection from a variety of *alta moda* designers.... *Tel 06/320-76-71. Via del Babuino 81. Metro Spagna. Mon–Sat 10am–7:30pm.*

See Map 13 on p. 144.

Ghezzi (p. 143) PANTHEON Clothing and colorful hosiery for Rome's ecclesiastical community.... *Tel 06/686-97-44. Via de' Cestari 32–33. Buses 30, 40, 46, 62, 64, 70, 87, 116, 492, or 571. Mon–Fri 10am–1pm, 4–7pm.*

See Map 14 on p. 145.

Gucci (p. 133) SPANISH STEPS Still sexy, even now that designer Tom Ford has passed the baton.... *Tel 06/678-93-40. www.gucci.com. Via Condotti 8. Metro Spagna. Mon–Sat 10am–7:30pm.*

See Map 13 on p. 144.

Jam Store (p. 138) VIA DEL CORSO High-energy sportswear boutique for trendy teens.... *Tel 06/678-1313. www.rinascente.it. Galleria Colonna (Alberto Sordi, at Via del Corso). Buses 62, 85, 95, 116, 175, or 492. Mon–Sat 10am–7:30pm; Sun noon–7pm.*

See Map 13 on p. 144.

La Rinascente (p. 136) SPANISH STEPS Rome's nicer department store, worth visiting for its accessories selection.... *Tel 06/679-76-91. www.rinascente.it. Largo Chigi 20. Buses 62, 85, 95, 116, 175, or 492. Mon–Sat 9:30am–10pm; Sun 10:30am–8pm.*

See Map 13 on p. 144.

L.E.I. (p. 136) VIA NAZIONALE Find Prince Charming (and his credit card), then come here for girly but gorgeous frocks worthy of Cinderella herself.... *Via Nazionale: Tel 06/482-17-00; Via Nazionale 88; buses 40, 60, 64, 70, 170, or H; Mon–Sat*

10am–7:30pm. Via dei Giubbonari: Tel 06/6875432; Via dei Giubbonari 103; buses 30, 40, 62, 70, 87, 116, or 492 to Campo de' Fiori; Tues–Sat 10am–2pm; Mon–Sat 4–8pm.

See Map 12 on p. 130.

Loco (p. 137) CAMPO DE' FIORI Totally unique shoes for women who simply don't have enough.... *Tel 06/688-08-216. Via dei Baullari 22. Buses 30, 40, 46, 62, 64, 70, 87, 116, 492, or 571. Tram 8. Mon 3–7:30pm; Tues–Sat 10am–8:30pm.*

See Map 14 on p. 145.

Mario Lucchesi (p. 137) SPANISH STEPS Hogan shoes and bags, Fay outerwear, and other Italo-preppy essentials, including golf equipment.... *Tel 06/361-41-59. Via del Babuino 162. Metro Spagna or Flaminio. Mon–Sat 10am–7:30pm.*

See Map 13 on p. 144.

Marmi Line (p. 142) PIAZZA NAVONA Wide selection of restored marble antiques. Will ship anywhere in the world.... *Tel 06/689-37-95. www.marmiline.com. Via de' Coronari 113–141/145. Buses 70, 87, 280, or 492. Mon–Sat 10am–7:30pm.*

See Map 14 on p. 145.

Martina Novelli (p. 137) VATICAN Tiny shoe store with all the latest and greatest designs, from flats to 4-inch stilettos.... *Tel 06/397-37-247. Piazza Risorgimento 38. Metro Ottaviano. Buses 23, 81, 271, or 492. Tram 19. Mon–Sat 10am–2pm, 3:30–8pm. Closed Jewish holidays.*

See Map 12 on p. 130.

Mercato delle Stampe (p. 142) PIAZZA DEL POPOLO Market of used and antiquarian books, prints, and magazines..... *No telephone. Largo della Fontanella di Borghese. Bus 119. Mon–Sat roughly 7:30am–noon.*

See Map 13 on p. 144.

Missoni (p. 134) SPANISH STEPS The originator of colorful Italian knitwear.... *Tel 06/679-25-55. www.missoni.com. Piazza di Spagna 78. Metro Spagna. Mon–Sat 10am–7:30pm.*

See Map 13 on p. 144.

Miss Sixty (p. 139) VATICAN/VIA DEL CORSO Jeans and party clothes for chicks with attitude.... *Via del Corso: Tel 06/678-1045; www.misssixty.com; Via del Corso 179; Metro Spagna. Via Cola di Rienzo: Tel 06/3200918; Via Cola di Rienzo 235; buses 23, 81, or 492 to Via Cola di Rienzo. Mon–Sat 10am–7:30pm.*

See Map 12 on p. 130.
See Map 13 on p. 144.

Modigliani (p. 136) SPANISH STEPS Home, gift, and wedding registry items in ceramic, stainless, and glass, in classic and modern designs. Will ship anywhere.... *Tel 06/678-5653. www.modigliani.it. Via Condotti 24. Metro Spagna. Mon–Sat 10am–7:30pm.*

See Map 13 on p. 144.

Mr. Wine (p. 141) PANTHEON The preferred wine seller of Rome's parliamentarians; across the street from the parliament building.... *Tel 06/68-13-41-41. Piazza del Parlamento 7. Buses 119 or 913. Mon–Sat 10am–1pm; Mon–Fri 3:30–8pm.*

See Map 14 on p. 145.

Murphy&Nye (p. 139) VIA DEL CORSO/VATICAN Stylish, sailing-inspired sportswear for Roman poseurs.... *Via del Corso: Tel 06/ 36004461; www.murphynye.com; Via del Corso 26; Metro Flaminio/Spagna. Via Cola di Rienzo: Tel 06/3265-1812; Via Cola di Rienzo 139; buses 23, 81, 492 to Via Cola di Rienzo. Mon–Sat 10am–7:30pm.*

See Map 12 on p. 130.
See Map 13 on p. 144.

Nuyorica (p. 135) CAMPO DE' FIORI Where *centro storico fashionistas* come for their Marc Jacobs, Chloe, and Balenciaga ready-to-wear and accessories.... *Tel 06/6889-1254. www.nuyorica.it. Piazza Pollarola 36–37. Buses 30, 40, 46, 62, 64, 70, 87, 116, 492, or 571. Tram 8. Mon–Sat 10:30am–8pm.*

See Map 14 on p. 145.

Onyx (p. 138) SPANISH STEPS Sportswear for junior-high girls and Hilton-sisters-in-training.... *Tel 06/679-15-09. www.onyx.it. Via del Corso 132/Via Frattina 91. Buses 62, 85, 95, 116, or 492. Metro Spagna. Mon–Sat 10am–7:30pm.*

See Map 13 on p. 144.

Piazza Testaccio (p. 140) TESTACCIO Covered produce market in a neighborhood off the tourist track.... *No telephone. Piazza Testaccio. Metro Piramide. Mon–Sat roughly 6am–2pm.*

See Map 12 on p. 130.

Pinko (p. 135) CAMPO DE' FIORI Well-made and (barely) affordable urban wear for daring women in their 20s and 30s.... *Tel 06/ 683-09-446. www.pinko.it. Via dei Giubbonari 76–77. Buses 30, 40, 46, 62, 64, 70, 87, 492, or 571. Tram 8. Mon–Sat 10am–8pm.*

See Map 14 on p. 145.

Porta Portese (p. 141) TRASTEVERE Vendors at Rome's biggest open-air flea market sell everything: secondhand clothes, plumbing fixtures, bicycles, and kittens.... *No telephone. Between Via Portuense and Via Ippolito Nievo. Metro Piramide. Buses 170, 280, 718, or 719. Tram 30. Sun roughly 6am–3pm.*

See Map 12 on p. 130.

Prada (p. 134) SPANISH STEPS Hipper-than-thou Italian design house catering to wealthy waifs and wallflowers.... *Tel 06/679-08-97. www.prada.com. Via Condotti 92–95. Metro Spagna. Mon–Sat 10am–7:30pm.*

See Map 13 on p. 144.

Prototype (p. 138) CAMPO DE' FIORI Hip T-shirts, jeans, and Converse high-tops. For men and women.... *Tel 06/683-00-330. Via dei Giubbonari 50. Buses 30, 40, 46, 62, 64, 70, 87, 492, or 571. Tram 8. Mon–Sat 10am–2pm, 4–7:30pm.*

See Map 14 on p. 145.

Roberto Cavalli (p. 134) SPANISH STEPS Veteran women's designer employs embellished denim, fur, and leather for in-your-face, body-hugging sex appeal... *Tel 06/6938-0130. www.robertocavalli.it. Via Borgognona 7A. Metro Spagna. Mon–Sat 10am–7:30pm.*

See Map 13 on p. 144.

Sermoneta (p. 139) SPANISH STEPS Leather gloves and accessories in every color of the rainbow.... *Tel 06/679-19-60. www.sermonetagloves.com. Piazza di Spagna 61. Metro Spagna. Mon–Sat 10am–7:30pm.*

See Map 13 on p. 144.

Sole (p. 136) CAMPO DE' FIORI Glam up your wardrobe with a hot leather trench or papal-chic tasseled belt from this tiny boutique.... *Tel 06/6880-6987. Via dei Baullari 21. Buses 30, 40, 62, 64, 70, 87, 116, 492, or 571. Tram 8. Mon 3:30–7:30pm; Tues–Sat 10am–1:30pm, 3:30–8pm.*

See Map 14 on p. 145.

Sportstaff (p. 135) SPANISH STEPS A fashion victim's paradise, with cheaply made trendy tops, pants, and accessories.... *Piazza di Spagna: Tel 06/678-15-99; www.sportstaff.com; Piazza di Spagna 86; Metro Spagna. Via del Corso: Tel 06/58200913; Via del Corso 172a; Metro Spagna. Daily 10am–7:30pm.*

See Map 13 on p. 144.

Stefanel (p. 135) CITYWIDE National clothing chain with basics and some fun stuff for men and women, a cut above Benetton.... *Tel 06/6992-5836. www.stefanel.it. Piazza Venezia 5. Mon–Sat 10am–7:30pm; Sun noon–7pm. Large branches at Via del Corso (Tel 06/6992-5783; Via del Corso 122) and Via Cola di Rienzo (Tel 06/321-1403; Via Cola di Rienzo 223); Mon–Sat 10am–7:30pm.*

See Map 14 on p. 145.

Trancanelli (p. 137) VATICAN Sneakers, stilettos, and other great shoes for the fashionable men and women of upscale Roma nord.... *Tel 06/323-45-03. Piazza Cola di Rienzo 84. Metro Lepanto. Buses 70, 81, or 280. Mon–Sat 10am–2pm, 4–7:30pm.*

See Map 12 on p. 130.

Trimani (p. 141) TERMINI Opened in 1821, this place knows wine. More than 3,000 varieties, plus a wine bar next door.... *Tel 06/446-96-61. www.trimani.com. Via Goito 20. Metro Termini. Mon–Sat 8:30am–1:30pm, 3:30–8pm.*

See Map 12 on p. 130.

Underground **(p. 141)** SPANISH STEPS Once-monthly market held in parking lot near the Spanish Steps. Lots of vintage jewelry; political and religious knickknacks like buttons, signs, and decorative plates; and everyday junk.... *Tel 06/36-00-53-45. Via Francesco Crispi 96. Metro Spagna or Barberini. Bus 95. Oct–April, 1st Sun of month 10am–8pm.*

See Map 13 on p. 144.

Valentino **(p. 134)** SPANISH STEPS The Roman couturier's flagship store.... *Tel 06/678-36-56. www.valentino.com. Via Condotti 13. Metro Spagna. Mon–Sat 10am–7:30pm.*

See Map 13 on p. 144.

Via Sannio **(p. 141)** SAN GIOVANNI Daily market selling both new and used items. Best buys are leather jackets, vintage cocktail dresses, and soccer jerseys.... *No telephone. Metro SanGiovanni. Mon–Sat 9am–2pm.*

See Map 12 on p. 130.

W Apolloni **(p. 142)** PIAZZA DEL POPOLO Antiques vendor of art and furniture from the 17th century, rare sculptures, and jewelry from various eras. One of Rome's most exclusive antiquarians.... *Tel 06/679-24-29. Via del Babuino 132. Metro Flaminio or Spagna. Mon–Sat 10am–8pm.*

See Map 13 on p. 144.

N I G H

TLIFE

6

Map 15: Rome Nightlife Orientation

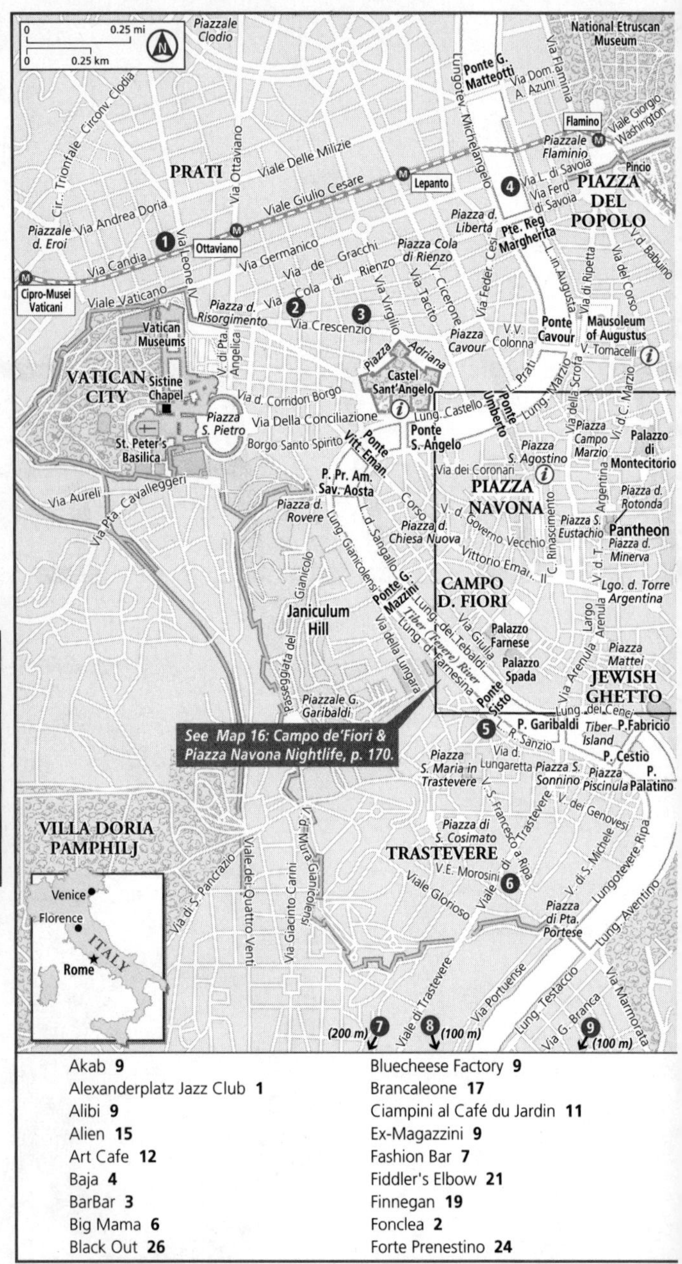

Akab **9**
Alexanderplatz Jazz Club **1**
Alibi **9**
Alien **15**
Art Cafe **12**
Baja **4**
BarBar **3**
Big Mama **6**
Black Out **26**
Bluecheese Factory **9**
Brancaleone **17**
Ciampini al Café du Jardin **11**
Ex-Magazzini **9**
Fashion Bar **7**
Fiddler's Elbow **21**
Finnegan **19**
Fonclea **2**
Forte Prenestino **24**

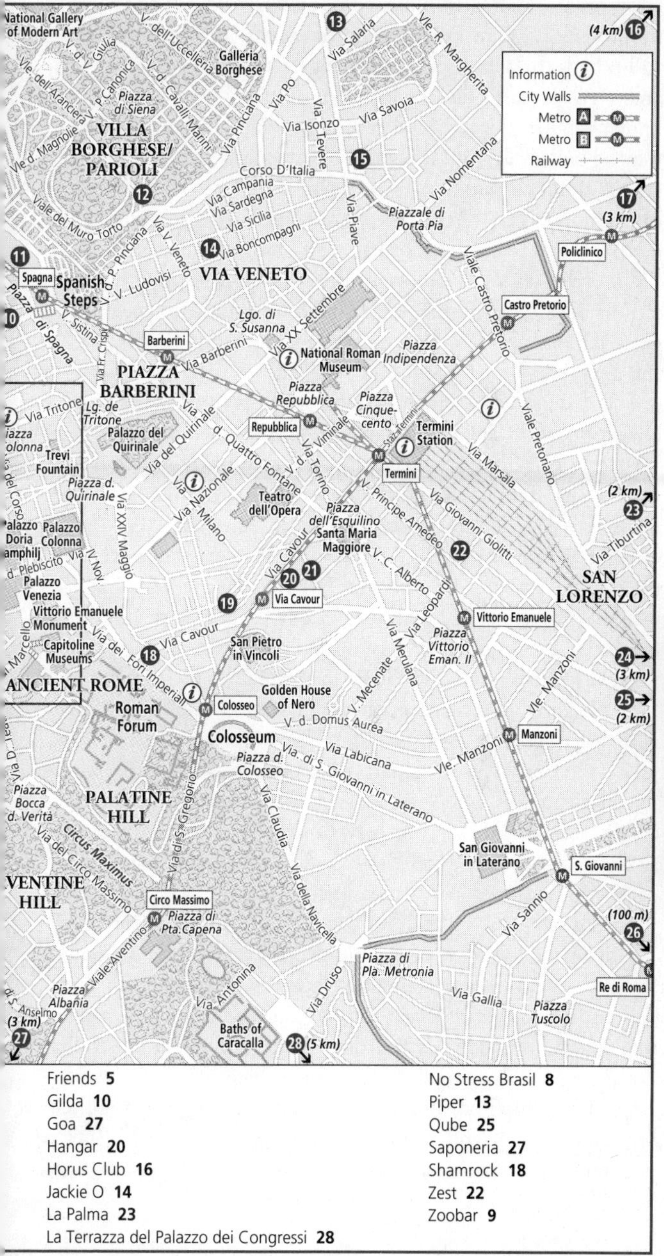

Friends **5**	No Stress Brasil **8**
Gilda **10**	Piper **13**
Goa **27**	Qube **25**
Hangar **20**	Saponeria **27**
Horus Club **16**	Shamrock **18**
Jackie O **14**	Zest **22**
La Palma **23**	Zoobar **9**
La Terrazza del Palazzo dei Congressi **28**	

Basic Stuff

Easy, breezy, and often cheesy are the keywords when it comes to most nightlife in Rome. There are plenty of great nights out to be had, for sure, but cutting edge clubs, international DJs, and a particularly diverse bar scene are not what this city is known for—though several recent openings indicate a change may be underway. Since most discos are a cab ride away, expensive, and not all that impressive, you're usually better off spending your *dopocena* (after dinner) hours making the rounds at the *centro storico*'s lively outdoor bars and lounges and seeing where the night takes you. Almost all the best spots are within walking distance of each other, so if you don't like the music or can't get a table at the first bar you try, you can simply sashay on to the next.

For those who demand strobe lights, pounding bass, and a chance to shake it on the dance floor, the once-working-class Testaccio and Ostiense quarters, south of the city, are club central, where defunct slaughterhouses and abandoned factories have been recycled into warehouse-style *discoteche.*

At the trendier clubs, bouncers wield velvet ropes with the gravity of bishops administering last rites, and a veritable catwalk of characters, all of whom seem to think they're still in the *dolce vita* 1960s, do their best to look blasé as they wait their turn. When club staff does deign to let you into their inner sanctum, you'll be hit for a cover charge of 10€ to 20€ ($13–$25)—and that might not even include a drink; expect to pay another 10€ ($13) or so per cocktail. Once you've cleared the whole selection process, you may well wonder what all the fuss was about; Roman DJs tend to play Beyoncé's latest hits in obsessively remixed loops, and the crowd is often too busy scoping each other out to dance, drink, or have a good time. No matter what the scene is, you're in for some great people-watching.

Romans are a very sociable people, and at many venues, straight or gay, the meat-market factor is present in full force. Roman guys, from the smooth to the awkward, see foreign females and immediately feel their inner stallion rumble to life. Ladies who've been patient enough to listen to their broken-English pick-up lines should have no qualms about letting them buy you a drink and then disappearing. Seem harsh? Italian women can be a hell of a lot bitchier. Alternatively, you can keep your suitors at arm's length all night so that at least they'll give you a ride home. Foreign guys looking to chat up local *ragazze* are in for more of a challenge, as Roman girls are almost tribal and notoriously difficult to hit on—though if you casually flash the keys to your yacht or your Screen Actors' Guild membership card, they might give you the time of day.

Vietato Fumare

For better or worse, the biggest thing to hit the nightlife scene in Rome was the smoking ban that went into effect throughout Italy in January 2005. Miraculously enough, people actually respect the law, which applies to all restaurants' and bars' indoor areas. Which isn't to say that Romans have quit smoking–most bars have an outdoor area where you can puff away unhassled.

So, what else is there to do in Rome if bars and clubs are not your scene? Plenty, actually. Italy has had a long-term love affair with jazz and blues, and Rome has several excellent venues, mellow and raucous, that bring top-notch local and international acts year-round. Alternatively, simply going out for a stroll through the floodlit piazzas of Rome, gelato in hand, can be a splendid way to pass the evening.

If you do venture out of the *centro storico,* getting back to your hotel at the end of your night can be frustrating. Few night buses serve the areas where the best clubs are located, so try to arrange for a taxi to pick you up later in the night (some places have taxi stands just outside or have staff who will call a cab for you, but don't count on it).

Events & Listings

To find out what's going on from night to night, pick up *Time-Out Roma* at any newsstand (2€/$2.50). The monthly magazine has special events listings for pubs, *discoteche, centri sociali,* and restaurants—though in Italian only. *Roma C'è* (1€/$1.25; www.romace.it) comes out each Thursday and includes nightlife listings categorized by neighborhood and genre. It also has a short broken-English-language section called "This Week in Rome," which often contains the same listings from week to week. The newspaper *La Repubblica* publishes its weekly *Trovaroma* events guide on Thursdays. *Zero6,* an independent glossy pamphlet, is available free in many bars and boutiques.

Drinking Prices & Practices

With glasses starting at 1.50€ ($1.90), wine makes for the cheapest night out—and at those prices, the most insidious hangover when you're trudging through the Vatican Museums the next day. Beer generally starts at 4€ ($5) for a pint, and prices for mixed drinks can range anywhere between 5€ and 10€ ($6.25–$13). *Mojitos,* Bloody Marys, and strawberry *caipiroskas* are all popular in Rome, but one of the best Italian bar drinks is a vodka lemon, a simple blend of vodka and *limonata* (lemon soda). Keep in mind that Italians, in general, don't drink to get loud and obnoxious. Unlike in, say, Edinburgh—where the nightly bar crawl is a spectacle of belligerent, vomiting students—public drunkenness in Rome is a major faux pas. Mirth, revelry, and a certain amount of alcohol-induced *joie de vivre* are fine, but no one likes an ugly American, sober or wasted.

What to Wear

Roman nights out can often run from the aperitivo hour straight through to late-night clubbing without a change of clothes. Lucky for you, Rome is not a formal city, and you can get away with wearing some sort of dressed-up jeans ensemble pretty much everywhere. For guys, a cool pair of sneakers will do the trick; for girls, just remember this mantra: The more accessories, the better. To see what kind of crowd you're up against in Rome's trendiest haunts, check out the photos at www.romadisconight.com.

The Lowdown

Opening ceremonies... A little bit civilized, a little bit decadent, the *aperitivo* hour is when you get a glass of something light and/or sparkly, along with a snack, a few hours before dinner. Rome's most famous market square, Campo de' Fiori, is the undisputed champion of this scene. Come 6pm, it's a dog-eat-dog scramble for the best outdoor tables—those at next-door neighbors Taverna del Campo and **La Vineria**—as legions of Romans descend on the piazza as if reenacting the siege of Carthage. Great for drinking on the cheap, the bars here are highly social and packed from early evening to 2am. In northern Italy, the *aperitivo* is a more established rite and includes a generous spread of tapas-style finger foods, offered at no extra charge to those who buy a drink; in Rome, it's more like free peanuts and potato chips. In recent years, however, a slew of Milan-style *aperitivo* joints have opened in

Rome—get a buffet along with your buzzing scene at **Friends** in Trastevere, **Fluid** near Piazza Navona, **Baja** on the river, or **BarBar** near the Vatican.

Bars for the *bella gente*... The preferred turf of the Roman *bella gente* (roughly, the young, rich, and fabulous) lies in the area, known to some as the "triangle of booze," east of Piazza Navona. This crowd is pretty cliquey, so if you want to be a part of it, you'll need a good tan and plenty of attitude. **Bar del Fico** is a classic, casual watering hole—the name means both "bar of the fig" and "bar of the cool"—where chic locals and visitors sip drinks alfresco under a gnarled canopy of fig branches or in the bar's less-glamorous indoor salon. On a beautiful ivy-draped corner nearby, **Bar della Pace** has indoor and outdoor tables and a fashionable clientele to match. Across the way is **Bar Bramante,** which is mostly a restaurant, but the bar gets going with a crowd of well-dressed 30-somethings after midnight. The late-night scene at **Bloom,** a former chapel with sumptuous red divans and wraparound Art Deco bar, is like an exclusive soiree—lively and full of beautiful people, but not too crowded. DJs spin the latest in whatever's the latest until 2am, and then everyone migrates en masse to **La Maison,** a dance club around the corner, which by that hour isn't charging its normal cover anymore. (Also in this 'hood, **Jonathan's Angels,** famous for the kitschy self-portraits of its owner, ex–circus acrobat Nino Madras, is dark and small and attracts more tourists than hipsters, but the toilet—a peaceful, trickling garden—is a must-see.) Near the Pantheon, **Le Coppelle** is where the stylish set come for a relaxing cocktail after dining at one of the fashionable restaurants on the same square. As long as there are *Buddha Bar* compilations, they will be played at **Le Bain,** a *luxe* restaurant/lounge/art gallery just off Largo Argentina. Get cozy on a plush banquette and enjoy an intimate drink or two as candlelight flickers off your champagne flute.

The new breed... When, a few years ago, Roman nightlife mavens suddenly realized there could be more to life than sidewalk cafes and commercial discos, a rash of modern-looking, design-led bars and lounges exploded around the *centro storico.* Many of these joints feature only the trappings of modernity (soulless metallic interiors and clean lines), but there are a few standouts that have really caught on among Rome's nocturnal tastemakers. Like a Habitrail for hipsters, uber-trendy **Supperclub** (a franchise of the Amsterdam original) consists of a series of long, narrow tunnels that terminate in various play areas—dining rooms with broad white sofas, cagelike bars, or swank dance floors. An improbably modern hiccup on 16th century Via del Governo Vecchio, **Fluid** has all kinds of over-the-top, new-fangled design elements, including the bar's namesake feature, a cascade of Windex-like solution that falls in viscous streams against the back wall. **Crudo,** a cocktail lounge and raw bar near Campo de' Fiori, is probably the most original-looking space in Rome; furnished with 1960s armchairs and coffee tables, its garage-y main room has exposed concrete and bold art on the walls. **Fashion Bar,** in the Marconi neighborhood south of Trastevere, has an appealing mix of modern design, *Brady Bunch*–house flagstones, and rosy '80s glow. Nonstop fashion shows on the bar's TV screens is a bit annoying, but the music is fun, and food is served until late. **Zest,** a sleek poolside bar atop the 3-year-old Radisson-SAS Es Hotel, affords quaffers an oddly hypnotic view of Termini station, with its De Chirico-esque travertine arches and night trains rolling in and out, abacus-like, over the railyard.

Livin' *la dolce vita*... For a brush with pathetic vestiges of "the sweet life" (or, to pick up a sugar daddy), look no further than **Jackie O.** This legendary club near Via Veneto was a favorite haunt of the glitterati in the 1960s and is enjoying something of a revival among the wealthy set. The club's undeniably glamorous interiors, however, are not enough to offset the sad wax-museum tableau of aging Romans caught in a vainglorious attempt to recapture some semblance of the fabulous life they probably never even led. Visiting celebs often end up being photographed here, but it's only because they don't know any better. Another place where paparazzi might come on a slow night is **Gilda,** near the Spanish Steps, whose clientele is like a good reality show—the cast is nauseating, yet you can't stop watching. Showbiz has-beens with too much plastic surgery and sleazy politicos hobnob here to show off their newest furs or flaunt their 20-something flavors-of-the-month. In a bizarre location, adjacent to the Hertz rental car office in the subterranean mall under Villa Borghese, **Art Cafe** is one of those preposterously outdated places that somehow still manages to hold relatively hip Romans in thrall. Despite crooners who mumble confidently through English-language standards and interior decor (metallics, neons, and bubble-shaped areas of raised banquettes) that seems to have been lifted directly off some glitzy 1980s cruise ship lounge, this place is hugely trendy—just surrender to the all-consuming cheesiness, and you'll have a great time.

A drink with a view... On the panoramic Pincio hill, just north of the Spanish Steps, **Ciampini al Café du Jardin** is a classy place to catch the sunset or stargaze with a lover. The Hotel Raphael and Hotel Eden (see the Accommodations chapter) both have romantic rooftop bars, though the scene is quiet to nonexistent much of the time. Still under construction at press time, the roof bar at Hotel Forty Seven (see the Accommodations chapter), with its 270-degree terrace overlooking the stunning ruins and famous hills of ancient Rome, looks poised to be a promising spot. For a striking view of 20th-century Rome, head to 21st-century **Zest,** atop the Es Hotel.

Disco inferno... In terms of patronage, discos are alive and well in the Eternal City, drawing huge crowds most nights of the week. However, sophisticated club kids who can intelligently

Summer in the City

By late May, just about every Roman club battens down its hatches and relocates to a summer venue on the beach at Ostia or Fregene, which stays open through early September. Within the city limits, the most unique summer spot has got to be ***La Terrazza del Palazzo dei Congressi****—an alfresco club on the roof of an office building in the Fascist-era EUR district. It's a trek, but there is some seriously fabulous partying to be done down here, against the stark silhouettes of Mussolini's dream cityscape. An even bigger pain to get to by public transportation, the* ***Fiesta!*** *summer music festival occupies a horse race track far south of the center. Featuring big-name soul, rock, and Latino concerts, multiple dance floors, half-naked Brazilian women, and opportunities to shoot tequila between every conga line, it's a good time, every time—except when it's 2am and there are no buses or cabs to take you home. For a truly lovely night out, Villa Celimontana park, just south of the Colosseum, is the impossibly gorgeous home of the* ***Jazz and Image*** *festival, with more than a few soul and blues acts thrown into the mix.*

describe the difference between "ambient" and "trance" will find most of what passes for the club scene in Rome pretty yawn-inducing. So long as you don't go out clubbing in Rome with high expectations, you won't be disappointed. Eternally popular Radio Londra and **Akab** are both good all-around bets on Testaccio's club strip, where the music is neither too commercial nor too esoteric. Dance music aficionados give props to **Bluecheese Factory,** also in Testaccio; Friday- and Saturday-only DJ sets are anything but cheesy. Nearby, **Ex-Magazzini** attracts a trendier crowd, with glass paneling on the second floor that lets you watch the crowd bump and grind below you, but music is less inspired. For Casey Kasem-era Top 40 rock and pop, and '80s funk and electronic, follow the Rubik's Cube flyers to **Zoobar** on Saturday for *Nonsolottanta* ("not only '80s"). One of the first Roman clubs to break from the mainstream, **Goa,** in the Ostiense quarter south of Testaccio, has vogue-ish Indian decor and attracts all kinds of dancers (gay, straight, and transgender) for serious trance and electronica. A stone's throw from Goa, **Saponeria** (a former soap factory) is a more commercial, single-floor disco that attracts a younger, well-scrubbed crowd. North of the center, **Piper** is like a Roman Studio 54, except that it's still open. Opened by Italian pop star Patty Pravo in the 1970s, this mainstay of the Roman nightlife circuit may have seen its glory days peak and crash, but it has managed to hang on to a mixed-age crowd with its diverse music and freewheeling disco-days aura. In the same 'hood, mainstream Roman youth frequents **Alien,** a multiroom disco with the kind of music and upbeat attitude you might find at a roller rink—DJs blast the Backstreet Boys, and no one walks off the dance floor in disgust. For "elite" members of society who don't care to slum it with the peons when they hit the discoteca, all Roman clubs are equipped with an obnoxious *sala privé* (private VIP room).

Meat markets... A fruit and vegetable market by day, **Campo de' Fiori** after dark is a buzzing social scene and pick-up central. Almost every address on the pedestrian square is an alcohol purveyor of some kind, and the cobblestones are always filled with locals and foreigners milling around and checking each other out. Half the patrons at disco-pub **Trinity College,** off Via del Corso, are horny Roman guys; the other half are American girls-gone-wild. Replace "American" with "Italian," and you've got the same crowd at **Baja,** a sleek, always festive *risto-disco* that floats (moored) on the Tiber. Just watch out for those flash floods.

The gay scene... Preening queens, muscle men, transvestites, and straight-acting gays all flock to Rome's premier gay disco, **Alibi,** which has two of the most happening dance floors in the city. In summer, the rooftop terrace (against Monte Testaccio) creates a third dance floor and a rather fabulous atmosphere for boozing and cruising. American-owned **Hangar** has also been around for quite some time and attracts fashionable young gays and lesbians despite its proximity to seedy Termini. The most notorious gay night in town is the Muccassassina ("killer cow") party, which goes from Friday evening well into Saturday morning at **Qube,** with performances by the finest drag queens in the land. For the ladies, Venus Rising is a monthly lesbian one-nighter at **Goa.** For a good night's cruising, boys can head for Monte Caprino (the west side of the Capitoline Hill). There are also a lot of one-off events in and around Rome for gay men, lesbians, and transsexuals, sponsored by the **Mario Mieli Gay Cultural Association** (Tel 06/541-39-85; www.mariomieli.org). Contact **Arci-Gay** (Tel 06/855-55-22; www.arcigay.it) and **ArciLesbica** (Tel 06/418-03-69) for the latest info on Rome's queer scene.

All that jazz (and blues)... The average Roman knows more about jazz than most Americans, and the brand-new **Casa del Jazz** (see the Entertainment chapter) is the most recent manifestation of Italy's affinity for the genre (and of Mayor Walter Veltroni's desire to endow his city with more modern cultural spaces). In a beautiful 1930s mansion that was once occupied by a gypsy clan boss, the *casa* features interactive multimedia libraries, recording studios, and a regular line-up of international jazz acts. For a more traditional venue, the highly respected **Alexanderplatz** has long been the last word in Roman jazz, hosting the biggest names in American and Italian jazz and blues. (Some acts can be catatonic; before you sign up for a night of live Muzak, check to see who's playing.) Way the hell out on the Via Tiburtina, **La Palma** is a refined club in an ugly part of town that also takes its jazz seriously. **Big Mama,** an if-the-house-is-a-rockin', don't-bother-knockin' blues joint in Trastevere, is down and dirtier, with daily performances from mostly local, top-quality artists—no cheesy crooners here. One of the best regular acts is Più Bestial Che Blues, who cover everything from Sam Cooke to Prince—a guaranteed good time (and singer Davide Gentili, a dentist in real life, looks like an Italian George Clooney). *I Bestiali* play at mellower, British-style **Fonclea** by the Vatican.

A good band is hard to find... While tons of big-name bands play Rome in summer (see the Entertainment chapter), the year-round live rock/pop scene isn't very consistent. For alternative tastes, your best bet is **Brancaleone,** a *centro sociale* that regularly hosts quality alternative and punk bands, home-grown DJs, and hugely well-attended drum n' bass nights known as "Agatha." Kids with mohawks and tattoos squat at **Forte Prenestino,** doing their best to look hard, until a good show comes around, which is fairly often: Famous names in the hard-core, punk, and ska scenes, like Fugazi and the Buzzcocks, have played here. **Black Out** is, for the most part, an alternative rock-playing disco, but it also occasionally features live rock and hip-hop acts from around Italy, the U.S., and the U.K. Out past the Via Nomentana, **Horus Club** is another cool venue (an Art Nouveau cinema stripped of its seats) that sometimes has rock and hip-hop shows. For something completely different, **No Stress Brasil,** an authentic restaurant/bar/disco/*churrascaria* in Trastevere, has live Brazilian music Tuesday to Sunday; they'll even let you try your hand at "Girl from Ipanema" on karaoke nights (Mon–Wed).

The local pub scene... A reliable option when you just want to relax with a beer or five, Rome's pubs all share that generic "Irish pub" look (Guinness memorabilia, soccer pennants, scratched-up wood-paneled bars with brass fixtures), and the best are found in the Monti neighborhood northeast of the Colosseum. Great for a cold draught after touring the ruins (or whenever, really), the **Shamrock** just gets louder and livelier as the night wears on. Nearby, **Finnegan** is the self-proclaimed "only real Irish pub in

Rome" and the second home of scores of beer-drinking, English-speaking expatriates. **Fiddler's Elbow,** a block from Santa Maria Maggiore, is also frequented by a jolly mix of expatriates, a few tourists, and those Romans who'll actually have more than a few pints in one sitting. Near Piazza Navona, **Abbey Theatre,** a pub named after the national theater of Ireland, broadcasts all kinds of sporting events (from the Super Bowl to the World Championship of Curling) and hops with Roman and expat kids at night.

Map 16: Campo De' Fiori & Piazza Navona Nightlife

NIGHTLIFE

The Index

Abbey Theatre (p. 169) PIAZZA NAVONA Pub/sports bar popular with Roman and foreign students. Broadcasts all major U.S. professional and college games.... *Tel 06/686-13-41. www.abbey-rome.com. Via del Governo Vecchio 51–53. Buses 30, 40, 62, 64, 70, 87, 116, 492, or 571. No cover. Sun–Thurs 11am–2am; Fri–Sat 11am–3am.*

See Map 16 on p. 170.

Akab (p. 166) TESTACCIO Well-established, cavelike disco/bar, usually with cutting-edge DJs.... *Tel 06/578-2390. www.akabcave.com. Via di Monte Testaccio 68–69. Metro Piramide. Buses 23, 30, 95, 170, 271, or 280. Tram 3. Cover 10€–20€ ($13–$25). Tues–Sat 10pm–4am.*

See Map 15 on p. 158.

Alexanderplatz Jazz Club (p. 167) VATICAN One of Italy's most renowned jazz clubs. From June to August, the club closes and sponsors the outdoor Jazz and Image festival at Villa Celimontana.... *Tel 06/397-42-171. www.romajazz.com. Via Ostia 9. Metro Ottaviano. Buses 23, 490, 492, 913, or 990. Daily 9pm–3am. Cover 6.50€ ($8.15) (monthly pass).*

See Map 15 on p. 158.

Alibi (p. 167) TESTACCIO Notorious gay disco with plenty of nongays; DJs play a requisite mix of house and techno. Fantastic rooftop terrace on Monte Testaccio open in summer.... *Tel 06/574-34-48. Via di Monte Testaccio 40–44. AE, MC, V. Metro Piramide. Buses 23, 30, 75, 95, or 170. Tram 3. Wed–Sun 11:45pm–5am. No cover Wed–Thurs and Sun; Fri 12€ ($15); Sat 15€ ($19).*

See Map 15 on p. 158.

Alien (p. 166) VENETO Mass-market disco plays energetic mix of pop and house; relocates to the beach at Fregene in summer.... *Via Velletri: Tel 06/841-22-12; www.aliendisco.it; Via Velletri 13–19; bus 63. Fregene: Tel 06/665-64-761; Piazzale Fregene 5. Tues–Sun 11pm–4am. Cover varies.*

See Map 15 on p. 158.

Art Cafe (p. 164) VIA VENETO The young and trendy are ga-ga for the '80s-style glamour of this sprawling club beneath Villa Borghese.... *Tel 06/3600-6578. Viale del Galoppatoio 33. Metro Spagna. Buses 95 or 116. Tues and Thurs–Sat 9pm–4am. Cover 15€–20€ ($19–$25).*

See Map 15 on p. 158.

Baja (p. 163) PIAZZA DEL POPOLO Meat market riverboat disco-bar on the Tiber with trick-happy bartenders.... *Tel 06/326-00-118. Lungotevere Arnaldo da Brescia, between Ponte Regina Margherita and Ponte Nenni. Metro Flaminio. Buses 81 or 628. Tues–Sun 8pm–3am. Closed during high water (occasionally Nov–March). No cover.*

See Map 15 on p. 158.

BarBar (p. 163) VATICAN Trendy, labyrinthine underground lounge, done up in slick '60s motifs and full of peppy and preppy locals. Hot *aperitivo* spot on Sunday.... *Tel 06/6880-5682. www.barbarroma.it. Via Ovidio 17. AE, DC, MC, V. Buses 23 or 492. Daily 7pm–3am. Cover varies.*

See Map 15 on p. 158.

Bar Bramante (p. 163) PIAZZA NAVONA Restaurant/cocktail bar; hip 30-something crowd spills over to Bar della Pace across the way.... *Tel 06/688-03-916. Via della Pace 25. Buses 30, 40, 62, 64, 70, 87, 116, 492, or 571. Daily 7:30pm–2am. No cover.*

See Map 15 on p. 158.

Bar del Fico (p. 163) PIAZZA NAVONA A hipster fixture: This unpretentious indoor/outdoor cocktail bar has a stylish, mixed-age crowd and the occasional celebrity.... *Tel 06/686-52-05. Piazza del Fico 26–28. Buses 30, 40, 62, 64, 70, 87, 116, 492, or 571. Daily 11am–3am. No cover.*

See Map 16 on p. 170.

Bar della Pace (p. 163) PIAZZA NAVONA By day, quiet and picturesque cafe; by night, de rigueur stop on the fashionable *centro storico* bar circuit.... *Tel 06/686-12-16. Via della Pace 3–7. Buses 30, 40, 62, 64, 70, 87, 116, 492, or 571. Daily 8am–3am. No cover.*

See Map 16 on p. 170.

Big Mama (p. 168) TRASTEVERE Home of the blues in Rome, with boisterous nightly performances by classy blues, funk, and rock acts. Call ahead to reserve a table.... *Tel 06/581-25-51. www.bigmama.it. Vicolo San Francesco a Ripa 18. Buses 23, 271, 280, 780, or H. Trams 3 or 8. Daily 9pm–2:30am. Closed July–Oct. Monthly membership card 7€ ($8.75), yearly card 13€ ($16).*

See Map 15 on p. 158.

Black Out (p. 168) SAN GIOVANNI Classic Roman rock venue, with live punk, garage, and indie bands (sometimes from the U.S. and the U.K.).... *Tel 06/704-96-791. www.blackoutrockclub.com. Via*

Saturnia 18. Metro Re di Roma. Bus 87. Wed–Sat 11pm–4am. Closed in summer. Cover varies.

See Map 15 on p. 158.

Bloom (p. 163) PIAZZA NAVONA Nouveau-cuisine restaurant until 11:30pm, then legitimately fun cocktail joint for good-looking, well-dressed men with women 10 years their junior. Stiff drinks and drink prices, but "BlooMonday" knocks 2€ ($2.50) off every cocktail.... *Tel 06/688-02-029. Via del Teatro Pace 29–30. Buses 30, 40, 62, 64, 70, 87, 116, 492, or 571. Tram 8. Open to non-diners 11:30pm–2am. No cover, but capricious selection at the door.*

See Map 16 on p. 170.

Bluecheese Factory (p. 166) ESTACCIO One Roman dance club that *isn't* cheesy. Weekend-only parties feature electronica and jungle sets.... *Tel 06/57287631. Via Caio Cestio 5b. Metro Piramide. Buses 23, 30, 75, 95, or 170. Tram 3. Fri–Sat 11:30pm–3am. Cover 5€ ($6.25).*

See Map 15 on p. 158.

Brancaleone (p. 168) EASTERN SUBURBS A *centro sociale* that boasts a cinema, a disco, and a recording studio. Friday "Agatha" nights have been known to attract crowds of more than a thousand during summer.... *Tel 06/820-00-959. www.brancaleone.it. Via Levanna 11. Bus 60. Wed–Sat 10:30pm–5am. Cover 5€ ($6.25).*

See Map 15 on p. 158.

Campo de' Fiori (p. 166) CAMPO DE' FIORI Packed with bars, Rome's most famous market square is ideal for socializing and drinking on the cheap.... *Campo de' Fiori. Buses 30, 40, 62, 64, 70, 87, 116, 492, or 571.*

See Map 16 on p. 170.

Casa del Jazz (p. 167) AVENTINE/SOUTHERN SUBURBS Brand-new multimedia space, music lab, concert venue—in a 1930s villa reclaimed from crime bosses.... *Tel 06/4894-1208. www.casajazz.it. Viale di Porta Ardeatina 55, near Via Cristoforo Colombo. Buses 175 or 714. Mon–Sat 10am–midnight; concerts most nights at 9pm. Free admission; concerts 12€–16€ ($15–$20).*

Ciampini al Café du Jardin (p. 165) SPANISH STEPS/VENETO Panoramic bar on the Pincio hill overlooks the *centro storico*, Vatican City, and points west.... *Tel 06/678-5678. Viale Trinita' dei Monti. Metro Spagna. Mid-March to April and mid-Sept to mid-Oct Thurs–Tues 8am–8pm; mid-May to mid-Sept Thurs–Tues 8am–1am. Closed mid-Oct to mid-March. No cover.*

See Map 15 on p. 158.

Crudo (p. 164) CAMPO DE' FIORI Industrial garage meets Eisenhower-era furniture and eclectic murals; snack and sip among

Rome's hippest.... *Tel 06/683-8989. www.crudoroma.it. Via degli Specchi 6. Buses 23, 30, 40, 62, 64, 70, 87, 116, 271, 280, or 492. Tram 8. Daily 6pm–3am. No cover.*

See Map 16 on p. 170.

Ex-Magazzini (p. 166) TESTACCIO One of Rome's hipper discos, with a see-through floor on the upper level, plush sofas, and catwalk-worthy clientele. Uninspired mix of almost all dance genres.... *Tel 0/575-80-40. Via Magazzini Generali 8. Metro Piramide. Buses 23, 30, 60, 75, 95, 170, or 280. Tram 3. Wed–Sun 10pm–4am. Closed June–Aug. Cover varies.*

See Map 15 on p. 158.

Fashion Bar (p. 164) SOUTHWESTERN SUBURBS California-inspired, pink-tinged living room, complete with "fireplace" and bi-level sitting areas; DJs play '70s, '80s, and R&B music.... *Tel 06/55300742. Piazza Meucci 4. Bus 170. Thurs–Sat 8pm–4am. Cover varies.*

See Map 15 on p. 158.

Fiddler's Elbow (p. 169) MONTI The oldest Irish pub in Rome, always packed with a lively crowd of locals, resident expats, and travelers.... *Tel 06/487-21-10. www.thefiddlerselbow.com. Via dell'Olmata 43. Metro Cavour or Termini. Buses 70, 75, or 714. Daily 5pm–2am. No cover.*

See Map 15 on p. 158.

Finnegan (p. 168) MONTI A favorite pub among expatriates, with Guinness, Harp, and Caffey's all on tap.... *Tel 06/474-7026. Via Leonina 66. Metro Cavour. Buses 71, 75, or 714. Daily 1pm–2am. No cover.*

See Map 15 on p. 158.

Fluid (p. 163) PIAZZA NAVONA *Aperitivo* cocktail bar brings a dash of modernity to old Rome with sculpted resin ceiling panels and ottomans that look like ice cubes.... *Tel 06/683-2361. Via del Governo Vecchio 46. Buses 30, 40, 62, 64, 70, 87, 116, 492, or 571. Daily 6pm–2am. No cover.*

See Map 16 on p. 170.

Fonclea (p. 168) VATICAN Has nightly happy hour (7–8pm) and live music most nights. Expect to hear soul, funk, jazz, and rock.... *Tel 06/689-63-02. www.fonclea.it. Via Crescenzio 82a. Metro Ottaviano. Buses 23, 81, or 271. Tram 19. Daily 6pm–2am. No cover Sun–Fri; Sat 6€ ($7.50).*

See Map 15 on p. 158.

Forte Prenestino (p. 168) EASTERN SUBURBS An old prison yard retooled into a *centro sociale* for the anti-establishment/punk-rock/Communist set. *Tel 06/218-07-855. www.forteprenestino.net. Via Federico Delpino. Trams 5 or 19. Daily 7pm–3am. Cover 4€ ($5).*

See Map 15 on p. 158.

Friends (p. 163) TRASTEVERE Modern chrome decor and good, free food during the buzzing *aperitivo* hour.... *Tel 06/581-6111. Piazza Trilussa 34. Buses 23, 271, or 280. Tram 8. Mon–Sat 7am–2am; Sun 6pm–2am.* Aperitivi *6–8:30pm. No cover.*

See Map 15 on p. 158.

Gilda (p. 164) SPANISH STEPS Exclusive club frequented by high rollers and trophy women who try to channel the glamorous Italian actresses of a bygone era. Try not to gag on the sleaze.... *Tel 06/678-48-38. www.gildabar.it. Via Mario de' Fiori 97. Metro Spagna. Daily 11pm–4am. Cover varies. Gilda-on-the-beach takes place each summer, Tues–Sun in Fregene.... Tel 06/665-60-649. Lungomare di Ponente 11.*

See Map 15 on p. 158.

Goa (p. 166) OSTIENSE Cavernous club with vaguely ethnic feel gets pumping with ambient, trance, electronic, and techno music by owner/DJ Giancarlino.... *Tel 06/574-82-77. Via Libetta 13. Metro Garbatella. Buses 23 or 271. Thurs–Tues 11pm–4am. Cover varies.*

See Map 15 on p. 158.

Hangar (p. 167) MONTI Rome's first gay bar opened in 1983 and is still a very popular hangout on weekends. Thursday features amateur striptease performances; Monday is porn video night.... *Tel 06/488-13-97. Via in Selci 69a. Metro Cavour. Buses 71, 75, or 714. Wed–Mon 10:30pm–2am. Cover varies.*

See Map 15 on p. 158.

Horus Club (p. 168) EASTERN SUBURBS Rock and hip-hop acts in a former Art Nouveau cinema.... *Tel 06/868-01-410. Corso Sempione 21. Buses 36, 60, 86, or 90. Tues–Sat 10:30pm–3am. Cover varies.*

See Map 15 on p. 158.

Jackie O (p. 164) VENETO The legendary 1960s disco has been revamped into a posh piano bar and lounge for aging members of the glitterati.... *Tel 06/428-85-457. www.jackieo.it. Via Boncompagni 11. Metro Barberini. Buses 95 or 116. Wed–Sat 9pm–4am. Cover varies.*

See Map 15 on p. 158.

Jonathan's Angels (p. 163) PIAZZA NAVONA Wall-to-wall kitsch and frescoes featuring "Jonathan" surrounded by his kids (the "angels") decorate this fun, if touristy, cocktail bar. The toilet is not to be missed.... *Tel 06/689-34-26. Via della Fossa 16. Buses 30, 40, 46, 62, 64, 70, 81, 87, 492, or 571. Mon 8pm–2am; Tues–Sun 5pm–2:30am. No cover.*

See Map 16 on p. 170.

La Maison (p. 163) PIAZZA NAVONA Where the posh crowd goes to boogie after Bloom (see above) closes for the night.... *Tel 06/683-33-12. Vicolo dei Granari 4. Buses 30, 40, 46, 62, 64, 70, 81,*

87, 116, 492, or 571. Tram 8. Tues–Sun 11pm–4am. No cover Tues–Fri; Sat–Sun 15€ ($19).

See Map 16 on p. 170.

La Palma (p. 167) EASTERN SUBURBS Class acts make it worth the cab fare to this great jazz club in an ugly part of town.... *Tel 06/435-99-029. www.lapalmaclub.it. Via G. Mirri 35. Metro Tiburtina, then bus 545. Mon–Thurs 10pm–2am; Fri–Sat 10pm–4am. Cover varies.*

See Map 15 on p. 158.

La Terrazza del Palazzo dei Congressi (p. 165) EUR Really, truly fabulous open-air summer party on top of an office building in Fascist-era EUR. Worth the trek.... *Tel 06/683-33-12. Piazzale Kennedy. Metro EUR Fermi. Buses 30, 170, or 714. June–Aug, Fri–Sun 10:30pm–4am. Cover varies.*

See Map 15 on p. 158.

La Vineria (p. 162) CAMPO DE' FIORI It's always a party at Rome's most social and least expensive indoor/outdoor wine bar.... *Tel 06/6880-3268. Campo de' Fiori 15. Buses 30, 40, 62, 64, 70 87, 116, 492, or 571. Mon–Sat 9am–1am; Sun 5pm–1am. No cover.*

See Map 16 on p. 170.

Le Bain (p. 163) LARGO ARGENTINA Comfy, glowing art gallery/cocktail bar for the chill-out-loving Eurotrash set.... *Tel 06/686-56-73. www.lebain.it. Via delle Botteghe Oscure 32a–33. Buses 30, 40, 46, 62, 64, 70, 81, 87, 492, or 571. Tues–Sun 7pm–2am. No cover.*

See Map 16 on p. 170.

Le Coppelle (p. 163) PANTHEON Sip and people-watch on lounge chairs overlooking a picturesque piazza—great for a mellow night-cap.... *Tel 06/683-2410. Piazza delle Coppelle 52. Buses 30, 70, 87, 116, or 492. Daily 6pm–2am. No cover.*

See Map 16 on p. 170.

No Stress Brasil (p. 168) TRASTEVERE Eat, drink, dance, and sing to the sounds of Rio at this haunt of Brazilian expats. Live orchestra Tuesday through Saturday.... *Tel 06/583-35-015. www.nostressbrasil.net. Via degli Stradivari 35. Buses 170 or 780. Trams 3 or 8. Daily 8pm–2am. Cover varies.*

See Map 15 on p. 158.

Piper (p. 166) VENETO/NORTHERNSUBURBS Historic disco venue where many Italian pop stars got their start; still a prime spot for all ages.... *Tel 06/841-44-59. Via Tagliamento 9. Bus 63. Sat–Sun 10:30pm–4:30am. Cover 18€ ($23).*

See Map 15 on p. 158.

Qube (p. 167) EASTERN SUBURBS A raver's haven in a rough neighborhood, also the host of Rome's most famous gay night,

Muccassassina.... *Tel 06/438-54-45. www.qubedisco.com. Via Portonaccio 212. Tram 5. Thurs–Sat 11pm–4am. Cover varies.*

See Map 15 on p. 158.

Saponeria (p. 166) OSTIENSE Soap factory turned dance factory attracts clean-cut 20-somethings.... *Tel 06/574-69-99. Via degli Argonauti 20. Metro Garbatella. Buses 23, 271, or 280. Tues–Sun 10:30pm–5am. Cover 20€ ($25).*

See Map 15 on p. 158.

Shamrock (p. 168) MONTI Cool down after touring the Colosseum with a pint at this friendly, high-energy Irish pub.... *Tel 06/679-1279. Via del Colosseo 1. Metro Colosseo. Buses 60, 75, 85, 87, or 175. Daily 5pm–3am. No cover.*

See Map 15 on p. 158.

Supperclub (p. 164) PANTHEON Multi-sensory, mazelike venue. Reserve well in advance for the 75€ ($94) *prix-fixe* dinner and stay all night, or show up after 11pm to catch the party already underway.... *Tel 06/6880-7207. www.supperclub.com. Via de' Nari 14. Buses 30, 40, 62, 64, 70, 87, 116, 492, or 571. Tram 8. Disco Mon–Sat 11pm–2am. Cover for disco 10€ ($13).*

See Map 16 on p. 170.

Trinity College (p. 166) PIAZZA VENEZIA An all-out meat market by night, where the ratio of drunk American college girls and ready-to-pounce Roman "studs" is 1:1. By day, a cozy stop during Rome's rare cold days, with Irish beers and pub food.... *Tel 06/678-64-72. Via del Collegio Romano 6. Buses 30, 40, 62, 64, 85, 95, 175, or 492. Daily 11am–3am. No cover.*

See Map 16 on p. 170.

Zest (p. 164) TERMINI On the seventh floor of Rome's most modern hotel, poolside drink spot with hypnotizing view of 1930s architecture and train tracks of Termini below.... *Tel 06/444-841. Via F. Turati 171. Metro Termini. Buses 70 or 71. Daily 10am–2am. No cover.*

See Map 15 on p. 158.

Zoobar (p. 166) TESTACCIO Aching to do the robot to "Situation"? Look no further than Saturday's new-wave-leaning '80s party.... *Tel 338/813-5081. www.zoobar.roma.it. Via di Monte Testaccio 22. Metro Piramide. Buses 23, 30, 95, 170, 271, or 280. Thurs–Sat 11pm–3:30am. Cover 2.50€–4€ ($3.15–$5).*

See Map 15 on p. 158.

ENTERTA

INMENT

7

Map 17: Rome Entertainment

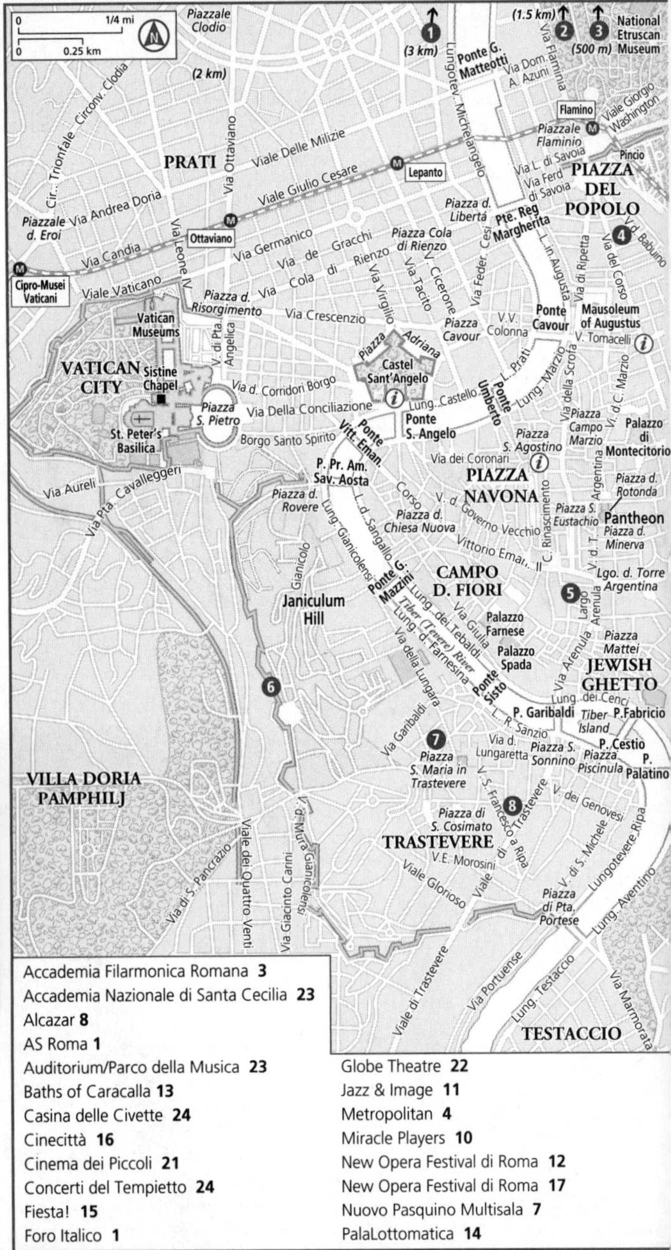

Accademia Filarmonica Romana **3**
Accademia Nazionale di Santa Cecilia **23**
Alcazar **8**
AS Roma **1**
Auditorium/Parco della Musica **23**
Baths of Caracalla **13**
Casina delle Civette **24**
Cinecittà **16**
Cinema dei Piccoli **21**
Concerti del Tempietto **24**
Fiesta! **15**
Foro Italico **1**
Globe Theatre **22**
Jazz & Image **11**
Metropolitan **4**
Miracle Players **10**
New Opera Festival di Roma **12**
New Opera Festival di Roma **17**
Nuovo Pasquino Multisala **7**
PalaLottomatica **14**

San Clemente **17**
SS Lazio **1**
Stadio Flaminio **2**
Stadio Olimpico **1**
Teatro dell'Opera **18**
Teatro di Marcello/Concerti del Tempietto **9**
Teatro di Roma-Argentina **5**
Teatro Olimpico **3**
Teatro Romano di Ostia Antica **12**
Teatro Sistina **20**
Teatro Verde **6**
Warner Village Moderno **19**

Basic Stuff

Sure, other Italian cities like Milan and Venice, and world capitals like New York and London, have better-funded, better-organized, and more varied fine arts scenes, but only Rome can deliver one-of-a-kind spectacles like full-scale opera at the Baths of Caracalla and live, edge-of-your-seat suspense like papal elections and puffs of smoke from the Sistine Chapel. In this city, the name of the game is take a dramatic setting and make it an entertainment venue. Unless you have very advanced tastes, you'll find Rome's classical music and other fine arts offerings more than satisfactory.

Many visitors come to Rome with visions of Pavarotti types on every corner—and, for the record, every self-respecting guy in town has his own soaring rendition of "Nessun Dorma" at the ready, should circumstances demand it—but the city's Teatro del'Opera has long been a source of embarrassment for local opera enthusiasts; it's seen numerous strikes, walkouts, and lackluster performances. More robust recent seasons, however, seem to suggest that things are on the mend for opera in Rome. Classical music performances abound in Rome and are generally high-quality, with frequent top-notch concerts from the Accademia Nazionale di Santa Cecilia at its new digs, the 3-year-old Auditorium-Parco della Musica. As for the stage, theaters are plentiful, but productions are almost always in Italian, and save for the odd revival of *Showboat,* too intellectually taxing for the average person to want to sit through while on vacation. Without a doubt, the performing arts scene in Rome is at its apogee in the summer, when the symphony and the opera play under the stars at archaeological sites and festivals of every genre bring big-time acts from all over the globe to breathtaking outdoor venues.

And if all that fancy-pants performing-arts stuff isn't for you, fear not: There are always sports. Well, one sport, anyway. *Calcio* (soccer) is a national pastime and a religion in Italy. Everyone, from senators to pizza chefs, follows the fate of their favorite team with the kind of fervor the Catholic church only wishes it could inspire. If you can get tickets, the home games of either of Rome's two *Serie A* (premier league) teams, archrivals **AS Roma** and **SS Lazio,** are an intensely emotional and wonderfully authentic cultural experience and a guaranteed good time. Among Italian *Serie A* league play, European cups, friendly matches, and summer tournaments, you can catch a Roma or Lazio game almost year-round.

Hollywood on the Tiber

Legends like Fellini, Gassman, and Mastroianni, who cut their teeth on the set of Rome in the dolce vita '50s and '60s, may be dead and gone, but thanks to them and other filmmakers of their era, Rome's prominent place in the world of cinema endures. These days, a steady flow of publicity-loving stars on the world movie promotion circuit (from the cast of Ocean's Twelve *to Tom Cruise and Katie Holmes) jets to Rome for premieres, awards ceremonies, and other red carpet photo ops, cementing a glamorous image for the city that is always ready for her close-up.* ***Cinecittà****—a dream of Mussolini and the production studio for such epics as* Ben-Hur *and* La Dolce Vita*—has fallen from the mythic status it once held, but the studio still churns out some winners, including Roberto Benigni's* Life is Beautiful *and Anthony Minghella's* The Talented Mr. Ripley. *Mostly, however, the lots have given way to campy variety shows, bad police dramas, and* Grande Fratello *(*Big Brother*, the only reality show that ever caught on in Italy). Located about 5 miles south of the city center, Cinecittà is not technically open to the public, but "student tours" are offered at 10am weekdays and must be booked at least a week in advance. Elaborate sets depicting the Old West, ancient Rome, and the canals of Venice are on view, as is the 19th-century lower Manhattan for Martin Scorsese's* Gangs of New York, *one of the most recent big-budget films shot here.*

If all else fails, remember that Rome is a city of constant posing and pageantry, and some of the best entertainment takes place on the street, where lovers' arguments often reach Shakespearean levels, or in the market, where old ladies' histrionic dialogue about the deadly effects of air-conditioning can be priceless theater. Each neighborhood has its favorite lunatic and so-bad-it's-good street performer—witness the enamored throngs at Campo de' Fiori when everyone's favorite *mago* (magician), a toupeed Pakistani gentleman, performs his goofy tricks.

Listings & Tickets

Roma C'è and *TimeOut Roma* have extensive listings in Italian for the city's film, theater, and musical performances. The tourist board also puts out the monthly *L' Evento,* which highlights upcoming performances. The **ORBIS** agency, Piazza Esquilino 37 (Tel 06/474-4776), sells tickets for many events, but not all—you'll often have to go to the specific, often far-flung venue to secure your seats. Credit cards are not always accepted, so make sure you have cash.

The Lowdown

Symphonies and stuff... Founded by 16th-century composer Palestrina and named for the patron saint of music, the **Accademia Nazionale di Santa Cecilia** has set the standard for the classical music scene in Rome, if not the world. Under the direction of Korean-born conductor Myung-Whun Chung since 1997, the Accademia moved to its new headquarters, the Renzo Piano-designed **Auditorium–Parco della Musica,** with its three beetle-shaped concert halls, in 2003. The Accademia's summer program takes place in the *Cavea,* the center's semicircular outdoor stage, and caters to the masses, hauling out warhorses like Beethoven's Ninth and Diana Ross year after year. Rome's other major classical troupe, the **Accademia Filarmonica Romana,** plays at the **Teatro Olimpico.** With a lineage going back to Verdi and Rossini, the Philharmonic stays mostly within the traditional realms of choral and chamber music but occasionally ventures into the provinces of blues, jazz, or experimental music.

A night at the opera... You would think that the city that was the setting for *Tosca* would be an opera powerhouse—but you would be mistaken, unfortunately. To begin with, Rome's **Teatro dell'Opera,** whose nondescript 1930s facade is dwarfed by surrounding buildings, lacks the exterior visual cred of Milan's La Scala, Venice's La Fenice, or the amphitheater at Verona. In defense of Rome's opera, the theater's interior is certainly operatic in its opulence, and the company does put on some beautiful performances, which seem to be getting more consistent now that management is stable. Long the ace in the hole of Roman opera, summer performances at the ancient **Baths of Caracalla** were suspended for a number of years after nit-picking archaeologists complained that the invasive productions—Verdi's *Aïda* brought live elephants and camels onto the site—and sopranos' high Cs might be damaging the 1,800-year-old ruins. Which, okay, was a valid point. Happily, the city council's history and opera buffs have since reconciled, and 2003 saw the triumphant return of full-scale summer opera at the baths, and it's still one of the more unforgettable ways to spend a balmy Roman evening.

The play's the thing... Unless you understand Italian, or are just really eccentric, Rome's varied theater scene will not be relevant to your visit here. But if you did, in fact, book your trip in the hopes of catching some sort of post-deconstructionist production of *Titus Andronicus,* read on: The best stage productions in town are usually at the **Teatro di Roma–Argentina,** opposite the Area Sacra ruins, a few blocks from Campo de' Fiori. Built in the 19th century, the Argentina has seen world-famous operas (including the premiere of Rossini's *Barber of Seville,* which flopped on opening night), theater productions, and dance troupes pass through as headline acts. Should you be in Rome when they're putting on *Julius Caesar,* buy a ticket: the Teatro Argentina sits on the very spot—for real—where Caesar was stabbed to death that fateful March 15 in 44 B.C. Speaking of the Bard, a faithful reproduction of the original **Globe Theatre** in London was built in Villa Borghese in 2002 and hosts various stage events beyond Shakespeare's *oeuvre.* Touring American and English theater groups often play in the **Teatro Olimpico,** which also attracts internationally acclaimed dance and musical troupes. Near Via Veneto, the **Teatro Sistina** occasionally gets off-Broadway productions. A fun way to learn about Roman history, the **Miracle Players** are a group of native English-speaking expats and experienced actors who perform their original comedies (written by repertory founding member Denise McNee, based on the writings of Livy, Tacitus, and all those guys) on Tuesday and Saturday nights in summer in front of the Mamertine Prison, overlooking the Roman Forum. For more serious, full-length *theatah,* the **English Theatre of Rome,** led by American Gaby Ford, puts on several plays in English each year.

Cinema Paradiso... Locals love to make fun of the U.S. film industry's output—*americanata* is the term used for any Hollywood-produced glossy action flick in which the hero dodges every bullet, cracks perfectly timed jokes, saves a kitten, and gets the girl—but deep down, as Roman box office numbers show, they can't get enough of the larger-than-lifeness and optimism of American movies. Romans also give props to their domestic filmmakers, like Nanni Moretti, Gabriele Muccino, and Turkish-transplant Fernan

Ozpetek, whose features are on a decidedly more human scale and among the most thoughtful and honest cinema out there. Unfortunately for non-Italian speakers, you'll have a tough time enjoying yourself at the cinema in this country, as all film imports are dubbed into Italian—and forget about subtitles. Expatriate movie goers who just want an English-language fix scan the newspaper listings for what's on at Pasquino (now officially called **Nuovo Pasquino Multisala,** a Trastevere cinema with three screens in *versione originale*), only to be disappointed by its pathologically blah-inspiring line-up of films no one would ever spend 7€ ($8.75) on at home. More appetizing features can be found at a few other Roman cinemas: **Metropolitan, Warner Village–Moderno,** and **Alcazar** (Mon only) have all woken up and smelled the expat community and often have at least one original-language film—look for "V.O." in newspaper listings. Wednesday night is discount-ticket night at cinemas citywide.

I love rock 'n' roll... Thanks in large part to the initiatives of its music-loving mayor, Walter Veltroni, Rome has made huge strides in becoming a top destination on the world tours of the biggest names in rock and pop. The overwhelming majority of these concerts take place in summer. In 2005, U2 and R.E.M. played to festive crowds at the **Stadio Olimpico,** Bruce Springsteen battled the mediocre acoustics at the **PalaLottomatica** in EUR, and **Fiesta!** (a horse racetrack-turned-sprawling summer music festival) saw Tori Amos, Joss Stone, Morcheeba, and Jamiroquai take to its main stage. The **Cornetto Free Music Festival** (sponsored by Italy's biggest ice-cream brand, Algida) comes every summer to Villa Borghese or the Circo Massimo, with acts like Sting, Duran Duran, and Black Eyed Peas. At least once a year, the city sponsors a huge free concert in one of the archaeological areas—Paul McCartney played in front of the Colosseum in 2003.

A kick in the balls (and other sports)... Rome is home to two major-league soccer teams—archrivals **AS Roma** and **SS Lazio**—and from late August to late May, one or the other will be playing on any given Sunday in the **Stadio Olimpico.** Hard-core (usually unemployed) fans show up at the stadium several hours before kick-off to set off firecrackers, taunt the police, and unfurl their huge, often polemic banners. Everyone else arrives 15 to 30 minutes before the game, team scarves around their necks (red and yellow for Roma, light blue and white for Lazio), and starts chain-smoking to cope with the emotional stress. The best view of the game is from the *tribuna* sections (above the sidelines), but you'll have more fun in the *curve* (behind the goals). If you're lucky, you'll be in town during the Roma-Lazio derby—there's one in the fall and one in the spring—which pits the city's home teams in a veritable fight to the death. Tensions on and off the field are incredibly high leading up to and during the derby, making for some of the most carnal moments in modern Roman culture you are likely to encounter. Depending on how well they've done the season before, Roma and Lazio sometimes also play in the UEFA Cup and Champions League tournaments, against the best in Europe. The World Cup will take place in Germany in the summer of 2006, at which time *romanisti* and *laziali* join in brotherhood for a month or so to cheer on the Italian national team, *gli azzurri* ("the blues").

Soccer isn't the only big sporting event in Rome, though it's certainly the most fanatically followed. **The Italian Open,** held each May at the Foro Italico complex, is a big draw and brings the world's top tennis players—and socialites—to town for an important clay-court event. It's the largest tournament before the French Open (also clay) and Wimbledon grand slams begin. And, believe it or not, Italy even fields a rugby team that competes in the Six Nations Championship, along with England, France, Ireland, Scotland, and Wales. Six Nations scrums are held in late winter each year, with home games played at the **Stadio Flaminio.**

Kidding around... Italy's low birthrate means children are a relative rarity in Rome, but those that do exist are such an integrated part of everyday life that there aren't too many special events or facilities geared to the tykes beyond, well, school. There are a few options, though. The **Teatro Verde** puppet theater, way up on the Janiculum hill (located there because of a nearby children's hospital), presents lively *Pulcinella* (the original Punch and Judy) shows every afternoon

In the Summertime

Under the aegis of the ***Estate Romana ("Roman summer")*** *program of cultural offerings, open-air festivals abound in Rome, with events running the gamut from outdoor classical and pops concerts to films and impromptu plays in picturesque piazze. Summer also brings the terrific* ***RomaEuropa Festival,*** *one of Italy's biggest and best, which takes place at the Villa Medici (on the grounds of Villa Borghese); its slate includes everything from acid jazz to Cirque du Soleil-ish ensembles of pensive saltimbanques and dancing animals. Many philharmonic troupes and classical orchestras also take their music outdoors during the summer. The* ***Baths of Caracalla*** *and the scenic Villa Giulia (the National Etruscan Museum, north of Villa Borghese) play host to summer concerts for the* ***Teatro dell'Opera*** *and the* ***Accademia Nazionale di Santa Cecilia,*** *while the basilica of* ***San Clemente****'s medieval courtyard hosts small-scale shows put on by the* ***New Opera Festival di Roma.*** *Nearby, Villa Celimontana (see the Getting Outside chapter) sets the gorgeous scene for the* ***Jazz and Image*** *festival. One of Europe's largest jazz festivals, this shindig has hosted such internationally renowned artists as Tito Puente, B. B. King, and Herbie Hancock, and its refreshment kiosks are operated by some of the city's top gourmet restaurants.* ***Fiesta!*** *is a summer-only music festival held at a horse-racing track south of Rome—once only Latin-American, Fiesta! now features more rock, soul, and reggae acts. If you're looking for music among the ruins, classical concerts run by* ***Concerti del Tempietto*** *are held nightly during the summer outside the* ***Teatro di Marcello*** *(see the Diversions chapter) or the charming* ***Casina delle Civette*** *at Villa Torlonia park, in an elegant suburb just northeast of the center. For Greek and Roman classics staged inside a real ancient theater, travel to the* ***Teatro Romano di Ostia Antica*** *(inside the archaeological site of Ostia Antica; see the Getting Outside chapter). Note that most summer festivals start in June, continue through July, take a break for a few weeks in August, and then pick up again for a few weeks in September.*

except Wednesday and also on weekend mornings. Another option for the wee ones is the **Cinema dei Piccoli** in Villa Borghese, which usually features old school family films or Disney cartoons dubbed in Italian, as well as the odd Nazi resistance documentary. Neither the Ice Capades nor the Ringling Brothers ever come to Rome—and somehow Roman kids survive—but summer often sees the arrival of small-time circuses on the outskirts of town.

The Index

See Map 17 on p. 180 for all Entertainment listings.

Accademia Filarmonica Romana (p. 184) NORTHERN SUBURBS The fall season of the Roman Philharmonic (founded in 1821) includes performances of chamber and choral music and dance. Concerts are held in the Teatro Olimpico (see below).... *Tel 06/320-17-52. www.filarmonicaromana.org. Via Flaminia 118. Tram 2. Tickets start at 15€ ($19).*

Accademia Nazionale di Santa Cecilia (p. 184) PIAZZA DEL POPOLO Rome's foremost symphony orchestra, with concerts year-round at the Auditorium-Parco della Musica's indoor halls or outdoor *cavea*.... *Tel 06/8024-2501. www.santacecilia.it. Largo Luciano Berio 3. Tickets start at 20€ ($25).*

Alcazar (p. 186) TRASTEVERE Small cinema shows films in V.O. *(versione originale)* on Monday only.... *Tel 06/588-00-99. Via Merry del Val 14. Tickets 4.50€–7€ ($5.65–$8.75).*

AS Roma (p. 186) NORTHERN SUBURBS One of Rome's *Serie A* soccer squads. Its colors are crimson and gold *(giallorosso)*.... *www.asromacalcio.it. Tickets can be purchased at the Stadio Olimpico on game day, at Lottomatica stores, or at the Official AS Roma store at Via Colonna 360 (Tel 06/678-65-14). Tickets 15€–90€ ($19–$113).*

Auditorium–Parco della Musica (p. 182) NORTHERN SUBURBS Exciting new performing arts center in the northern suburbs; the Renzo Piano–designed complex has three concert halls, used primarily by the symphonic performances of the Accademia di Santa Cecilia.... *Tel 06/802-411. www.auditoriumroma.com. Viale Pietro de Coubertin 30. Buses 52, 217, or 910. Tram 2. Ticket prices vary.*

Baths of Caracalla (p. 184) AVENTINE Dramatic summer venue for the Teatro dell'Opera. *www.opera.roma.it. Metro Circo Massimo. Buses 30, 60, 75, or 118. Tram 3. Tickets 16€–119€ ($20–$149).*

Casina delle Civette (p. 188) NORTHEASTERN SUBURBS In Villa Torlonia park, venue for Concerti del Tempietto classical recitals.... *Buses 36 or 60.*

Cinecittà (p. 183) SOUTHERN SUBURBS Rome's major film studios, where Fellini worked much of his magic. Tours are sporadic but can always be arranged for film students (and they're free!).... *Tel 06/7229-3780. www.cinecittastudios.it. Via Tuscolana 1055. Metro Cinecittà.*

Cinema dei Piccoli (p. 188) VILLA BORGHESE Small, mostly children's cinema featuring old-school cartoons and family films, as well as some darker, more grown-up didactic fare.... *Tel 06/855-34-85. Via della Pineta 15. Buses 116, 490, or 495. Tickets 4.50€ ($5.65).*

Concerti del Tempietto (p. 188) GHETTO/EASTERN SUBURBS Summer program of classical music under the stars at the ruins of the Teatro di Marcello and the Casina delle Civette in Villa Torlonia.... *Tel 06/8713-1590. www.tempietto.it. Tickets 15€–18€ ($19–$23).*

English Theatre of Rome (p. 185) CITYWIDE Formerly known as the Off-Night Repertory, this theater group led by American Gaby Ford stages several excellent, often hilarious English-language plays each season.... *Tel 06/444-1375. www.rometheatre.com. Via Castelfidardo 31, int. 11. Venues vary. Tickets 12€–15€ ($15–$19).*

Estate Romana (p. 188) CITYWIDE Rome's summertime cultural festival, featuring art exhibitions, dance, music, theater, and children's programs. Varying locations.... *Tel 06/488-991. www.estateromana.it. Ticket prices vary; many events are free.*

Fiesta! (p. 186) SOUTHERN SUBURBS This popular music festival occupies the Capannelle racetrack every summer. Live rock, soul, and reggae, Latin and Caribbean DJs, plus international snacks and boutiques.... *Tel 06/6618-3542. www.fiesta.it. Via Appia Nuova 1245, Ippodromo delle Capannelle. Metro to Colli Albani, then bus 664. Tickets 8€ ($10).*

Foro Italico (p. 187) NORTHERN SUBURBS Huge Fascist-era sports complex, home to soccer games at the Stadio Olimpico and annual Italian Open tennis tournament.... *Tel 06/368-58-218. Viale dei Gladiatori 31. Buses 32, 271, or 280. Tram 2. Ticket prices vary.*

Globe Theatre (p. 185) VILLA BORGHESE Faithful reproduction of the London original stages Shakespeare and more.... *Tel 06/8207-7304. www.globetheatreroma.com. Largo Aqua Felix. Buses 116, 490, or 495. Ticket prices vary.*

Jazz and Image (p. 188) COLOSSEUM/FORUM Summer-long jazz and blues festival at Villa Celimontana park, organized by Alexanderplatz jazz club.... *Tel 06/589-78-07. www.romajazz.com. Piazza della Navicella. Metro Colosseo. Buses 60, 75, 81, 87, 175, or 271. Tram 3. Tickets 15€–20€ ($19–$25).*

Metropolitan (p. 186) PIAZZA DEL POPOLO Recently renovated movie theater often has one screen in V.O.... *Tel 06/326-00-500. Via del Corso 7. Metro Flaminio. Tickets 5€–7€ ($6.25–$8.75).*

Miracle Players (p. 185) ROMAN FORUM Fun, informative, and original comedies about Roman history performed in English above the Roman Forum. Mid-June to mid-August, Tuesday and Saturday at 7:30pm.... *Tel 06/446-9867 or 06/70393427. www.miracleplayers.org. Mamertine Prison (Clivo Argentario/Roman Forum). Buses 60, 75, 85, 87, or 175. Free.*

New Opera Festival (p. 188) ANCIENT ROME/OUTSIDE ROME Summer opera company puts on endearingly intimate productions in the courtyard of the church of San Clemente and at the ancient Teatro Romano di Ostia Antica. Seating can be uncomfortable.... *Tel 06/561-1519 or 347/852-4241. www.newopera festivaldiroma.com. Tickets 25€ ($31).*

Nuovo Pasquino Multisala (p. 186) TRASTEVERE The "premier" English-language cinema in Trastevere, showing a usually undesirable assortment of general releases and the occasional indie film.... *Tel 06/580-36-22. Piazza Sant'Egidio 10. Buses 23, 271, 280, or H. Tram 8. Tickets 4.15€–6.20€ ($5.20–$7.75).*

PalaLottomatica (p. 186) EUR Flying-saucer like venue designed by Pierluigi Nervi in the 1930s as the *Palazzo dello Sport*, home to indoor rock concerts.... *Tel 199-128-800. www.palalottomatica.it. Piazzale dello Sport. Metro EUR Palasport. Ticket prices vary.*

RomaEuropa Festival (p. 188) CITYWIDE One of Italy's biggest and best modern-leaning performing-arts festivals, with seasons lasting June through July and September through mid-November. Offerings include everything from acid jazz concerts to New Age, Cirque du Soleil–type troupes.... *Tel 06/474-22-86. www.roma europa.net. Venues and ticket prices vary.*

San Clemente (p. 188) COLOSSEUM Medieval church courtyard home to small-time productions staged by the New Opera Festival (see above for more info). *Via di San Giovanni in Laterano. Metro Colosseo. Buses 85 or 87. Tram 3.*

SS Lazio (p. 182) NORTHERN SUBURBS Rome's other big-deal soccer team and AS Roma's fierce intercity rival. The team's colors are light blue and white *(biancoceleste)*.... *Tel 06/323-73-33. www.sslazio.it. Tickets can be purchased at the Stadio Olimpico on game day or at the Lazio Point on Via Farini 34, Tel 06/482-67-68. Tickets 15€–90€ ($19–$113).*

Stadio Flaminio (p. 187) NORTHERN SUBURBS Stadium north of Piazza del Popolo where the Italian rugby squad and minor city sports leagues play.... *Tel 06/368-57-832. Via Flaminia. Tram 2. Ticket prices vary.*

Stadio Olimpico (p. 186) NORTHERN SUBURBS Site of the 1960 Olympic games and current home of the AS Roma and SS Lazio soccer squads on alternating Sundays. In summer, big-name rock concert venue.... *Tel 06/323-73-33 (ticket office). Viale dello Stadio Olimpico. Buses 32, 271, or 280. Tram 2. Tickets for matches 15€–90€ ($19–$113).*

Teatro dell'Opera (p. 184) TERMINI The city opera company, trying to shed its tarnished reputation, stages several productions each season. Summer performances take place at the Baths of Caracalla.... *Tel 06/481-601. www.opera.roma.it. Via Firenze 72. Metro Repubblica. Tickets 16€–119€ ($20–$149).*

Teatro di Marcello (p. 188) GHETTO Magnificent, 1st century B.C. backdrop for nightly classical concerts offered by Concerti del Tempietto in summer.... *Tel 06/87-13-15-90. www.tempietto.it. Buses 30, 40, 62, 63, 64, 70, 87, 95, 170, 492, or 628. Tickets 15€ ($19).*

Teatro di Roma–Argentina (p. 185) LARGO ARGENTINA A theater with a past, the Argentina was where Rossini's *Barber of Seville* debuted—to jeers and boos. Today, look for first-rate dance, musical, and theater productions.... *Tel 06/688-04-601. www.teatrodiroma.net. Largo Argentina 52. Buses 30, 40, 46, 62, 64, 70, 87, or 492. Tram 8. Tickets 10€–26€ ($13–$33).*

Teatro Olimpico (p. 184) NORTHERN SUBURBS Home auditorium of the Roman Philarmonic; also offers a wide range of alternative and classic theater, as well as dance.... *Tel 06/326-5991. Piazza Gentile da Fabriano. Bus 280. Tram 2. Tickets start at 20€ ($25).*

Teatro Romano di Ostia Antica (p. 184) OSTIA ANTICA/OUTSIDE ROME Classic comedies and tragedies and operas are performed among the ruins of a real, 1st century A.D. theater.... *Tel 06/6880-4601. www.newoperafestivaldiroma.com. From Metro Piramide, then Ostia Lido train to Ostia Antica. Tickets start at 15€ ($19).*

Teatro Sistina (p. 185) VENETO Playhouse hosting English-language plays and musicals, as well as Italian adaptations of shows like *Grease* and *Hello Dolly!*... *Tel 06/482-6841. www.ilsistina.com. Via Sistina 129. Metro Spagna or Barberini. Ticket prices vary.*

Teatro Verde (p. 187) TRASTEVERE Home of Punch and Judy puppet shows and other Italian-language plays for children. Performances October to April, Saturday and Sunday only, at 5pm.... *Tel 06/588-2034. www.teatroverde.it. Circonvallazione Gianicolense 10. Trams 3 or 8. Tickets 7€–8€ ($8.75–$10).*

Warner Village–Moderno (p. 186) TERMINI One screen at this high-tech multiplex is usually dedicated to films in V.O.... *Tel 06/477-79-202. Piazza della Repubblica 45. Metro Repubblica. Tickets 5.50€–7.50€ ($6.90–$9.40).*

HOTLINES & OTHER BASICS

Airport... **Fiumicino (FCO),** also known as Leonardo da Vinci, is Rome's main airport and is open 24 hours a day. Overhauled in 1999, Fiumicino is modern, bright, and user-friendly, with clear signage and extensive duty-free shopping opportunities. If your bags do not arrive at the same time you do (this happens somewhat frequently, especially if you've made a connection at another European airport), try not to freak out—just file a claim with the baggage people, and most likely the airline will deliver your luggage to your hotel within half a day. There is also a left luggage desk in Terminal C (International Arrivals). Rome's other airport, **Ciampino,** is mainly a hub for military flights, but it also handles charter and budget airline flights from within Europe. For more information, Aeroporti di Roma's official website (**www.adr.it**) is quite helpful. Operators at Fiumicino's main switchboard (Tel 06/659-51) can tell you whether flights are on time.

Airport transportation to downtown... Two train services run directly from Fiumicino into the city. The **Leonardo Express** train to Termini Station takes 35 minutes, costs 9.50€ ($12) and runs about every half-hour between 7am and 10pm. Local service (destination Fara Sabina-Orte) is 5€ ($6.25), runs about every 15 minutes, and makes stops at Trastevere (20 min.), Ostiense (25 min.), Tuscolana (35 min.), and Tiburtina (40 min.) stations, but not Termini. If you're traveling in a group or lugging around a couple of suitcases, skip the train hassle and take a taxi. Cab fare to or from Fiumicino is around 45€ ($56), including surcharges for baggage. From Ciampino airport, you can reach central Rome by taking a **COTRAL** bus to Anagnina, and from there, the Metro (2€/$2.50 one-way), or **Terravision**'s direct coach (8€/$10 one-way) to Stazione Termini, Rome's main train station. Licensed taxis are white and metered (you can't, and shouldn't, negotiate a fixed rate beforehand) and are found at a well-organized taxi stand just outside the terminal. Some cabs accept credit cards, but they are the minority. Hacks posing as taxicab drivers are always lurking outside the customs area, waiting to prey on weary international arrivals. They'll offer you a ride into town in an air-conditioned Mercedes or similarly flashy car and sometimes demand upwards of 100€ ($125). However, if you can negotiate a firm and reasonable price (say, 50€/$63 with no "extras"), this can be a comfortable option, and you can often pay with a credit card.

Babysitters... Most hotels do not provide childcare. If you're in a bind, call **United Babies** at Piazza Nicoloso da Recco 9 (Tel 06/589-94-81), a licensed daytime play group run by American Lucy Gardner. The service is open from 8am to 2:30pm, and babysitting is available until 6pm. Americans who plan to be in Rome for a longer period of time may want to contact the United States Embassy, which can provide you with a list of other English-speaking babysitters in the city.

Banks and currency exchange offices... ATMs are plentiful around the city and are by far the best option for getting cash while abroad. You will be charged $5 or so by your home bank for each withdrawal, but the exchange rate is quite advantageous. Banks in central Rome are open Monday through Friday from 9am to 1pm and 3 to 5pm, Saturday from 9am to 1pm. Most will handle currency exchanges and credit card cash advances for a nominal fee, but bear in mind that you may have to wait in a line—and Roman lines can be a little stressful, especially when money is involved. Currency exchange offices are also located throughout the *centro storico,* as well as the airports and Termini Train Station, though they tend to gouge you either with hefty fees or inflated exchange rates.

Car rentals... **Hertz** at Via Veneto 156 (Tel 06/321-68-31) and **Avis** at Via Sardegna 38a (Tel 06/428-24-728) have offices in the city center. Many rental companies have offices at Fiumicino airport, including **Avis** (Tel 06/650-11-531), **Thrifty** (Tel 06/793-40-137), and **Hertz** (Tel 06/650-11-553). All three are open daily until midnight. **Europcar** (Tel 06/488-28-54), **Avis** (Tel 06/481-43-73), and Italian chain **Maggiore** (Tel 06/488-00-49) operate rental offices at Termini Station.

Consulates and embassies... **United States Embassy:** Via Veneto 119a–121 (Tel 06/467-41). **Embassy of Canada:** Via Zara 30 (Tel 06/445-981). **Embassy of the United Kingdom:** Via XX Settembre 80a (Tel 06/482-54-41). **Embassy of Australia:** Via Alessandria 215 (Tel 06/852-721). **Embassy of New Zealand:** Via Zara 28 (Tel 06/440-29-28).

Currency... Italy said *arrivederci* to the lira in February 2002. Now, the euro is the official currency of Italy (and 12 other European Union members). Unfortunately, the changeover drove up prices all over the Continent. That, combined with the currently weak dollar, has made travel in Europe much more expensive than ever before. All price conversions in this guide are based on 1€ = US$1.25.

Driving and parking... For the average tourist, driving a car in Rome makes as much sense as shooting yourself in the foot with a poison dart. With diabolical traffic restrictions in the historic center and an agonizing parking situation citywide, a car is a serious liability. On the other hand, if you plan to venture out of town, a car is often handy, and once you're outside the city, Italian highways are very user-friendly. If your destination is served by train, however, go by rail—it's almost always faster. If you do bring a car, some useful parking garages are located in the Villa Borghese (Viale del Muro Torto), at the Lepanto Metro Station (Via Lepanto), and in Piazza del Popolo. The controversial Vatican Parking Garage (Via Aurelia), built atop ancient ruins, was inaugurated for the Holy Year and Jubilee in 2000.

Electricity... Italy's electrical outlets put out 220 volts, whereas the United States system is wired for 110 volts. Small appliances (like laptops) from the States will function fine in Italy—you just need to get a two-pronged adapter, available for 4€ ($5) or so at most Roman hardware stores (*ferramenta* or *casalinghe*). Bulky transformers are needed to operate higher voltage appliances like hairdryers, but even transformers aren't always reliable. If your hotel bathroom doesn't provide a hairdryer, ask the front desk for a *phon* or *asciugacapelli.*

Emergencies and police... For general emergencies, you have your choice of dialing **112** for the **Carabinieri,** or **113** for the **Polizia.** *Carabinieri* are the army police; *polizia* are a civilian force. Both are generally helpful, though mountains of paperwork, stamps, and seals can be involved for even minor claims. For **fire emergencies,** dial the **Vigili del Fuoco** at **115.** For auto assistance, call the **Automobile Club d'Italia (ACI)** at **116.** It has a reciprocal agreement with AAA. The most centrally located police office *(questura)* is at Piazza del Collegio Romano 3, reached by buses 30, 40, 46, 62, 64, 70, 85, 87, or 492.

Events information... For information on concerts, theater performances, or other types of entertainment, you can buy the weekly magazine ***Roma C'è,*** which has an English-language section, or the monthly ***TimeOut Roma.*** All the Italian daily newspapers have events sections, and *La Repubblica*'s Thursday ***TrovaRoma*** insert is especially thorough. Free info on selected events is available from tourist kiosks, which are scattered around the city center. Ask for ***L'Evento*** and/or ***Un Ospite a Roma.*** The latter is also available at upscale hotels.

Festivals & Special Events

JANUARY: Children get a visit and gifts from ***La Befana*** (the Old Witch) on January 6 (Epiphany), which marks the end of the Christmas season.

FEBRUARY: Pranksters don masks and children dress as if it is Halloween for **Carnevale** (Feb or Mar). There is also an adorable children's parade near the Colosseum on *Martedì Grasso* (Fat Tuesday). When the Vatican's Christmas tree is taken down mid-month, tourists can often make off with free souvenir ornaments.

MARCH: March 8, **La Festa delle Donne (Women's Day),** is when Roman girls get wild and paint the town like bachelorettes, and men give the women in their lives bouquets of yellow mimosa flowers or risk eternal damnation. Nonstop religious services, hordes of pilgrims, and gluttonous feasting are the highlights of the **Settimana Santa,** the week leading up to Easter (March or April); the pope celebrates the **Via Crucis** at a dramatically lit Colosseum on Good Friday, and an outdoor Mass in St. Peter's Square on Easter Sunday draws tens of thousands. The third Sunday in March sees the main streets closed to traffic for the **Rome City Marathon** (www.maratonadiroma.it).

APRIL: The **Natale di Roma** (Rome's birthday, 753 B.C.) is celebrated on the Campidoglio on April 21, with fireworks set off over the Circus Maximus. A sea of azaleas replaces the lounging masses on the Spanish Steps on the **Festa della Primavera** during the beginning of the month. The **Settimana dei Beni Culturali** (April or May) is one of the best times to visit Rome, when all state-owned museums and archaeological sites are open free of charge.

MAY: Rock concerts in Piazza San Giovanni in Laterano and labor demonstrations mark **Primo Maggio** (May 1). **The Italian Open,** Italy's closest thing to a Grand Slam tennis tournament, takes place at the Foro Italico in mid-May. For equestrian fans, there's show-jumping at the Piazza di Siena, in Villa Borghese, in late May.

JUNE: **Pentecost Sunday** is the best day of the year to visit the Pantheon—firemen pour enormous barrels of red rose petals through the hole in the dome, blanketing the congregation below. The **Estate Romana** and **RomaEuropa** cultural festivals begin in June and last throughout the summer. A military parade down Via dei Fori Imperiali commemorates the **Anniversary of the Republic** on June 2.

June 23 is the **Festa di San Giovanni,** which calls for huge feasts of snails and suckling pig. Rome's patron saints—Peter and Paul—are celebrated at their respective basilicas (St. Peter's and San Paolo Fuori le Mura) on **San Pietro e San Paolo** on June 29.

JULY: Estate Romana and RomaEuropa festivals are in full swing; Trastevere holds the **Festa de' Noantri** street fair during the last 2 weeks of July. Also in late July, **Donne Sotte Le Stelle** is a big-time international fashion show at the Spanish Steps.

AUGUST: The **Festa della Madonna della Neve** at Santa Maria Maggiore on August 5 recalls (with white flower petals) a miraculous summer snow in the 4th century, which prompted the building of the basilica. **Ferragosto** (Aug 15) sees the city empty out and all but shut down until early September.

NOVEMBER: Romans visit the great Verano cemetery in droves to remember their dead on **Ognissanti** (All Saints' Day, Nov 1). The **Vino Novello** (like Beaujolais nouveau) wine tasting takes place in late November in Campo de' Fiori, as well as at restaurants city-wide.

DECEMBER: The **Vatican Christmas tree** and ***presepe*** (nativity scene) go up and stay up until mid-February. On December 8, the **Day of the Immaculate Conception,** the pope rides down Via Condotti to the Trinità dei Monti church, where he holds Mass. Saccharine treats and sundry bric-a-brac are available at the **Christmas Market** in Piazza Navona until January 6; and, throughout the month of December, all major basilicas and many local churches display their nativity scenes *(presepi).* On **Christmas Eve,** the pope says midnight Mass from the balcony overlooking St. Peter's square.

Gay and lesbian sources... For info on the latest happenings, including nightlife, events, lectures, and counseling services for AIDS/HIV, look to the **Circolo Mario Mieli di Cultura Omosessuale** (Tel 06/541-39-85; fax 06/541-39-71; www.mariomieli.org). **ArciGay** (Tel 06/855-55-22; www.arcigay.it) and **ArciLesbica** (Tel 06/418-03-69) offer help lines for gay men and lesbians, respectively, as well as political and social forums. **Libreria Babele** at Via dei Banchi Vecchi 116 (Tel 06/687-66-28; buses 23, 30, 40, 46, 64, 271, or 571), the city's only gay and lesbian bookstore, sells the *Gay and Lesbian Map of Rome.* Also available for purchase is the *Guida Gay,* an annual Italian/ English guide that provides information on queer venues and events.

Health matters... If you have an emergency medical problem, you can go to the *pronto soccorso* (emergency room) of any local hospital. The most centrally located hospitals are **Ospedale Fatebenefratelli,** Isola Tiberina, north end. (Tel 06/683-72-99; buses 23, 271, 280, 780, or H), and **Ospedale San Giacomo** at Via Canova 29 (Tel 06/362-61; Metro Flaminio). There's also a major hospital near San Giovanni in Laterano: **Ospedale San Giovanni,** at Via Amba Aradam 8 (Tel 06/770-51; Metro San Giovanni). All doctors at the **MEDline** (Tel 06/808-09-95) speak English. Most pharmacies in Rome are open from 8:30am to 1pm and 4 to 8pm, and can fill almost any prescription. Outside of normal operating hours, pharmacies stay open on a rotating basis; most local papers print a list of these, and each pharmacy is also required to post information about the nearest open pharmacy. There are a few 24-hour pharmacies, as well: **Farmacia della Stazione,** Piazza dei Cinquecento, near Termini (Tel 06/488-00-19), and **Piram,** Via Nazionale 228 (Tel 06/488-07-54). If you're near Vatican City, the **Farmacia del Vaticano,** Porta Sant' Anna (Tel 06/698-83-422), is open Monday through Friday from 8:30am to 6pm and Saturday from 7:30am to 1pm. It stocks many drugs that are hard to find in Italian pharmacies—often at cheaper prices.

Holidays... Italy observes a number of federal and religious holidays: January 1 (New Year's Day), January 6 (Epiphany), Easter and Easter Monday (March or April), April 25 (Liberation Day), May 1 (Labor Day), June 2 (Anniversary of the Republic), August 15 (Ferragosto/Assumption of the Blessed Virgin Mary), November 1 (All Saints' Day), November 4 (World War I Victory Anniversary Day), December 8 (Immaculate Conception), December 25 (Christmas Day), and December 26 (Santo Stefano). Rome also observes St. Peter and St. Paul's Day on June 29.

Internet access... **Easy Everything,** Via Barberini 2–16 (Tel 06/429-03-388; Metro Barberini), open 24 hours, has three floors with approximately 350 Internet-equipped computer terminals. Before plopping down at one of the computers, you'll have to buy a ticket with a pass code; 1€ ($1.25) will get you about 20 minutes of Internet time—cheaper than at most Internet cafes in the city, but mouses are often broken, and the smell of Subway sandwiches (they've opened a franchise inside the building) pervades your online experience. **Verba,** at Via Cardinale Merry del Val 20 (Tel 06/581-32-08; www.verbaweb.com; buses 44, 75, 780, or H; trams 3 or 8), is a well-kept secret and an oasis of calm in Trastevere, with indoor and outdoor terminals, printing and scanning, and competitive prices (5€/$6.25 per hour; cheaper for students). The place is immaculate, the staff super-friendly, and DSL connections fast. Internet "hotspots" (wi-fi areas) are almost unheard of in Rome, but if you've brought your own laptop, one option is **La Caffettiera** (Tel 06/679-1847; Piazza di Pietra 65; buses 62, 85, 95, 116, 175, or 492), an old-school, dark-wood-panelled coffee bar and tea room near the Pantheon.

Newspapers... You can pick up the *Wall Street Journal, USA Today,* and the *Financial Times* from almost all kiosks, though they tend to be at least 1 day old. A local edition of the *International Herald Tribune* is edited and printed in Italy and includes the "Italy Daily" supplement, a good local news summary in English. As for news in Italian, the main Roman dailies are *Il Messaggero* and *La Repubblica,* whose Thursday *Trovaroma* booklet provides weekly info on cultural events. *Corriere della Sera* is the foremost national daily, with a section on news and happenings in Rome.

Opening and closing times... Opening and closing times in Rome can be highly irregular and tend to change with the season or at the whims of the owner. Most cafes and *tabacchi* shops open around 7am and stay open until 10pm. Most boutiques in the tourist center are open from 10am to 7:30pm, with no midday closing, but other smaller shops close from 2 to 4pm. Many shops stay open until 8:30 or 9pm in the summer. Almost all restaurants take a *riposo settimanale* (day off), usually on Sunday or Monday. The main archaeological sites are open daily, but state-owned museums are closed on Mondays; private museums are also closed 1 day of the week. The Vatican museums and Sistine Chapel are closed on Sundays and Catholic holidays; they also have reduced hours in winter and on Saturdays year-round. To avoid any disappointment, call ahead.

Passports and visas... Citizens of the United States, Canada, Australia, and New Zealand do not need a visa to visit Italy, nor do citizens of the European Union. If you are staying for longer than 3 months, you are required to apply for a *permesso di soggiorno,* available from the main police station at Via Genova. Be prepared for miles of red tape.

Post office... It used to be that you were far better off sending mail through the excellent, trustworthy, and often uncrowded **Poste Vaticane.** Two branches of the Vatican's post office are located on either side of St. Peter's Square, and one branch is located within the Vatican Museums. However, the **Poste Italiane** got its act together in 2002 and now delivers mail in a timely fashion. All postal services can be taken care of at the Terme di Diocleziano branch (Viale delle Terme di Diocleziano 30, near Termini), but if you're just mailing out a few postcards, you can buy stamps *(francobolli)* from the local *tabacchi* store. Postage is .62€ (78¢) for postcards or 1.03€ ($1.29) for letters to the U.S.

Public transportation... If you can get past the fact that the Metro and buses are slow and packed to capacity, public transportation in Rome is fairly reliable, with a number of convenient cross-town routes (buses 40, 60, 70, 87, 170, 271, 492, or 571—the famed 64, known for its high incidences of pickpocketing and perverted behavior, is best avoided altogether); clean, effective tram service; and the **Metropolitana** subway, which covers many tourist sites as well as outlying areas. Bus routes and stops, while marked, can be confusing for out-of-towners, but bus drivers and fellow riders are usually helpful in telling you when to get off. **ATAC,** the city's transportation agency, has a very handy website (www.atac.roma.it) for figuring out which lines to take to get from point A to point B; otherwise, call the ATAC hotline (Tel 800/431-784), and an operator will assist you. One-way tickets (Biglietto Integrato a Tempo—BIT), good for 75 minutes of travel on buses, trams, or the Metro, cost 1€ ($1.25) and are available at *tabacchi* bars and some newsstands. Also available are daily tickets (Biglietto Integrato Giornaliero—BIG) for 4€ ($5), a 3-day tourist pass (BTI) for 11€ ($14), and weekly tickets (Carta Integrata Settimanale—CIS) for 16€ ($20). You must stamp your tickets on the bus or at the Metro turnstiles upon entry. (Transport inspectors rarely show up to check your tickets, but if you're caught, put on the best stupid-American act you can muster, and you might get away with it. If not, it's a fine of 51€/$64 and heaps of public humiliation.) ATAC also runs night buses *(autobus notturni)* at major stops. These are indicated on signposts by an N after the bus number and by the symbol of an owl—cute, huh? Times are irregular, though, so try to avoid waiting at stops if you're traveling alone.

Religious services... Each month brings ample opportunities to see *Sua Santità* (His Holiness) **Papa Benedetto XVI.** The last Sunday of every month, the pope gives an address—often in Italian and another language, depending on the crowd—from his apartment overlooking St. Peter's Square. Check with your local diocese or the Vatican's website (www.vatican.va) for info on major Masses and events at St. Peter's. Most other churches offer at least one Mass on Sunday (9am or so) and often daily Masses at 7am, noon, and 6pm; check the schedule posted near the main entrance. For Mass in English, go to **Santa Susanna,** Via XX Settembre 14 (Tel 06/488-27-48; Metro Repubblica), the American parish in Rome, or to **San Silvestro** in Capite, Piazza San Silvestro 17a (Tel 06/679-77-75), the British parish. To accommodate Rome's international and growing immigrant communities, there are also a few non-Catholic places of worship in the city. Attend **Jewish** services at the Sinagoga, Lungotevere Cenci (Tel 06/684-00-61; www.romacer.org); **Muslim** services at the Moschea, Viale della Moschea (Tel 06/808-21-67); **Methodist** services at Via Firenze 38 (Tel 06/481-48-11); or **Presbyterian** services at St. Andrew's, Via XX Settembre 7 (Tel 06/482-76-27).

Standards of measure... Forget about memorizing complicated conversion formulas—all you need to know about the metric system are a few simple equivalents:

Distance/Height: A meter is just over 3 feet; a kilometer is just over half a mile.

Temperature: 0°C is freezing (rare in Rome, except for a few days in Feb); 10°C is 50°F; 20°C is a very pleasant 68°F; 30°C is 86°F and quite common from June to August; 40°C is 104°F (rare, but you'll hear this—*quaranta gradi*—all the time when Italians are exaggerating about the heat).

Weight: A kilogram (kg, or *chilo*) is 2.2 lbs; an *etto* (you'll see this on menus) is 100g, or about 4 oz.

Apparel: Most Roman clothing stores do not carry sizes larger than a women's 46 (U.S. 10), although Benetton goes up to 48 (U.S. 12). Likewise, big and tall men should seek out stores advertising *tagli forti* ("strong sizes"). Unfortunately, both men and women with larger feet will have to be shod elsewhere, as almost all Italian shoes max out at 45 for men (U.S. 12) or 41 for women (U.S. 9.5).

Taxes and duty free... As required by the European Union, Italy imposes a sales tax or **Value Added Tax** (VAT, or *IVA* in Italian) of 12% to 35% on all goods and services (already included in the listed price, not applied at the cash register). If you're purchasing more than 155€ ($194) worth of goods at one store, be sure to ask for the **Tax Free for Tourists** form. When you present this form, along with your passport, receipts, and purchases, upon your departure from the E.U., you will get a cash refund (in euros) of the VAT tax on the spot (or a credit card adjustment, which may take up to 6 months to process) at the border Customs office. Note that items that have been used in any way are not eligible for these rebates.

Taxis... By most other cities' standards, Roman taxis are a bit of a rip-off—even the legal ones. The fare structure is ridiculously complicated, with surcharges for luggage, for travel to and from the airport, and for rides between the hours of 10pm and 7am. On average, however, a cab ride within the city center should cost anywhere from 5€ to 12€ ($6.25–$15). Hailing a cab sometimes works, but usually the driver will just whiz by and shake his finger at you,

you crazy foreigner; instead, go to a cab stand (located near major sites) and assert your place in line—there is nothing quite as subversive and shifty as a cab queue in Rome. Watch out for car jockeys who lurk near taxi stands at the train station; if the cab name and number are not painted on a car, the driver is not legally sanctioned and will likely gouge you. The concierge at any hotel should call a cab for you, as should maitre d's at nicer restaurants. However, if you need to call one on your own, contact Tel 06/3570, 06/4157, 06/4994, 06/6645, or 06/5551. Note that when you call a taxi, the meter starts running at the time of the call, not when the cab arrives. If you suspect you're the victim of a dishonest cabbie ("Haven't we just driven around the same building 20 times?"), make a note of his *sigla* (medallion number) and taxi consortium phone number, posted on the outside of both front doors, and have a local call in the complaint.

Telephones... Italians can't live without their *cellulari,* especially the SMS function. In a culture where e-mail and IM have yet to become as commonplace as they are in the U.S. or U.K., text messages are used in Italy to broker deals, break off engagements, or simply chat inanely. If you want to fit in, you'll need a GSM mobile phone. (American AMPS phones do not work in Italy.) Otherwise, you're stuck with the *cabina* (pay phone)—a thoroughly old-world concept here and a common source of frustration for locals and visitors alike. Pay phones do not accept coins (if you find one that does, congratulations, you have an antique on your hands); instead, you must first purchase a phone card from a *tabacchi* shop. The cards come in denominations of 2.50€ ($3.15) and higher; note that the card will not work until you break off the perforated corner. To rent a cellphone for your trip, U.K.-based Cellhire (www.cellhire.com) is a handy service, but read the fine print regarding usage fees.

Time... Rome is 1 hour ahead of (that is, later than) Greenwich Mean Time (London) and 6 hours ahead of Eastern Standard Time (New York). Daylight savings begins in early April and lasts through late October.

Tipping... Tipping is not obligatory but perfectly acceptable in Italy, and it's expected of tourists who are used to tipping in their home countries. However, in many cases, an automatic service charge of 10% to 15% is already tacked onto restaurant checks—known as the *pane e coperto* (bread and cover) charge—so check first before laying down any extra cash. If you've received extraordinary service, an additional tip of approximately 10% is customary. Ten or so *centesimi* on top of your receipt, presented while you order your *caffè* or cappuccino at a bar, is standard and will usually get you speedier service, too. You should also tip porters, cab drivers, and maids 1€ ($1.25) for their efforts.

Tourist lines... On a sunny day, a great way to get oriented is with the city-run **110 Open** (Tel 06/4695-2252), an open-air, double-decker sightseeing bus. Departing from Piazza dei Cinquecento (in front of Termini) every 20 minutes, the 2-hour loop includes stops at the Colosseum, the Mouth of Truth, Piazza Navona, St. Peter's, Trevi Fountain, and Via Veneto. Tickets (13€/$16) include a multilingual audio guide and are valid for hop-on/hop-off travel all day. To visit the Appian Way, the **Archeobus** (Tel 06/4695-2252) is another hop-on/hop-off service (with some commentary in Italian and English), traveling every hour on the hour from Piazza Cinquecento to sites along the Via Appia Antica like the catacombs and the aqueduct park. Archeobus tickets are 8€ ($10), which does not include the price of admission at the catacombs. A **combo ticket** for the 110 Open and Archeobus is 20€ ($25), which saves you a whopping 1€ ($1.25). For more info about either, visit www.trambus.com/roma.htm (in Italian only). The **COTRAL** network (Tel 800/150-008) handles regional bus transportation outside Rome (like buses to Tivoli and the beach at Fregene). COTRAL's blue buses depart from Metro Lepanto, Metro Ponte Mammolo, Metro Anagnina, and Metro EUR-Fermi.

Travelers with disabilities... With streets of uneven cobblestones, churches with tall marble staircases, and uncertain elevator access in hotels, Rome is probably one of the worst imaginable cities for travelers with disabilities. However, changes are in progress to make it easier for the wheelchair-bound. **Roma Accessibile,** produced by the

Consorzio Cooperative Integrate (COIN) at Via Enrico Giglioli 54a (Tel 06/232-67-504), contains information on accessibility in hotels, museums, restaurants, and other sites. Information is also available 24 hours a day in English on its hotline. Check also www.coinsociale.it for some of the same information.

Visitor information... For information on Rome and Italy before you leave home, visit the website of the **Italian National Tourist Board** (www.italiantourism.com); bear in mind that listings here are often vague and not up-to-date. Rome's own tourism site, **www.romaturismo.com**, is much better, with tons of free downloadable brochures. Tourist information kiosks are located in Fiumicino Airport and Termini Station, as well near the Spanish Steps, Piazza Navona, Trastevere, and other densely touristed areas. The city's main tourist office is located at Via Parigi 5 (Tel 06/488-99-253); it's open Monday through Friday from 8:15am to 7:15pm, Saturday from 8:15am to 1:45pm. Here, you can pick up free city maps and guides and learn about current exhibitions, musical events, and more. Agents at the kiosks tend to be quite helpful, and most speak English well enough to get you where you're going. **Enjoy Rome** (Tel 06/445-18-43), open Monday through Friday from 8:30am to 2pm and 3:30 to 6pm, Saturday from 8:30am to 2pm, is a private tourist office staffed by native English speakers. They offer all kinds of great walking tours and bus excursions and can also help you out with accommodations and entertainment suggestions, as well as provide city maps. Visit www.enjoyrome.com to get acquainted with their services.

Weather... January and February are chilly but often clear, with lows rarely dropping below freezing. March brings equal parts springlike days and miserable rain. The warm weather arrives in late April and stays through October. The most glorious months for sightseeing, by far, are May and late September to mid-October because of the light and temperature. June and July can get quite hot and humid, but August is the least desirable month of all—the city is oppressively hot and depressingly empty. November is the rainiest month, but there are often a few

Indian-summer days. December is also cold, but the festivities surrounding Christmas make everything seem a little warmer.

Women's Rome... Women who need gynecological care can visit **Artemide** at Via Sannio 61 (Tel 06/704-76-220), a private clinic with moderate fees. Pregnancy tests *(test di gravidanza)* can be purchased easily and discreetly at any *farmacia.* **Telefono Rosa** (Tel 06/683-26-90 or 06/683-28-20) is an emergency help line for women who need counseling or advice regarding sexual abuse or harassment.

GENERAL INDEX

Accommodations

Restaurants

ROMMER'S® COMPLETE TRAVEL GUIDES

ska
ska Cruises & Ports of Call
erican Southwest
sterdam
entina & Chile
zona
anta
tralia
tria
amas
celona
ing
gium, Holland & Luxembourg
muda
ton
zil
ish Columbia & the Canadian
ockies
ssels & Bruges
dapest & the Best of Hungary
gary
ifornia
nada
ncún, Cozumel & the Yucatán
pe Cod, Nantucket & Martha's
ineyard
ibbean
ibbean Ports of Call
olinas & Georgia
cago
na
orado
sta Rica
ises & Ports of Call
ba
nmark
nver, Boulder & Colorado Springs
nburgh & Glasgow
gland
rope
rope by Rail
ropean Cruises & Ports of Call
rence, Tuscany & Umbria
Florida
France
Germany
Great Britain
Greece
Greek Islands
Halifax
Hawaii
Hong Kong
Honolulu, Waikiki & Oahu
India
Ireland
Italy
Jamaica
Japan
Kauai
Las Vegas
London
Los Angeles
Madrid
Maine Coast
Maryland & Delaware
Maui
Mexico
Montana & Wyoming
Montréal & Québec City
Munich & the Bavarian Alps
Nashville & Memphis
New England
Newfoundland & Labrador
New Mexico
New Orleans
New York City
New York State
New Zealand
Northern Italy
Norway
Nova Scotia, New Brunswick & Prince Edward Island
Oregon
Ottawa
Paris
Peru
Philadelphia & the Amish Country
Portugal
Prague & the Best of the Czech Republic
Provence & the Riviera
Puerto Rico
Rome
San Antonio & Austin
San Diego
San Francisco
Santa Fe, Taos & Albuquerque
Scandinavia
Scotland
Seattle
Seville, Granada & the Best of Andalusia
Shanghai
Sicily
Singapore & Malaysia
South Africa
South America
South Florida
South Pacific
Southeast Asia
Spain
Sweden
Switzerland
Texas
Thailand
Tokyo
Toronto
Turkey
USA
Utah
Vancouver & Victoria
Vermont, New Hampshire & Maine
Vienna & the Danube Valley
Virgin Islands
Virginia
Walt Disney World® & Orlando
Washington, D.C.
Washington State

ROMMER'S® DOLLAR-A-DAY GUIDES

stralia from $50 a Day
lifornia from $70 a Day
gland from $75 a Day
rope from $85 a Day
rida from $70 a Day
waii from $80 a Day
Ireland from $80 a Day
Italy from $70 a Day
London from $90 a Day
New York City from $90 a Day
Paris from $90 a Day
San Francisco from $70 a Day
Washington, D.C. from $80 a Day
Portable London from $90 a Day
Portable New York City from $90 a Day
Portable Paris from $90 a Day

ROMMER'S® PORTABLE GUIDES

apulco, Ixtapa & Zihuatanejo
nsterdam
uba
stralia's Great Barrier Reef
hamas
rlin
Island of Hawaii
ston
lifornia Wine Country
ncún
yman Islands
arleston
icago
neyland®
minican Republic
Dublin
Florence
Frankfurt
Hong Kong
Las Vegas
Las Vegas for Non-Gamblers
London
Los Angeles
Los Cabos & Baja
Maui
Miami
Nantucket & Martha's Vineyard
New Orleans
New York City
Paris
Phoenix & Scottsdale
Portland
Puerto Rico
Puerto Vallarta, Manzanillo & Guadalajara
Rio de Janeiro
San Diego
San Francisco
Savannah
Vancouver Island
Venice
Virgin Islands
Washington, D.C.
Whistler

Frommer's® National Park Guides

Algonquin Provincial Park
Banff & Jasper
Family Vacations in the National Parks
Grand Canyon
National Parks of the American West
Rocky Mountain
Yellowstone & Grand Teton
Yosemite & Sequoia/Kings Canyon
Zion & Bryce Canyon

Frommer's® Memorable Walks

Chicago
London
New York
Paris
San Francisco

Frommer's® With Kids Guides

Chicago
Hawaii
Las Vegas
New York City
Ottawa
San Francisco
Toronto
Vancouver
Walt Disney World® & Orlando
Washington, D.C.

Suzy Gershman's Born to Shop Guides

Born to Shop: France
Born to Shop: Hong Kong, Shanghai & Beijing
Born to Shop: Italy
Born to Shop: London
Born to Shop: New York
Born to Shop: Paris

Frommer's® Irreverent Guides

Amsterdam
Boston
Chicago
Las Vegas
London
Los Angeles
Manhattan
New Orleans
Paris
Rome
San Francisco
Seattle & Portland
Vancouver
Walt Disney World®
Washington, D.C.

Frommer's® Best-Loved Driving Tours

Austria
Britain
California
France
Germany
Ireland
Italy
New England
Northern Italy
Scotland
Spain
Tuscany & Umbria

The Unofficial Guides®

Beyond Disney
California with Kids
Central Italy
Chicago
Cruises
Disneyland®
England
Florida
Florida with Kids
Inside Disney
Hawaii
Las Vegas
London
Maui
Mexico's Best Beach Resorts
Mini Las Vegas
Mini Mickey
New Orleans
New York City
Paris
San Francisco
Skiing & Snowboarding in the We
South Florida including Miami & the Keys
Walt Disney World®
Walt Disney World® for Grown-ups
Walt Disney World® with Kids
Washington, D.C.

Special-Interest Titles

Athens Past & Present
Cities Ranked & Rated
Frommer's Best Day Trips from London
Frommer's Best RV & Tent Campgrounds in the U.S.A.
Frommer's Caribbean Hideaways
Frommer's China: The 50 Most Memorable Trips
Frommer's Exploring America by RV
Frommer's Gay & Lesbian Europe
Frommer's NYC Free & Dirt Cheap
Frommer's Road Atlas Europe
Frommer's Road Atlas France
Frommer's Road Atlas Ireland
Frommer's Wonderful Weekends from New York City
Retirement Places Rated
Rome Past & Present